Conversational AI

Dialogue Systems, Conversational Agents, and Chatbots

Synthesis Lectures on Human Language Technologies

Editor
Graeme Hirst, *University of Toronto*

Synthesis Lectures on Human Language Technologies is edited by Graeme Hirst of the University of Toronto. The series consists of 50- to 150-page monographs on topics relating to natural language processing, computational linguistics, information retrieval, and spoken language understanding. Emphasis is on important new techniques, on new applications, and on topics that combine two or more HLT subfields.

Conversational AI: Dialogue Systems, Conversational Agents, and Chatbots
Michael McTear
2020

Embeddings in Natural Language Processing: Theory and Advances in Vector Representations of Meaning
Mohammad Taher Pilehvar and Jose Camacho-Collados
2020

Natural Language Processing for Social Media, Third Edition
Anna Atefeh Farzindar and Diana Inkpen
2020

Statistical Significance Testing for Natural Language Processing
Rotem Dror, Lotem Peled, Segev Shlomov, and Roi Reichart
2020

Deep Learning Approaches to Text Production
Shashi Narayan and Claire Gardent
2020

Linguistic Fundamentals for Natural Language Processing II: 100 Essentials from Semantics and Pragmatics
Emily M. Bender and Alex Lascarides
2019

Cross-Lingual Word Embeddings
Anders Søgaard, Ivan Vulić, Sebastian Ruder, Manaal Faruqui
2019

Bayesian Analysis in Natural Language Processing, Second Edition
Shay Cohen
2019

Argumentation Mining
Manfred Stede and Jodi Schneider
2018

Quality Estimation for Machine Translation
Lucia Specia, Carolina Scarton, and Gustavo Henrique Paetzold
2018

Natural Language Processing for Social Media, Second Edition
Atefeh Farzindar and Diana Inkpen
2017

Automatic Text Simplification
Horacio Saggion
2017

Neural Network Methods for Natural Language Processing
Yoav Goldberg
2017

Syntax-based Statistical Machine Translation
Philip Williams, Rico Sennrich, Matt Post, and Philipp Koehn
2016

Domain-Sensitive Temporal Tagging
Jannik Strötgen and Michael Gertz
2016

Linked Lexical Knowledge Bases: Foundations and Applications
Iryna Gurevych, Judith Eckle-Kohler, and Michael Matuschek
2016

Bayesian Analysis in Natural Language Processing
Shay Cohen
2016

Metaphor: A Computational Perspective
Tony Veale, Ekaterina Shutova, and Beata Beigman Klebanov
2016

Grammatical Inference for Computational Linguistics
Jeffrey Heinz, Colin de la Higuera, and Menno van Zaanen
2015

Automatic Detection of Verbal Deception
Eileen Fitzpatrick, Joan Bachenko, and Tommaso Fornaciari
2015

Natural Language Processing for Social Media
Atefeh Farzindar and Diana Inkpen
2015

Semantic Similarity from Natural Language and Ontology Analysis
Sébastien Harispe, Sylvie Ranwez, Stefan Janaqi, and Jacky Montmain
2015

Learning to Rank for Information Retrieval and Natural Language Processing, Second Edition
Hang Li
2014

Ontology-Based Interpretation of Natural Language
Philipp Cimiano, Christina Unger, and John McCrae
2014

Automated Grammatical Error Detection for Language Learners, Second Edition
Claudia Leacock, Martin Chodorow, Michael Gamon, and Joel Tetreault
2014

Web Corpus Construction
Roland Schäfer and Felix Bildhauer
2013

Recognizing Textual Entailment: Models and Applications
Ido Dagan, Dan Roth, Mark Sammons, and Fabio Massimo Zanzotto
2013

Linguistic Fundamentals for Natural Language Processing: 100 Essentials from Morphology and Syntax
Emily M. Bender
2013

Semi-Supervised Learning and Domain Adaptation in Natural Language Processing
Anders Søgaard
2013

Semantic Relations Between Nominals
Vivi Nastase, Preslav Nakov, Diarmuid Ó Séaghdha, and Stan Szpakowicz
2013

Computational Modeling of Narrative
Inderjeet Mani
2012

Natural Language Processing for Historical Texts
Michael Piotrowski
2012

Sentiment Analysis and Opinion Mining
Bing Liu
2012

Discourse Processing
Manfred Stede
2011

Bitext Alignment
Jörg Tiedemann
2011

Linguistic Structure Prediction
Noah A. Smith
2011

Learning to Rank for Information Retrieval and Natural Language Processing
Hang Li
2011

Computational Modeling of Human Language Acquisition
Afra Alishahi
2010

Introduction to Arabic Natural Language Processing
Nizar Y. Habash
2010

Cross-Language Information Retrieval
Jian-Yun Nie
2010

Automated Grammatical Error Detection for Language Learners
Claudia Leacock, Martin Chodorow, Michael Gamon, and Joel Tetreault
2010

Conversational AI: Dialogue Systems, Conversational Agents, and Chatbots

Michael McTear

ISBN: 978-3-031-01048-4 paperback
ISBN: 978-3-031-02176-3 ebook
ISBN: 978-3-031-00187-1 hardcover

DOI 10.1007/978-3-031-02176-3

A Publication in the Springer series
SYNTHESIS LECTURES ON ADVANCES IN AUTOMOTIVE TECHNOLOGY

Lecture #48
Series Editor: Graeme Hirst, *University of Toronto*
Series ISSN
Print 1947-4040 Electronic 1947-4059

Conversational AI

Dialogue Systems, Conversational Agents, and Chatbots

Michael McTear
Ulster University

SYNTHESIS LECTURES ON HUMAN LANGUAGE TECHNOLOGIES #48

ABSTRACT

This book provides a comprehensive introduction to Conversational AI. While the idea of interacting with a computer using voice or text goes back a long way, it is only in recent years that this idea has become a reality with the emergence of digital personal assistants, smart speakers, and chatbots. Advances in AI, particularly in deep learning, along with the availability of massive computing power and vast amounts of data, have led to a new generation of dialogue systems and conversational interfaces. Current research in Conversational AI focuses mainly on the application of machine learning and statistical data-driven approaches to the development of dialogue systems. However, it is important to be aware of previous achievements in dialogue technology and to consider to what extent they might be relevant to current research and development. Three main approaches to the development of dialogue systems are reviewed: rule-based systems that are handcrafted using best practice guidelines; statistical data-driven systems based on machine learning; and neural dialogue systems based on end-to-end learning. Evaluating the performance and usability of dialogue systems has become an important topic in its own right, and a variety of evaluation metrics and frameworks are described. Finally, a number of challenges for future research are considered, including: multimodality in dialogue systems, visual dialogue; data efficient dialogue model learning; using knowledge graphs; discourse and dialogue phenomena; hybrid approaches to dialogue systems development; dialogue with social robots and in the Internet of Things; and social and ethical issues.

KEYWORDS

conversational interface, dialogue system, voice user interface, embodied conversational agent, chatbot, deep learning, data-driven, statistical, end-to-end learning, evaluation metrics, performance evaluation, usability, multimodality, hybrid systems, ethical issues

Contents

Preface

Conversational AI has been defined as "the study of techniques for creating software agents that can engage in natural conversational interactions with humans" [Khatri et al., 2018a]. While the idea of interacting with a computer using text or voice has been around for a long time, it is only recently that it has become a reality. Nowadays, people can talk to digital personal assistants on their smartphones, they can ask questions or issue commands to voice-enabled smart speakers, and they can navigate using voice-based systems in their cars. In other words, Conversational AI has become ubiquitous. Various terms are used in the literature to describe these systems, for example, *Dialogue System*, *Voice User Interface*, *Conversational Agent*, and *Chatbot*. In this book, the generic term *Dialogue System* will be used.

The aim of the book is to provide a readable introduction to the various concepts, issues, and technologies of Conversational AI along with a comprehensive list of references for those who wish to delve further. The book is mainly targeted at researchers and graduate students in Artificial Intelligence, Natural Language Processing, Human-Computer Interaction, and Conversational AI.

The structure of the book is as follows. Chapter 1 provides an introduction to dialogue systems, beginning with a brief history of different types of systems and then looking at present-day systems and what is required to model conversational interaction. Traditionally, dialogue systems were handcrafted: designers created rules for conversational interaction based on best practice guidelines. Chapter 2 describes the rule-based approach, presenting first the sub-components of a typical modularised architecture, then looking at the processes of development and reviewing some currently available toolkits that can be used to develop dialogue systems.

While the rule-based approach is still used extensively, particularly for commercially deployed dialogue systems, the current trend in academic research as well as in industrial research laboratories is dominated by statistical approaches using machine learning and large corpora of conversational data. Chapter 3 describes statistical approaches applied to the sub-components of the typical modular architecture, including Reinforcement Learning for dialogue management.

Chapter 4 looks at the question of how to evaluate a dialogue system, beginning with a comparison of laboratory-based evaluations and those conducted in more realistic settings. Until recently, task-oriented dialogue systems have been the focus of academic research and also in commercially deployed voice user interfaces, and a variety of evaluation metrics have been devised for these applications. With a new focus on open-domain non-task-oriented dialogue systems new metrics have been proposed and applied in various challenges and competitions for Conversational AI. The chapter concludes by reviewing some frameworks that aim to integrate some of these metrics into a unified system of evaluation.

Chapter 5 reviews the latest research in neural dialogue systems that have come to dominate the field. Neural dialogue systems are trained end-to-end using the Sequence-to-Sequence (seq2seq) approach. The chapter provides a fairly non-technical overview of the technology of neural dialogue and examines what has been achieved within this new paradigm as well as issues that are the focus of ongoing research.

Conversational AI is a rapidly developing field, with a lot of open issues and opportunities. Chapter 6 explores some challenges and areas for further development, including multimodal dialogue systems, visual dialogue, data efficiency in dialogue model learning, the use of external knowledge, how to make dialogue systems more intelligent by incorporating reasoning and collaborative problem solving, discourse and dialogue phenomena, hybrid approaches to dialogue systems development, dialogues with social robots and with the Internet of Things, and social and ethical issues.

Michael McTear
October 2020

Acknowledgments

During the course of writing this book, I have seen how Conversational AI has developed into a fast-moving field with new research papers appearing on a weekly basis. The field has come a long way since when I published a book on conversational computers in the 1980s. At that time, I was seen as a bit of an oddity for thinking that some day we would be able to talk to computers the way we now interact with our smartphones and smart speakers.

Over the years, I have learned a lot about conversational computers. I have benefited from meeting colleagues and friends at academic conferences such as Interspeech, SigDial, and IWSDS, including: Zoraida Callejas, David Griol, Kristiina Jokinen, Ramón López-Cózar, Wolfgang Minker, Sebastian Möller, Oliver Lemon, Verena Rieser, Alex Rudnicky, Gabriel Skantze, David Traum, Stefan Ultes, Jason Williams, and Steve Young.

In recent years, I have attended and presented at industrial conferences such as SpeechTEK, Conversational Interaction, ProjectVoice, and the RE·WORK AI Assistant Summits, where I have met and learned from colleagues including: David Attwater, Gérard Chollet, Deborah Dahl, Jim Larson, William Meisel, Robert J. Moore, Andy Peart, Wolf Paulus, and Bill Scholz.

I have also received support and encouragement from colleagues at Ulster University, in particular Maurice Mulvenna, Raymond Bond, Paul McKevitt, and Jonathan Wallace, as well as researchers Gillian Cameron, Sam Holmes, Paddy McAllister, Courtney Potts, Bronagh Quigley, and Shay van Dam.

A first draft of the book was reviewed by Oliver Lemon and an anonymous second reviewer, who both provided detailed comments and suggestions for improvements. I also received helpful comments from my close colleagues Zoraida Callejas and David Griol. Kristiina Jokinen provided comments on an earlier version of Chapters 1 and 2. Any deficiencies that remain are mine.

I would also like to acknowledge the ongoing support I received from Morgan & Claypool, including Michael Morgan, Publisher, Christine Kiilerich, Assistant Editor, and Graeme Hirst, Series Editor of the Synthesis Lectures on Human Language Technologies. Dr. C.L. Tondo helped me out on numerous occasions with problems I was encountering in LaTeX.

My wife, Sandra, supported and encouraged me throughout and never complained when I withdrew to my study in the attic to work on the book.

Finally, I would like to dedicate the book to my children Siobhan, Paul, Anna, and Rachel, and grandchildren Dylan, Sofia, Ethan, Olivia, and Cillian.

Michael McTear
October 2020

Glossary

alignment Alignment is where two words, phrases, or sentences are compared to discover relationships and similarities between them. Alignment is used extensively in machine translation to find relationships between the words and phrases in two languages and to evaluate the accuracy of the translation. Alignment is less applicable in dialogue systems as typically there can be a wide range of responses to a previous utterance in a dialogue and the responses do not usually use the same words as the previous utterance. For this reason alignment is less useful for evaluating the system's responses in a dialogue. 136

AMT Amazon Mechanical Turk is a crowdsourcing application for researchers and businesses through which they can recruit temporary workers to conduct research and other tasks virtually. 95

anaphoric reference Anaphoric reference is when a word or phrase refers to something mentioned previously. The use of pronouns and words such as *there* to refer back are examples of anaphoric reference. 15, 21, 32, 39, 64, 160

backchannels In conversation a backchannel is when one participant is speaking and the other produces verbal expressions such as *yeah*, *uh-huh*, and *right*, or nonverbal behaviors such as nodding, or combinations of verbal and nonverbal behaviors. Backchannel behaviors indicate agreement, understanding, acknowledgement, or attention and are not intended as attempts to take the turn from the current speaker. 176

beam search Beam search is an algorithm that expands the most promising node in a graph, optimizing the search and reducing memory requirements. Beam search is often used to maintain tractability in applications where the search would otherwise become intractable. For example, beam search may be used in response generation in a dialogue system where decoding the most likely sequence would require searching through all possible output sequences. Beam search returns a list of the most likely output sequences up to a predetermined limit. In contrast, greedy search selects the most likely word at each step in the decoding, with the result that the search is fast but not necessarily optimal. 144

CFG A Context-Free Grammar, also known as Phrase Structure Grammar, analyses sentences in terms of phrases and words and models sentence structure hierarchically in a parse tree. For examples, see Figures 2.2 and 3.3. 46

coherence Coherence is what makes a text meaningful where ideas are connected logically to create meaning and maintain consistency. 64, 99, 109, 111, 145, 146, 148

cohesion Cohesion refers to features in a text that link items together. Lexical cohesion involves the use of repetition or words that are synonyms, hyponyms, or antonyms. Grammatical cohesion involves the use of expressions for anaphoric reference such as pronouns. 64

conditional random fields Conditional random fields (CRFs) are used in pattern recognition and machine learning for structured prediction, for example, in sequence tagging to identify elements in a sentence such as parts-of-speech or entities. 75

conversation flow Conversation flow, also known as dialogue flow, can be represented visually as a graph. Conversation flow specifies the flow of a conversation from a starting point to a finishing point, including branches where the conversation can go in different directions. Conversation flow graphs are used widely by designers to specify the actions and steps in a conversation. 40, 53–55, 64, 107, 136

cosine similarity Cosine similarity is used to calculate the similarity between word vectors in multidimensional space by measuring the cosine of the angle between them. Vectors that are more similar have a smaller angle between them. 132, 147

deictic A deictic expression is a word or phrase that points to the time, place, or situation in which a speaker is speaking. Resolving deictic expressions depends on context. In a physical setting a deictic expression may be accompanied by pointing. Deixis is expressed in English using demonstratives such as *this* and *that*, personal pronouns such as *he* and *she*, adverbs such as *here* and *there*, expressions of time, e.g., *now* and *when* and tense, e.g., *he had gone*, which describes a time relative to some other time. 174

dialogue flow Dialogue flow, which can be represented visually as a graph, specifies the flow of a dialogue from a starting point to a finishing point, including branches where the dialogue can go in different directions. Dialogue flow graphs are used widely by designers to specify the actions and steps in a dialogue. 25, 49, 54, 61, 94

dialogue policy Dialogue policy refers to the decision-making component of a Dialogue Manager (DM). A policy is a mapping from states in the dialogue to actions to be taken in those states. DM takes an action in each state and receives a reward. The aim is to maximize the final reward. Reinforcement Learning (RL) is used to learn a policy that maximizes the rewards by learning to take the best actions in each state of the dialogue. 66, 71, 72, 79, 88, 99

dialogue state tracking Dialogue state tracking, also known as belief state tracking, is a core element of the dialogue management component. The dialogue state represents all aspects of the interaction that are relevant for the system's choice of its next action. The dialogue state tracker updates the dialogue state as a result of new observations, such as the user's utterances or other events that are relevant to the dialogue. Dialogue state tracking becomes intractable in large dialogue systems as the number of states to be tracked becomes very large. Addressing this issue has been a major focus in dialogue systems research. Dialogue state tracking has been investigated in a number of challenges Dialogue State Tracking Challenge (DSTC) in which different approaches to Dialogue state tracking are compared and evaluated. 18, 72, 77, 84, 86, 99, 153, 154

discriminative A discriminative model is used for classification and regression tasks in supervised machine learning tasks. The model finds a decision boundary between classes. For example, if a classification task involves distinguishing between pictures of cars and vans, the model will be able to decide if a given picture shows a car or a van based on the most similar examples from the training data. Discriminative models are contrasted with generative models. 4, 99

entity In Natural Language Processing an entity is an object that is named in an utterance that is relevant to the application. For example, in a flight booking application there would be entities for **destination**, **origin**, **date**, **time**, and so on. The Natural Language Understanding component extracts values for these entities during the dialogue. Some platforms use the term *slot*. Extracting entities in a text is called *Entity Extraction*. See also named entity. 5, 32, 68, 69, 97, 112

F1 In statistical analysis F1 (also known as F-score or F-measure) is a measure of the accuracy of a test. F1 measures the balance (or harmonic mean) between precision and recall, where adjusting one of the measures to improve it will often result in lowering the score for the other. For example, improving precision can result in a lower score for recall, and vice versa. The highest possible value of F1 is 1, indicating perfect precision and recall. 98, 113, 121, 180

few-shot learning Few-shot learning in natural language processing refers to the learning of tasks using a small number of examples. Few-shot learning addresses the problem of data sparseness in machine learning. A more extreme case is one-shot learning in which one, or a few, examples are used to create a model capable of classifying many examples in the future. 78, 144, 166

FIA The form interpretation algorithm (FIA) is used in VoiceXML to process forms. There are three phases. In the *select* phase the next unfilled form is selected. In the *collect* phase the user is prompted for input using appropriate grammars and the system waits for the user's input. In the *process* phase the input is processed by filling form items (e.g., fields) and executing other actions such as input validation or response to events. Platforms such as Dialogflow, Amazon Lex, and IBM Watson Assistant use a similar a algorithm in slot-filling dialogues. 57

finite state dialogue In a finite state dialogue the flow of the dialogue is modeled as a finite-state-machine that specifies the complete dialogue flow. The finite state machine specifies all the states that the dialogue can be in and all possible transitions between the states. A dialogue flow graph is a visual representation of a finite state dialogue. 18

finite state grammar A finite state grammar is a simple grammar that analyses sentences word by word in a linear fashion. A finite state grammar can be used to analyze simple inputs in a dialogue system. 45

Gaussian Process A Gaussian process (GP) is a nonparametric model that is used when the distribution of data cannot be defined in terms of a finite set of parameters. GP is useful for modeling uncertainty. 88

generative A generative model is used in classification tasks in supervised machine learning. In contrast to a discriminative model that distinguishes between classes, e.g., to separate pictures of cars from pictures of vans, a generative model is able to produce a new picture of either class. Generative models are often used to find the hidden parameters of a distribution, whereas discriminative models are used to find the boundary that separates the data into different classes. 3, 99

intent An intent is a representation of the intention of the user in an application. For example, the utterance *I want to book a flight to London* could be labeled as the intent **book_flight**. Generally, the developer defines the intents to be used in an application and supplies a list of utterances that can express each intent. Most toolkits offer system intents for commonly used intents. Intents are detected from utterances using machine learning, i.e., classification, which is a probabilistic approach with the advantage that the utterances of the user do not have to exactly match the utterances defined for an intent, thus providing greater flexibility than a rule-based grammar. 47, 60–62, 65, 67, 68, 70, 75, 76, 85, 97, 139

knowledge graph A knowledge graph represents relationships between objects, concepts, or events in a domain. A knowledge graph models specific items and their relationships in contrast to an ontology which models general items and their relationships. In other words, a knowledge graph is an ontology with data. Large knowledge graphs model billions of entities and their relationships and are usually multi-domain. 5, 49, 167, 168, 170, 177

language model A language model is a probability distribution over sequences of words. A language model is used to estimate how probable different words and phrases are. Language models have been used extensively in speech recognition and in natural language understanding to help distinguish between words and phrases that sound similar. For example, *to*, *too*, and *two* sound the same but have different meanings and different usage in a text. Very large language models have been created, such as Google's BERT, Microsoft's Turing NLG, and OpenAI's GPT-3, and are now being used in a wide variety of Natural Language Processing tasks. These language models are able to produce text that is in many cases indistinguishable from human-produced text. 5, 45, 128, 149, 158

language modeling See language model. 134, 139, 144

maximum likelihood Maximum likelihood estimation (MLE) is a method (or function) that is used to determine the values of the parameters of a machine learning model from a data sample so that under the model the observed data is most probable. 129, 147

N-best An N-best list is an ordered list of hypotheses, for example, of recognition results from the speech recognition component. In many cases the 1st-best hypothesis is selected by default, but it is also possible to re-score the N-best list to retrieve the correct word based on information from other component of the system, such as semantic or contextual information. 44, 45, 48, 83

N-gram An N-gram is a sequence of N words, e.g., a bigram is a sequence of two words, a trigram is a sequence of three words, etc. N-grams are used in language modeling to predict the probability of the next word in a sequence. The probabilities are learned from a large corpus of data (sentences). N-grams are used in applications such as auto-completion in emails and spell checking. 45, 79, 128, 147

named entity A named entity is a real word object such as a person, location, organization, etc. that is referred to with a proper name, e.g., Boris Johnston, London, etc. Named entities are instances of entities. For example, in the sentence *Boris Johnston is an instance of Prime Minister of the UK*, *Boris Johnston* and *UK* are examples of named entities and *Prime Minister* is an example of an entity. Recognizing named entities in a text is called *Named Entity Recognition*. See also entity. 3, 68

ontology An ontology, as used in computer science and the Semantic Web, is a formal representation of the relationship between concepts or entities within a domain. For example, in medicine an ontology would represent knowledge about symptoms, diseases, and treatments. An ontology models general entities and their relationships and is typically curated by hand for a specific domain, whereas a knowledge graph models specific items and their relationships, often in multiple domains. However, often the terms are used interchangeably. 4, 49, 168, 177, 178

overfitting Overfitting in machine learning is when a model is too closely fit to the training data. In particular, the model might learn irrelevant details and noise in the training data that are included as concepts in the model. As a result these concepts will not apply when the model is applied to new data so that the performance of the model is adversely affected in terms of its ability to generalize. 161

parse Parsing is a process in which a string of text such as a sentence is analyzed according to the rules of a grammar. Parsing determines if the sentence is correct according to the grammar rules and, in the case of semantic parsing, returns the meaning of the sentence. The result of parsing can be shown in a parse tree, as in Figures 2.2 and 3.3 that show the relationships between phrases and words in the parsed sentence. 1, 6, 46, 73–75, 97

parser A parser is a computer program that creates a parse of a sentence. 47, 73, 75

perplexity Perplexity measures the uncertainty of a language model in terms of the number of choices available when selecting the next token in a sequence, where a lower perplexity indicates greater confidence. 106, 113, 121, 128, 141, 149

precision Precision is the ratio of correctly identified items over all the items detected, reflecting the accuracy of the classification. For example, if 60 items were identified and 40 of them were correct, precision would be 40/60, i.e., 2/3. Precision is usually measured along with recall. 6, 61, 98, 105, 113

Q-function The Q-function in Reinforcement Learning estimates the overall expected reward of taking a particular action in a given state and then following the optimal policy. 6, 83, 87, 88

Q-learning In Reinforcement Learning Q-learning is an algorithm that is used to estimate an optimal policy using the Q-function. The "Q" in Q-learning stands for quality, in other words, it represents how useful an action is in achieving a future reward. Q-learning is applied to and adjusts the Q-values in the system's state space. 87

Q-values Q-values in Reinforcement Learning are the values of each state-action pair. At the start of the learning process the Q-values are initialized to zero and are then updated after each learning episode. 6, 87

recall Recall is the ratio of the items that the system has correctly classified over all the items that should have been identified, reflecting the system's ability to identify as many correct items as possible. For example, if 60 items were identified out of a total of 100 relevant items, recall would be 60/100, i.e., 3/5. Recall is usually measured along with precision. 6, 98, 113

SVM A Support Vector Machine (SVM) is a supervised learning model used in machine learning tasks such as classification and regression tasks. In classification the objective is to separate two classes of data points using a hyperplane (i.e., decision boundary) that shows the maximum distance between the two classes of data points. An SVM model is given sets of training examples for each category and once trained can classify new text. 75

ultimate default category The Ultimate Default Category in Artificial Intelligence Markup Language (AIML) is matched when the dialogue system cannot match the user's utterance against one of its list of categories. The system's response is specified in the <template>, for example, *Sorry I didn't understand that, can you please repeat?* , or *tell me more*. The term **fallback intent** is used on most other platforms. 58–60

Wizard of Oz The Wizard of Oz (WoZ) technique is used in studies of human-computer interaction to collect data about how users interact with an automated system, such as a dialogue system. In the technique the wizard, who is concealed from the user in a laboratory setting, simulates the dialogue system and the user believes that they are interacting with the system. The technique is particularly useful for observing the use and effectiveness of a user interface. The wizard may perform the role of part of the system. For example, the wizard might take the role of the dialogue manager to test different strategies before they have been implemented in the system. 53, 70, 77, 139

zero-shot learning Zero-shot learning in natural language processing refers to the learning of tasks for examples that have never been seen during training. Zero-shot learning provides a way to understand the generalization power of the learned representations. 165, 166

Acronyms

AI Artificial Intelligence. 15, 16, 19, 29, 54, 65, 130, 146

AIML Artificial Intelligence Markup Language. 7, 21, 55, 58–60, 67, 69, 179

AMT Amazon Mechanical Turk. 95, 105, 113, *Glossary:* AMT

ASR Automatic Speech Recognition. 17, 18, 29, 45, 46, 48–50, 57, 68, 72, 76, 82, 83, 85, 89, 94, 98, 101, 102

BLEU Bilingual Evaluation Understudy. 104, 105, 149

CFG Context-Free Grammar. 46, 73, *Glossary:* CFG

CSLU Center for Spoken Language Understanding. 18

DAMSL Dialog Markup in Several Layers. 48

DBDC Dialogue Breakdown Detection Challenge. 110, 157

DM Dialogue Manager. 2, 49, 50, 60, 65, 66, 71, 72, 75–78, 82, 88, 98, 99, 101, 175

DNNs Deep Neural Networks. 45, 52, 71, 125

DR Dialogue Register. 77, 78

DSTC Dialogue State Tracking Challenge. 3, 86, 99, 152, 154

ECA Embodied Conversational Agent. 22

FIA Form Interpretation Algorithm. 57, 67, *Glossary:* FIA

GP Gaussian Process. 88, *Glossary:* Gaussian Process

GPT Generative Pre-Training. 21, 130, 139, 140, 144

GRU Gated Recurrent Unit. 135

HMIHY How May I Help You. 19

HMMs Hidden Markov Models. 45

IQ Interaction Quality. 113, 118–120, 122

LSTM Long Short-term Memory. 80, 134, 135, 137, 149, 174

MDP Markov Decision Process. 81–83, 86, 87, 140

ML Machine Learning. 29

MT Machine Translation. 104, 105, 126

NLG Natural Language Generation. 50, 51, 60, 66, 71, 78–81, 99, 100, 175

NLP Natural Language Processing. 3, 5, 29, 144, 145

NLU Natural Language Understanding. 3, 17, 25, 29, 45, 46, 48–51, 57, 60, 61, 66–68, 71–73, 75, 76, 82, 85, 86, 89, 94, 97, 98, 101, 102, 140, 175, 182

NP Noun Phrase. 73

NUC Next Utterance Classification. 105, 106

PARADISE PARAdigm for Dialogue System Evaluation. 82, 113, 114, 116, 122

PDA Personal Digital Assistant. 13, 26, 181, 182

POMDP Partially Observable Markov Decision Process. 83, 84, 86–88, 120

QoE Quality of Experience. 113, 116, 122

RL Reinforcement Learning. 2, 43, 71, 72, 77, 79, 81, 82, 84–86, 88, 99, 140

RNN Recurrent Neural Network. 69, 76, 80, 127, 132–134, 136, 137, 139, 162, 164, 173, 174

SASSI Subjective Assessment of Speech System Interfaces. 102, 103

Seq2Seq Sequence to Sequence. 71, 81, 100, 104, 106, 125–127, 136, 141, 147, 149

SMS Short Messaging Service. 24

SSA Sensibleness and Specificity Average. 106, 112, 121, 122, 141, 142

SSML Speech Synthesis Markup Language. 51, 52, 69

SVM Support Vector Machine. 75, 120, *Glossary:* SVM

TTS Text to Speech Synthesis. 18, 51, 52, 69, 100, 101, 126

US User Satisfaction. 114, 116, 118

UX User Experience. 103

VoiceXML Voice Extensible Markup Language. 20, 35, 47, 52, 54, 55, 57, 58, 63, 66, 67

VP Verb Phrase. 73

VUI Voice User Interfaces. 19, 20

W3C World Wide Web Consortium. 20

WER Word Error Rate. 29, 97, 112

CHAPTER 1
Introducing Dialogue Systems

A dialogue system is a computer program that supports spoken, text-based, or multimodal conversational interactions with humans. Generally, a distinction is made between task-oriented and non-task-oriented dialogue systems. In task-oriented dialogues the human user and the system engage in an interaction to accomplish some task. Example 1.1 is taken from a demo in which Paul Cutsinger (PC), Head of Amazon Alexa Voice Design Education, initiates a dialogue with Alexa to plan a trip and Alexa asks him a series of questions to obtain the information required to complete the task[1]:

Example 1.1

PC: Alexa, open plan my trip.
ALEXA: Where are you planning to go?
PC: I'm going to Portland.
ALEXA: What city are you leaving from?
PC: Seattle.
ALEXA: What date are you flying out?
PC: Next Thursday.
ALEXA: This will be fun. You go from Seattle to Portland on April 27th, 2017.

In non-task-oriented dialogues the human user and the system engage in general conversational interaction (also known as *chit-chat*). Example 1.2 is taken from a conversation with the Mitsuku chatbot.[2]

Example 1.2

USER: How are you today?
MITSUKU: Ah. Everything is going extremely well. How are you?
USER: Not too bad.
MITSUKU: Glad to hear it. What's new?
USER: The weather is not so great today.
MITSUKU: Ah. Where would you rather be?
USER: Somewhere warm and sunny.

[1]The demo can be viewed in this video https://youtu.be/0V_rNKx-P1I.
[2]Conversation recorded at https://www.pandorabots.com/mitsuku/.

MITSUKU: Where? Not too hot I hope.
USER: Perhaps Spain.
MITSUKU: You seem uncertain. Tell me a little about your life in Spain.

In this example Mitsuku engages in a general conversation. Mitsuku reacts to the user's utterances and prompts for further input, simulating the way humans engage in everyday conversations.

This book is about dialogues such as these and the technologies that are used to design, develop, and evaluate them. The current chapter begins with a brief discussion of what a dialogue system is and why researchers and developers are fascinated with the dream of creating a conversational computer. Section 1.2 provides a brief historical review, describing some of the achievements as well as the limitations of earlier dialogue systems. Section 1.3 looks at examples of current systems and how they are deployed on different types of platform and device. Section 1.4 examines what is required for a system to be able to engage in dialogue with human users and to what extent current systems meet this requirement. Finally, Section 1.5 introduces three different approaches that will be described in greater detail in later chapters: the traditional approach in which systems are developed using handcrafted rules; an approach that emerged in the late 1990s in which aspects of dialogue behavior are learned from data rather than handcrafted; and an approach that has come to dominate current dialogue systems research from around 2014 in which dialogue systems are learned from data in an end-to-end fashion using deep neural networks.

1.1 WHAT IS A DIALOGUE SYSTEM?

Although dialogue systems have been around for a long time, it is only recently that they have become mainstream and a part of everyday life for billions of users. It is generally agreed that dialogue systems came of age in 2011 when Apple launched Siri, a personal assistant that supports spoken interactions with smartphone users. Since then dialogue systems have appeared in various forms, as chatbots on channels such as Facebook Messenger, as personal digital assistants on smartphones, for example, Apple's Siri,[3] Google Assistant,[4] Microsoft's Cortana,[5] and Samsung's Bixby;[6] on smart speakers such as Amazon Echo[7] and Google Nest;[8] and as social robots such as Pepper[9] and Furhat [Al Moubayed et al., 2012].

Various terms have been used to describe the dialogue systems that operate on these devices, including: *Personal Digital Assistant*, *Virtual Personal Assistant*, *Conversational Agent*, *Chat-*

[3]https://www.apple.com/siri/
[4]https://assistant.google.com/
[5]https://www.microsoft.com/en-us/cortana
[6]https://www.samsung.com/global/galaxy/what-is/bixby/
[7]https://www.amazon.com/smart-home-devices/b?ie=UTF8&node=9818047011
[8]https://store.google.com/magazine/compare_nest_speakers_displays
[9]https://softbankrobotics.com/

bot, and *Conversational User Interface*. Indeed, the website *chatbots.org* lists 161 synonyms for Conversational AI systems.[10] There is little consistency in the use of these various terms in the research literature and in the media. For example, Chen et al. [2017] use the term *dialogue system* to describe both task-oriented and non-task-oriented systems, while Jurafsky and Martin [2020] distinguish between *dialogue systems* that engage in conversations with users to help complete tasks, and *chatbots* that mimic the conversations characteristic of casual, social interactions between humans. Sarikaya [2017] prefers the term *Personal Digital Assistant (PDA)* to describe multi-purpose dialogue systems that can answer questions from any domain, help with a variety of goal-oriented tasks, and engage in casual conversation. Others, especially in the media, use the term *chatbot* to describe this sort of system.

Rather than attempting to tease out fine distinctions between all these different terms, it is more productive to focus on what all of the terms mentioned here have in common, i.e., that they provide a new type of interface—a *conversational user interface*—that replaces the traditional graphical user interface [McTear et al., 2016]. So now, instead of responding to text and images on a computer screen by clicking and selecting with a mouse, or on a mobile phone screen by using their fingers to tap, pinch, and scroll, users can interact with an interface that allows them to engage with applications in a conversational manner, i.e., by taking turns as in a dialogue.

1.1.1 WHY DEVELOP A DIALOGUE SYSTEM?

There are several reasons why researchers should wish to develop a dialogue system:

- To provide a low barrier entry for users, enabling them to interact in an intuitive way with services, resources, and data on the internet. With dialogue systems there is no need to learn an interface—in theory, at least. The user can say what they want and the assistant can act as a social companion, providing support and entertainment, or in commercial environments, providing customer self service and automated help.

- From a Cognitive Science point of view to address the challenge of how to model human conversational competence computationally as a means of understanding and studying human behavior and social interaction. The ability to converse in a natural manner, provide relevant responses, and understand the partner's emotional state is one of the high-level cognitive skills that enables social bonding and coordination of actions. Communication is based on the agent's cognitive capabilities such as memory, perception, and the ability to plan and learn. Modeling these capabilities computationally is a key challenge in Cognitive Science research.

- To simulate human conversational behavior so that the dialogue system might pass as a human, as in the Turing test and competitions such as the Loebner prize (see Section 1.2.3). Note, however, that being able to fool humans into believing they are talking to a human

[10] https://www.chatbots.org/synonyms/

is not necessarily a requirement for an effective dialogue system. Moreover, there are also ethical concerns with this approach, as people may feel uncomfortable with a dialogue system that is too human-like or that deceives them into thinking that they are interacting with a human. See, for example, initial reactions to Google's Duplex system that sounded so human-like that some users believed they were talking with another human [O'Leary, 2019]. In order to address these concerns, Duplex now starts each voice call by identifying itself as a virtual assistant from Google.

1.2 A BRIEF HISTORY OF DIALOGUE SYSTEMS

Currently, there is a lot of hype about dialogue systems and conversational user interfaces, but it is important to realize that the idea of creating a conversational computer has been around for a long time. For example, Pieraccini [2012] states that the dream of building a machine that could speak, understand speech, and display intelligent behavior can be traced back at least to the early 1700s, while Mayor [2018] describes how the Ancient Greeks imagined robots and other forms of artificial life, and even invented real automated machines.

Historically there have been five distinct traditions in dialogue systems research involving communities that have largely worked independently of one another. These are:

- Text-based and Spoken Dialogue Systems.
- Voice User Interfaces.
- Chatbots.
- Embodied Conversational Agents.
- Social Robots and Situated Agents.

It will be helpful to review the achievements as well as the limitations of these different traditions and to assess their relevance for dialogue systems research and development.

1.2.1 TEXT-BASED AND SPOKEN DIALOGUE SYSTEMS

The term *dialogue system* is generally used to refer to systems developed in research laboratories in universities and industry with the aim of automating text-based and voice-based interactions between machines and human users.

Dialogue systems that appeared in the 1960s and 1970s were text-based. BASEBALL [Green et al., 1961], SHRDLU [Winograd, 1972], and GUS [Bobrow et al., 1977] are some well-known examples. BASEBALL was a question-answering system that could answer questions about baseball games. The system was able to handle questions with a limited syntactic structure and simply rejected questions that it was not able to answer. SHRDLU was linguistically more advanced, incorporating a large grammar of English, semantic knowledge about objects in its domain (a blocks world), and a pragmatic component that processed non-linguistic information about the domain. GUS was a system for booking flights that was able to handle linguistic phenomena such as indirect speech acts and anaphoric reference. For example, the utterance *I want to go to San Diego on May 28* was interpreted as a request to make a flight reservation, and the utterance *the next flight* was interpreted with reference to a previously mentioned flight. GUS used frames to guide the dialogue, for example, with slots for the values of the travel date, destination and so on that the system had to elicit from the user—a technique that is still used widely in today's task-oriented dialogue systems. See McTear [1987] for an overview of these early text-based dialogue systems.

During the late 1970s and early 1980s, dialogue researchers turned their attention to more advanced aspects of dialogue, such as how to recognize the intentions behind a user's utterances, how to behave cooperatively, and how to deal with different types of miscommunication such as misconceptions and false assumptions [Reilly, 1987]. This work was inspired by philosophers of language such as Grice, Austin, and Searle, as well as research in Artificial Intelligence (AI) on plan recognition and plan generation.

Grice [1975] developed a theory of conversation in which he proposed that participants in conversation are expected to observe the Cooperative Principle (CP) which he formulated as follows:

> *Make your contribution such as is required, at the stage at which it occurs, by the accepted purpose or direction of the talk exchange in which you are engaged.*

Based on the CP Grice proposed four conversational maxims: Quantity, Quality, Relation, and Manner that cover, respectively: how much we should say in a conversation; the truth of what we say; how what we say should be relevant; and how we should communicate clearly. These maxims are still being used widely by dialogue designers as general recommendations for how to design conversations with automated systems, for example, by the conversation designers at the Actions on Google website.[11,12]

Austin [1962] and Searle [1969] developed a theory of speech acts based on the observation that when people engage in conversation they do more than simply produce utterances—they perform actions. For example, they ask questions, make promises, pay compliments, and so on. One important insight from Speech Act Theory is that the performance of a speech act requires that certain conditions be fulfilled. For example, for an utterance to be intended as a command by a speaker and understood as such by an addressee, various pre-conditions are required, including the following [Searle, 1969]:

- The hearer is able to perform the requested act.

[11] https://designguidelines.withgoogle.com/conversation/conversation-design/learn-about-conversation.html

[12] Note that Grice's main intention was to use the maxims and the CP as a basis for his theory of *conversational implicature* in order to explain how speakers could flout the maxims in order to convey meanings beyond the literal meanings of their utterances (see discussion in Levinson [1983]).

- The speaker believes that the hearer is able to perform the requested act.
- The speaker wants the hearer to perform the act.
- It is not obvious to the speaker and hearer that the hearer would have done the act in the normal course of events.

In the plan-based model of dialogue that became prominent in the 1980s, speech acts such as requests were formalized as *action schemas* similar to those used in AI models of planning [Allen and Perrault, 1980], [Cohen and Perrault, 1979]. This early work on planning in dialogue was the basis for subsequent theoretical work in dialogue technology such as the BDI (Belief, Desire, Intention) model [Allen, 1995], Information State Update Theory [Traum and Larsson, 2003], and the Constructive Dialogue Modeling theory [Jokinen, 2009]. However, one of the problems with the plan-based approach was that it was computationally complex and in the worst case intractable.

Around the late 1980s and early 1990s, with the emergence of more powerful and more accurate speech recognition engines, Spoken Dialogue Systems (SDSs) began to appear, such as: ATIS (Air Travel Information Service) in the U.S. [Hemphill et al., 1990], and SUNDIAL, a major project funded by the European community [McGlashan et al., 1992]. Later systems include MIT's Mercury [Seneff and Polifroni, 2000], Ravenclaw [Bohus and Rudnicky, 2009], and TRIPS [Allen et al., 2001]. These systems were usually restricted to a single domain, such as flight enquiries or train timetable information, where the system had to elicit several items of information from the user such as departure place, date, and time, destination, and so on, in order to construct a query to retrieve a suitable flight or train from a database. The DARPA Communicator systems were an exception as they investigated multi-domain dialogues involving flight information, hotels, and car rentals [Walker et al., 2001]. These systems often suffered from speech recognition errors and so a major focus was on avoiding miscommunication, for example, by employing various strategies for error detection and correction, including different forms of confirmation. See utterances S2, S3, and S5 in Example 1.3, taken from an interaction with the MIT Mercury system that provides telephone access to an online flights database [Seneff and Polifroni, 2000].

Example 1.3 (U=User, S=System)

S1: How may I help you?
U1: I want to travel to Washington Dulles on November fourth.
S2: From Boston to Washington Dulles on November 4. Can you provide the approximate departure time or airline preference?
U2: I need to arrive at around nine a.m.
S3: Okay. Flights from Boston to Washington Dulles arriving at 9:00 am on November 4.
One moment please.

The best matching flight is a US Airways flight arriving at 8:59 a.m. I also have a United flight arriving at 8:36 a.m.
U3: What time does the United flight leave?
S4: United flight 1819 departs at 7:00 am from Boston. Shall I book this flight for you?
U4: Yes please.
S5: United flight 1819 has been added to your itinerary. You depart Boston at 7:00 am and arrive in Washington Dulles at 8:36 am. Where would you like to go next?
U5: I would like to return to Boston.
S6: What date will you be returning on?
U6: The same day.

The dialogue begins with an open-ended question and continues with questions to elicit further information from the user. Generally, the system controls the dialogue by asking questions but the user is also allowed to take the initiative as in U3. This type of interaction is known as *mixed-initiative dialogue* as both the system and the user can ask questions or add additional information. However, although mixed-initiative dialogue offers a more natural style of interaction, this comes at the cost of more complex processing for the Automatic Speech Recognition (ASR) and Natural Language Understanding (NLU) components, increasing the potential for errors.

Example 1.4 shows an interaction that goes wrong, due mainly to speech recognition errors [Bohus, 2007]. The system's interpretation of the user's input is in square brackets and uppercase).

Example 1.4

S1: What city are you leaving from?
U1: Urbana Champaign [OKAY IN THAT SAME PAY].
S2: Sorry I'm not sure I understood what you said. What city are you leaving from?
U2: Urbana Champaign [FOR MINUTE SINCE HEY].
S3: I'm still having trouble understanding you. To go on, I need you to answer the following question. What city are you leaving from?
U3: Chicago [CHICAGO].
S4: Traveling from Chicago. Where would you like to go?
U4: Huntsville [SEOUL].
S5: Traveling to Seoul. What day did you need to travel?
U5: No no I'm traveling to Birmingham [THE TRAVELING TO BERLIN PM].
S6: Traveling in the afternoon. Okay what day would you be departing Chicago?
U6: Uh the tenth of august [AT THE TENTH OF AUGUST].
S7: A flight tomorrow. I have a Korean Airlines flight departing Chicago at 1:40 p.m., arrives Seoul at 5 p.m. the next day.

In this example the system is unable to correctly recognize the user's spoken input for the departure and arrival cities and also makes errors with the time and date. While speech recognition has improved considerably since this dialogue was recorded, it is still the case that the performance of deployed dialogue systems degrades when dealing with unusual accents, interference on the channel, or background noise [Sahu et al., 2018].

In addition to developments in dialogue theory, one of the major contributions of this earlier research was the production of toolkits to support developers of spoken dialogue systems, including: the Center for Spoken Language Understanding (CSLU) Toolkit [Sutton and Cole, 1997], Trindikit [Larsson and Traum, 2000], and DIPPER [Bos et al., 2003].

The CSLU toolkit was developed as an integration of core speech technologies (Automatic Speech Recognition (ASR) and Text to Speech Synthesis (TTS)) along with facial animation and RAD (Rapid Application Development)—a graphically based authoring environment for designing and implementing spoken dialogue systems using a simple drag-and-drop interface. Thus, researchers with little technical knowledge of speech technology could develop simple spoken dialogue systems quickly and with little effort. The toolkit was used widely in academia to support the teaching of spoken dialogue technology [Cole, 1999], [McTear, 1999]. See also Heeman's course on spoken dialogue systems at CSLU.[13] However, over time the toolkit was superseded by other technologies. RAD supported the development of finite state dialogues but could not be easily extended to include dialogues requiring more complex representations. Moreover, the underlying programming language was Tcl/Tk, which is less familiar to developers, while more recent toolkits are based on languages such as Java, Python, and Node.js.

The aim of Trindikit was to support developers wishing to implement dialogue systems involving Information State Update Theory. DIPPER borrowed many of the core ideas from TrindiKit but also simplified the technology in various ways, for example, by using a revised update language and enabling greater flexibility by integrating the system more tightly with the Object Oriented Architecture (OAA).[14] However, this work on representing the dialogue state has been largely superseded by more recent developments in Dialogue state tracking (see Section 3.3.3).

There are also practical reasons why these early toolkits have not been more widely adopted. In some cases the researchers moved to new positions and became engaged in other projects, or funding dried up so that the project could no longer be maintained. Another factor was a major change in research direction in dialogue technology from symbolic to statistical and machine learning-based approaches, so that more recent toolkits are based on the new paradigm, for example, OpenDial [Lison and Kennington, 2016] and PyDial [Ultes et al., 2017]. Finally, as a consequence of the increased interest of major software companies in this area, new toolkits and development platforms have been created that, while incorporating some of the features

[13] https://cslu.ohsu.edu/~heeman/cs550/
[14] http://www.ai.sri.com/~oaa/main.html

of these earlier examples, are generally easier to use, are more readily available, are not tied to proprietary platforms, and are more robust in performance (see Chapter 2, Section 2.3).

Around 2000 the emphasis in spoken dialogue systems research moved from handcrafted systems using techniques from symbolic and logic-based AI to statistical, data-driven systems using machine learning (see further Chapters 3 and 5). For comprehensive overviews of dialogue systems up to around 2010, see McTear [2004], Jurafsky and Martin [2009], and Jokinen and McTear [2009]. For developments since then, see Rieser and Lemon [2011b], McTear et al. [2016], Celikyilmaz et al. [2018], Gao et al. [2019], and Jurafsky and Martin [2020, Chapter 26].

1.2.2 VOICE USER INTERFACES

Alongside the text-based and spoken dialogue systems from academic and industrial research laboratories, various companies and enterprises were developing systems for commercial deployment to support automated telephone-based customer self-service tasks such as directory assistance, information enquiries, and other routine transactions. These systems became known as *Voice User Interfaces (VUI)* and are still being used widely to provide automated customer support over the telephone.

AT&T's How May I Help You (HMIHY) system is an early example [Gorin et al., 1997]. HMIHY supported call routing by classifying customer calls and routing them to the correct destination, thus reducing the costs of human agents and allowing them to handle more complex interactions. For example, by the end of 2001 HMIHY was handling more than 2 million calls per month and showing significant improvements in customer satisfaction over alternative solutions. HMIHY greets users with an open-ended prompt that encourages fairly free-form spoken language input. The system determines the class of the call from a set of 14 possible classes and one additional class for tasks not covered by the 14 classes and that require transfer to a human operator. The system extracts data relevant to the query either from the initial utterance or from a sub-dialogue. For example: given the user query *I have a query about my bill for October* the system would classify the query as the type **Ask(Bill)** and extract the item **Date** with the value *Ask(October)*. In many cases the dialogues are short: for example, 23% of the dialogues consisted of only two exchanges in a corpus of 4692 dialogues collected in several experimental trials of the system in use with real customers [Walker et al., 2002]. Example 1.5 shows a successful interaction with the HMIHY system [Walker et al., 2002]:

Example 1.5

S1: AT&T: How may I help you?
U1: I need to [uh] put a call on my calling card please.
S2: May I have your card number please?
U2: 7 6 5 4 3 2 1 0 9 8 7 6 5 4
S3: What number would you like to call?

U3: 8 1 4 7 7 7 6 6 6 6 (misunderstood)
S4: May I have that number again?
U4: 8 1 4 7 7 7 6 6 6 6
S5: Thank you.

This example illustrates a more extended dialogue in which, following the classification of the call, the system enters a sub-dialogue to collect values for a set number of attributes relevant to this type of call. The example also illustrates how the system can recover from a misunderstood utterance (U3-S4).

The following are some of the achievements of the Voice User Interface community:

- the development of design and evaluation guidelines for commercially deployed VUI [Cohen et al., 2004], [Lewis, 2016a], [Pearl, 2016];
- the development of standards, such as Voice Extensible Markup Language (VoiceXML)[15,16] for scripting spoken dialogues, and EMMA (Extensible Multimodal Annotation Markup Language)[17] for annotating multi-modal user input (see further, Chapter 2). For a recent book on World Wide Web Consortium (W3C) standards for VUI, see Dahl [2017];
- toolkits such as Voxeo Evolution[18] for developing VoiceXML-based applications;
- speech analytics: the process of mining recorded conversations between a company's service agents and customers to obtain information about the quality of the interaction, agent performance, customer engagement, and other factors that determine customer satisfaction and loyalty;[19] and
- usability testing: the application of effective metrics and methods for testing the usability of VUI [Hura, 2017].

1.2.3 CHATBOTS

Chatbots, also known as chatterbots, were created originally as attempts to simulate human conversations. ELIZA is generally viewed as the first chatbot [Weizenbaum, 1966]. ELIZA simulates a Rogerian psychotherapist, often in a convincing way, and has inspired many generations of chatbot authors for whom a major motivation is to develop a system that can pass Turing's Imitation Game [Turing, 1950]. The aim of the Imitation Game is to see if a machine can display intelligent behavior by fooling observers of a conversation between a human and a

[15] https://www.w3.org/TR/voicexml20/
[16] https://www.w3.org/TR/voicexml21/
[17] https://www.w3.org/TR/emma/
[18] https://evolution.voxeo.com/
[19] https://www.aspect.com/globalassets/10-best-practices-for-speech-analytics-wp.pdf

chatbot into thinking that the utterances from the chatbot were actually from another human participant. The Loebner Prize Competition,[20] launched in 1991 by Dr. Hugh Loebner, is an implementation of the Turing test. In this competition human users (known as the "judges") take part in text-based conversations on computer terminals with two different unseen conversational partners, one of which is another human (known as the "confederate") and the other a chatbot. After 25 minutes of questioning the judge must decide which conversational partner is the human and which is the chatbot. If a system can fool half the judges that it is human under these conditions, a solid Silver Medal is awarded to the creator of that chatbot, otherwise prizes are awarded to the creators of the chatbots according to the ranked scores of the judges.

The chatbot Mitsuku, which was introduced at the beginning of this chapter, has won the Loebner prize five times. Mitsuku was developed by Steve Worswick using the dialogue scripting language Artificial Intelligence Markup Language (AIML) (see Chapter 2, Section 2.3.2). Examples of chat logs with Mitsuku and additional information can be found at the Mitsuku chatbot website.[21]

Chatbots are being used increasingly in areas such as education, information retrieval, business, and e-commerce, where they act as automated online assistants to complement or even replace the services provided by humans in call centers.

Traditionally, chatbots like Mitsuku as well as the business chatbots developed for e-commerce have been handcrafted using scripting languages such as AIML[22] and ChatScript.[23] A new development that has become a hot topic in Conversational AI is to train open-domain chatbots such as Google's Meena [Adiwardana et al., 2020], Facebook's BlenderBot [Roller et al., 2020], and Open AI's Generative Pre-Training (GPT) models[24] from very large datasets of conversations using neural dialogue technologies (see further Section 1.4.3, and Chapter 5). The achievements of the chatbot community include the following:

- the development of scripting languages such as AIML and ChatScript;
- toolkits and platforms, for example, Pandorabots[25] and PullString;[26]
- advances in technology, such as the use of knowledge repositories to provide some degree of world knowledge as well as discourse mechanisms to provide limited support for and topic tracking;
- the incorporation of mobile functions to enable the deployment of chatbots on smartphones and other smart devices;

[20] https://en.wikipedia.org/wiki/Loebner_Prize
[21] http://www.square-bear.co.uk/mitsuku/home.htm
[22] http://www.aiml.foundation/
[23] https://sourceforge.net/projects/chatscript/
[24] https://openai.com/blog/openai-api/
[25] https://home.pandorabots.com/home.html
[26] https://www.facebook.com/pullstringinc/

- machine learning of conversational patterns from corpora of conversational data [Shawar and Atwell, 2005]; and
- within the past few years the use of neural dialogue technologies to train open-domain chatbots from large datasets of dialogues (see Chapter 5).

1.2.4 EMBODIED CONVERSATIONAL AGENTS

An Embodied Conversational Agent (ECA) is a computer-generated animated character that combines facial expression, body stance, hand gestures, and speech to provide a more human-like and more engaging interaction [André and Pelachaud, 2010],[Cassell et al., 2000]. An ECA takes the form of virtual agents and screen-based characters. Examples are:

- Smartakus, an animated character used in the SmartKom project to present information [Wahlster, 2006];
- REA, a real-time, multi-modal, life-sized ECA that plays the role of a real estate agent [Bickmore and Cassell, 2005]; and
- GRETA, a real-time three dimensional ECA that talks and displays facial expressions, gestures, gaze, and head movements [Niewiadomski et al., 2009].

The achievements of the ECA community include the following:

- advances in technology, such as: how to handle multi-modal input and output, the development of avatars and talking heads, and the production and interpretation of gestures and emotions;
- the development of standards and annotation schemes, such as SAIBA (Situation, Agent, Intention, Behavior, Animation), BML (Behavior Markup Language), FML (Functional Markup Language), MURML (Multi-modal Utterance Representation Language), and EML (Emotion Markup Language). See Dahl [2017] and [Jokinen and Pelachaud, 2013] for descriptions of many of these standards; and
- toolkits, for example, the Virtual Human Toolkit [Gratch et al., 2013] and ACE (Articulated Communicator Engine) [Salem et al., 2010].

For more detailed descriptions of ECAs, see McTear et al. [2016], especially Chapters 13–16.

1.2.5 ROBOTS AND SITUATED AGENTS

Social robots are becoming increasingly popular as companions for the elderly, as educational and entertainment toys for children, as self-service aids in public places, and more. Social robots allow users to perform tasks similar to those provided by a virtual personal assistant on a smartphone or smart speaker. Additionally, because of their physical embodiment, they are expected to possess social qualities such as the ability to recognize and display emotions, and other human-like social cues [Graaf et al., 2015].

Pepper is an example of a social robot that can recognize emotions based on characteristics of the user's voice, facial expression, and body movements.[27] Pepper can adapt its behavior to suit the situation and display empathy. For example, Pepper is used to greet guests in a hotel lobby to perform check-in either through dialogue or by getting the guest to use a touchscreen on its chest, which is useful if Pepper is unable to understand the guest's spoken input. Pepper can also engage in basic conversation. For example, in the hotel lobby scenario it can handle questions about room confirmation or enquire whether the guest requires help with their bags.

Mummer (MultiModal Mall Entertainment Robot)[28] is a four-year European Union (EU)-funded project with the overall goal of developing a social robot based on Softbank's Pepper platform [Foster et al., 2019]. The robot is designed to interact with users in a public shopping mall in a natural and engaging manner, combining spoken interaction with non-verbal communication and human-aware navigation. The technologies being investigated include: audio-visual sensing, social signal processing, conversational interaction, perspective taking, geometric reasoning, and motion planning.

SARA (Socially Aware Robot Assistant), developed in Carnegie Mellon University's ArticuLab, also recognizes and displays emotions [Matsuyama et al., 2016]. SARA studies the words a person says during a conversation as well as the tone of their voice, and feeds these cues into a program that determines an appropriate response designed to build a feeling of rapport with a person and to improve task performance.

Other examples of social robots are Professor Einstein, a physics tutor,[29] Leka, a robot that provides help and companionship for children with autism,[30] and Furhat, a robotic head based on a projection system that renders facial expressions, with motors to move the neck and head [Al Moubayed et al., 2012].

1.2.6 LIMITATIONS OF EARLY DIALOGUE SYSTEMS

While there is much to be learned from the achievements of these early dialogue systems, in many cases they suffered from one or more of the following limitations:

- they were often extremely brittle and would fall over or crash if there was the slightest deviation from the expected input;
- the systems worked well for the purposes for which they were designed but did not scale up or transfer easily to other domains;
- dialogue decisions were handcrafted and could not be guaranteed to be optimal;

[27] https://www.wired.com/story/pepper-the-humanoid-robot/
[28] http://mummer-project.eu/
[29] https://www.hansonrobotics.com/professor-einstein/
[30] https://www.leka.io/

- the systems were often developed using proprietary toolkits and languages that were not always openly available and that were often based on particular theories of dialogue;
- they were deployed on specialized platforms and could not be easily ported to other domains or deployed on other platforms; and
- they focused only on spoken or written language and didn't consider other modalities that are important in natural communication.

Many of these issues have been addressed in the current generation of dialogue systems.

1.3 PRESENT-DAY DIALOGUE SYSTEMS

Whereas dialogue systems previously existed either on specially dedicated servers in academic and industrial research laboratories or as telephone-based voice user interfaces, now they can be encountered on a wide variety of platforms and devices that are available to the general public. Dialogue systems can take the form of messaging apps on smartphones, PCs, and tablets; they can act as personal digital assistants on smartphones; and more recently they are to be found as voice-based assistants on smart speakers. We can also have dialogues with social robots and with smart devices in the home, in the car, and elsewhere.

1.3.1 DIALOGUE SYSTEMS ON MESSAGING PLATFORMS

In his keynote address at Microsoft Build 2016, Microsoft CEO Satya Nadella announced that "chatbots are the new app". Also in 2016, Facebook launched their Messenger-based chatbot platform. Suddenly the term *chatbot* re-emerged as the label for a new type of user interface that allows users to interact with services and brands using a conversational interface on their favorite messaging apps [Shevat, 2017].

One of the advantages of chatbots is that they can run on messaging applications such as Facebook Messenger, Telegram, Slack, Skype, Line, and WhatsApp that are widely used by millions of people to interact with friends, colleagues, and the services of companies. This means that it is not necessary to download and install a different app for each new service. Furthermore, since chatbots live within messaging applications, there is no need to worry about platform issues, as each chatbot can be available on all operating systems that are supported by the messaging app. In contrast, native mobile apps have to be adapted or rewritten for each mobile operating system and they need to be frequently updated to keep up with upgrades to the host system and its features. Since chatbots are implemented server-side, any updates can be propagated almost immediately to all users. The chatbot interface is similar to text messaging (SMS), except that the interaction takes place synchronously in real time and the other participant in the conversation is a chatbot and not a human. Generally, chatbot dialogues on messaging platforms are system-led and the user's responses are often limited to clicking on buttons containing pre-defined words and phrases (known as *Quick Replies* or *Suggestion Chips*). In

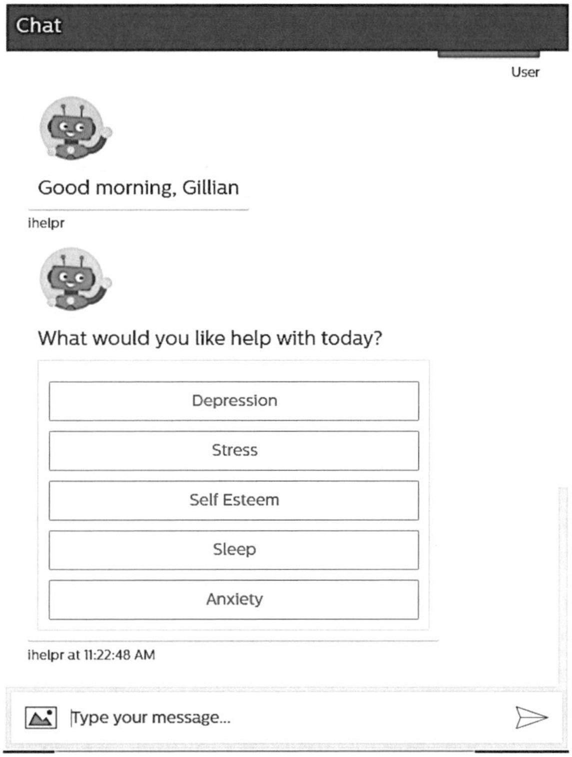

Figure 1.1: A chatbot with Quick Replies. Used with permission.

some cases the user can also type in a few words from a fixed set of possible inputs. Figure 1.1 shows an example from the iHelpr chatbot that provides guided self-assessment and advice in areas of mental health [Cameron et al., 2018]. Natural Language Understanding (NLU) can be used in more advanced systems to interpret the user's free text inputs, giving the user the opportunity to "say what they want and how they want", without being restricted to a fixed set of commands or queries. For example, in iHelpr Microsoft's Language Understanding Intelligent Service (LUIS)[31] was used to extract intents from the free-form utterances of the users.

In many simple chatbots the output takes the form of text, although nowadays many chatbot platforms support rich messages for delivering audio, video, images, maps, charts, buttons, emojis, and persistent menus.

The dialogue flow can vary across applications. In the simplest cases the entire dialogue flow is pre-determined and designed using a graphical flow chart (see Chapter 2). In other cases the dialogue flow may be more open-ended and evolve dynamically according to the context.

[31] https://www.luis.ai/

Chatbot conversation on messaging platforms is thread-centric. Messages are grouped automatically according to the sender, so that the thread of a conversation can be maintained and users can easily locate all the messages from a particular sender. In this way the dialogues maintain some permanence in contrast to voice-only dialogues that are transient.

Most chatbots are designed to connect to a specific service, such as news, weather, hotel bookings, or flight reservations. A notable exception is WeChat, a Chinese multi-purpose chatbot developed by Tencent.[32] With WeChat it is possible to accomplish many tasks, such as ordering flowers, making dinner reservations, ordering pizza, and making payments, all within the same interface.

1.3.2 DIALOGUE SYSTEMS ON SMARTPHONES

Dialogue systems on smartphones are often known as Personal Digital Assistants (PDAs) [Sarikaya, 2017] or Voicebots [Batish, 2018]. Examples include Apple's Siri, Microsoft's Cortana, Google Assistant, Samsung's Bixby, and others. A PDA on a smartphone supports a range of modes of interaction, including text input and output, speech-to-text, text-to-speech, as well as direct manipulation, for example, by allowing the user to make selections from a set of options by tapping. A PDA can also display images, and play audio or video clips.

PDAs on smartphones can also make use of information about the user, for example, user preferences, location, and information from sensors that has been collected on the phone. This enables the PDA to provide more intelligent and more personalized assistance, both proactively (for example, to provide reminders) and reactively (for example, to respond to the user's queries). Ideally, according to Sarikaya [2017], PDAs should be able to answer questions from any domain by accessing a range of different knowledge sources. They should also support the execution of goal-oriented tasks and they should have the ability to engage in conversations involving chit-chat. Current PDAs only support these functionalities to a limited extent.

Dialogues with PDAs can take a variety of different forms. When answering the user's questions, the dialogue takes the form of a *one-shot exchange* involving the user's question and the system's response. More recently, follow-up questions have been supported (see Section 1.4.1 and Chapter 2, Section 2.3.2). For task-oriented dialogues, once the user has activated a particular service, the system takes over and asks a series of questions to elicit required information from the user—for example, with a hotel booking application the dates of the booking, how many guests, the type of room, etc. This is known as *slot-filling*, since the information required to complete the transaction is gathered into a data structure containing a number of slots to be filled. Finally, in chit-chat type interactions the dialogue may continue for as long as the user wishes, resulting in a *multi-turn dialogue*.

[32] https://web.wechat.com/

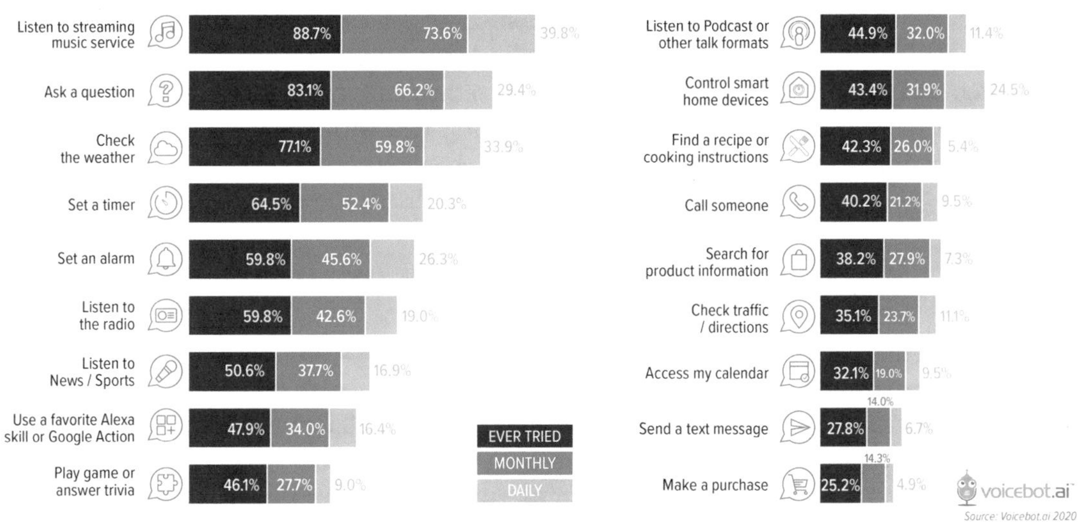

Figure 1.2: Smart Speaker Use Case Frequency, January 2020. Source: Voicebot Smart Speaker Consumer Adoption Report Executive Summary p. 9, April 2020. Used with permission.

1.3.3 DIALOGUE SYSTEMS ON SMART SPEAKERS AND OTHER DEVICES

Dialogues on smart speakers with assistants such as Amazon Alexa or Google Assistant are similar to those provided by PDAs on smartphones except that on some of the devices the interaction mode is voice-only. Naturally this places some restrictions on the interactions as everything has to be communicated by voice, including dealing with recognition issues and other problems that previously also affected telephone-based voice user interfaces. Recently, both Amazon and Google have released smart speakers with displays, such as Amazon Echo Show and Google Nest Hub in which voice interaction is integrated with a visual display on touch-sensitive screens. Smart speakers have become extremely popular. In a recent survey it was reported that in 2019 nearly 1 in 3 U.S. adults, i.e., 88.7 million adults, have access to a smart speaker.[33] Smart speakers are used for a wide variety of tasks, as shown in Figure 1.2. The most frequent tasks are similar to those provided by assistants on smartphones, such as requesting music, asking questions, and checking the weather. In the future it is predicted that voice assistants will be used increasingly to control smart appliances in the home such as thermostats, cookers, and dishwashers. For example, at CES2019, the world's largest exhibition for new consumer technologies, various

[33] https://research.voicebot.ai/download-smart-speaker-consumer-adoption-2020-executive-summary/

voice-activated devices were displayed, such as an Alexa-activated toilet flush, voice-controlled pianos, heart rate monitors, lawnmowers, and motorcycle helmets, and for the kitchen, a smart speaker with display providing visual and audio walkthroughs of cooking recipes.

Dialogue is also available on a number of wearable devices. For example, smart watches provide many of the functions that are also available on smartphones, such as notifications, messaging, navigation, and search. Users can speak to their smart watches as well as tapping on items on the screen and swiping displayed cards. Compared with smartphones the display on a smart watch is much smaller. This has a bearing on how much information can be displayed visually. See McTear et al. [2016], Chapter 13 for more discussion of dialogues with wearable devices.

1.3.4 DIALOGUE SYSTEMS IN CARS

Voice-based systems have become a standard feature in many new vehicles, motivated primarily by a need to keep people safe by allowing drivers to communicate with devices in the car without taking their eyes off the road or their hands off the steering wheel. Drivers can obtain directions, send emails, make phone calls, and play music using voice commands.

There are several voice-based systems for cars, including Apple CarPlay,[34] which contains a fully integrated version of Siri; Google Android Auto;[35] Nuance Dragon Drive,[36] and several brand-specific devices.

Dialogue in cars is more or less limited at present to voice commands that activate and control some of the car's features, such as environmental controls. Recently, Amazon Alexa and Google Assistant have been integrated into certain cars. In Fiat Chrysler cars Alexa can be used to start the car remotely, lock and unlock the doors, find the nearest gas station, say how much gas is left in the car, and provide information about the car's type pressures.[37] Similar commands are available in Ford cars. Google Assistant is integrated into the Android Auto smartphone projection technology and is available in a number of cars, including Acura, Alfa Romeo, Audi, Hyundai, Jeep, Kia, and Mercedes-Benz.[38] Google Assistant can be used to carry out several tasks, including navigation, finding gas stations, consulting the driver's calendar, reading incoming text messages, issuing reminders from the calendar, playing music and accessing radio stations, providing opening hours of businesses and restaurants and providing information on topics such as music and sports. It is also possible with Alexa and Google Assistant to control devices in the home such as thermostats, lights, and intruder alarms remotely from the car.

[34] https://www.apple.com/uk/ios/carplay/

[35] https://www.android.com/auto/

[36] https://www.nuance.com/about-us/newsroom/press-releases/nuance-announces-new-ai-powered-dragon-drive-features.html

[37] https://www.amazon.com/FCA-Chrysler/dp/B07DD2NSSW

[38] https://assistant.google.com/platforms/cars/

1.3.5 HOW CURRENT DIALOGUE SYSTEMS ARE DIFFERENT

Current dialogue systems have addressed many of the limitations of earlier systems:

- they can be developed and deployed on messaging apps such as Facebook Messenger, Slack, or Skype that users are already familiar with;
- they work seamlessly across multiple devices and platforms;
- the user does not need to download and install separate apps for each application;
- in many cases the systems have access to contextual information about users, such as their location, health, and other data that may have been acquired through sensors. This allows them to provide a more personalized experience for each user;
- the systems can often learn from experience in contrast with earlier systems that were static and did not alter or improve their behavior over time;
- many systems, especially robot agents, have multi-modal interaction capability and they can effectively analyze gaze signals, gesturing, nodding, and body posture. Generating appropriate multi-modal behavior has been extensively studied with ECAs and social robots; and
- a number of toolkits have become available that incorporate the latest developments in Artificial Intelligence (AI), Machine Learning (ML), and Natural Language Processing (NLP), and provide an intuitive and easy-to-learn resource for developers (see Chapter 2, Section 2.3.3).

There are also various technological drivers that have facilitated the development and deployment of this new generation of dialogue systems:

- advances in ASR, driven by the application of deep learning and resulting in dramatic reductions in Word Error Rate (WER), making spoken dialogue systems really possible;
- advances in NLU, also as a result of the application of deep neural networks;
- greater computing processing power to support the massive parallel computations required to run deep neural networks;
- the availability of vast amounts of data that enable AI systems to learn and become increasingly more intelligent;
- increased connectivity, allowing users to connect their smart devices to vast cloud-based resources;
- advances in computer vision, eye-tracking, and video processing; and

- the interest of the major technology companies in chatbots and conversational interfaces, enabling them to more accurately profile their users and thus gain a competitive advantage in the promotion of their e-commerce services. For example, the global research and advisory firm Gartner has predicted that 25% of all customer services operations will use virtual customer assistants by 2020.

1.4 MODELING CONVERSATION IN DIALOGUE SYSTEMS

Conversational interactions in current systems fall into three distinct types in terms of the types of interaction they support and which participant initiates and controls the dialogue.

- *User-initiated dialogues*: Interactions initiated by the user are typical of the way users interact with smart speakers and virtual assistants. The interaction is usually brief, consisting of a two-turn exchange in which the user asks a question or issues a command and the system responds.
- *System-directed dialogues*: In these interactions the system controls the dialogue. There are several types of system-directed dialogue:
    1. dialogues in which the system initiates the interaction proactively, for example, to deliver a reminder to a care recipient to take their medication;
    2. dialogues initiated by a user seeking instructions, for example, in an online recipe application, where the system provides a set of instructions with little input from the user, except to ask for the next instruction or for an instruction to be repeated; and
    3. dialogues initiated by a user requesting a service, for example, to make a hotel reservation. The system takes control of the interaction and asks a series of questions to determine the user's requirements and help complete the task. This is known as a *slot-filling dialogue*.
- *Multi-turn open-domain dialogues*: These are extended interactions in which both the system and the user take turns as in natural conversations between humans, where the conversation extends over potentially many turns and can involve a range of topics. This type of dialogue is generally not supported in currently deployed systems[39] but is the focus of much research in Conversational AI.

1.4.1 USER-INITIATED DIALOGUES

Examples 1.6 and 1.7 show one-shot exchanges in which the user asks a question or issues a command and the system responds.

[39]A notable exception is XiaoIce [Zhou et al., 2020], a social chatbot developed in China by Microsoft that can engage in extended dialogues with users.

Example 1.6 Asking for information

U: What's the weather forecast for tomorrow in Frankfurt?
S: In Frankfurt tomorrow it will be mostly sunny with a high of 23 and a low of 9

Example 1.7 Issuing a command

U: Set the alarm for 7 tomorrow morning.
S: Alarm set for 7 a.m. on Friday August 28th.

There are certain requirements for one-shot exchanges to be successful.

- The user's input has to be in a form that the system can interpret.
- The user has to include all the necessary information in a single utterance for the system to be able to interpret it successfully and answer the question or fulfil the command.
- The user needs to be able to deliver the utterance without any disfluencies.[40]
- The system needs to be able to answer the query or be able to carry out the command.

Recently, some dialogue platforms such as Amazon Alexa and Google Assistant have extended one-shot exchanges by allowing the user to make a follow-up query or command. These take two different forms:

- slot replacement and
- anaphora resolution

Slot Replacement

Here the follow-up utterance is the same as the original utterance but with a different slot value. Examples 1.8 and 1.9 are from interactions with Google Assistant:

Example 1.8

U1: What's the weather in Berlin?
S1: Currently in Berlin there is rain and a high of 10 degrees.
U2: What about Frankfurt?

[40]Note that some systems such as Google Assistant can successfully handle a certain amount of disfluency in the user's utterance.

In Example 1.8 the utterance about the weather in Berlin is replaced by an utterance about the weather in Frankfurt, i.e., the value of the location slot in the original utterance has been replaced. Example 1.9 is a longer interaction involving a series of follow-up utterances with slot replacements:

Example 1.9

U1: What's the weather forecast for Frankfurt for tomorrow?
S1: In Frankfurt tomorrow it will be mostly sunny with a high of 23 and a low of 9.
U2: What about Belfast?
S2: In Belfast tomorrow there will be scattered showers with a high of 17 and a low of 12.
U3: I meant London.
S3: Tomorrow in London it will be cloudy with a high of 19 and a low of 14.
U4: What about Sunday.
S4: In London on Sunday it will be partly cloudy with a high of 22 and a low of 12.

Anaphora Resolution

Anaphoric reference is similar to slot replacement except that in the follow-up utterance an entity in a slot is referred to using an anaphoric reference, such as a pronoun or a word such as *there*, as shown in Example 1.10, taken from a dialogue with Amazon Alexa:

Example 1.10

U1: What's the weather in London?
S1: In London it's 8 degrees with mostly cloudy skies.
U2: What's the population there?
S2: The population of London is about eight million seven hundred and ninety thousand.

Anaphora resolution is a very hard problem, especially in long multi-turn conversations, as it requires contextual inference to find expressions that refer to the same entity in current or past utterances [Khatri et al., 2018a]. In the Alexa Prize 2018 most teams used StanfordCoreNLP's Coreference Resolution System for anaphora resolution [Manning et al., 2014].

One-shot exchanges that complete successfully in this way follow a so-called *happy path* in which the user behaves as expected. But what happens when the utterances do not follow the happy path? The following are some use cases.

- The system is unable to interpret the user's utterance and says something like *Sorry I do not understand* and asks the user to repeat.

- The system does not know the answer to the user's question and says something like *Sorry I do not know the answer to that.*

- The system is not able to or does not know how to carry out the user's command and says something like *Sorry I can't do that* or *Sorry I do not know how to do that.*

- There is something missing or ambiguous in the user's utterance and the system inserts a request for clarification, as in Example 1.11:

  Example 1.11

  U: I am looking for a restaurant nearby.

  S: What kind of food would you like?

Most systems are able to handle use cases such as these in a fairly simple way. A more advanced and more helpful approach would be to guide the user, for example, by saying something like *I can answer questions about sport and entertainment.* Responses such as these and other responses such as clarification requests are usually handcrafted to meet the requirements of a specific use case but are difficult to apply more generally.

1.4.2 SYSTEM-DIRECTED DIALOGUE

Pro-Active Dialogues

Pro-active dialogues are an extensive of push notifications on smart phones where a message is sent to the user to remind them of an upcoming meeting, or in the case of a care receiver, a reminder to take medication. In contrast to push notifications pro-active dialogues engage the user in a dialogue, thus ensuring that they have received the reminder. As an example, Life-Pod[41] provides a proactive voice-based service that contacts care recipients such as elderly adults, chronically ill or special needs users in their homes to check-in, issue reminders, and engage in care plan dialogues. Figure 1.3 shows an example of a template for a simple proactive dialogue in which the system checks whether the user has taken water to prevent dehydration. This dialogue only requires a *yes* or *no* response from the user. In the future more extended dialogues could involve discussion of routines, medication plans, etc.

Instructional Dialogues

Car navigation is a common example of an instructional dialogue in which the system gives step-by-step directions to a specified destination. In currently deployed systems no user input is possible except in some cases to initiate the directions by stating the destination. Another example is cooking instructions on smart speakers in which the system helps users follow the steps

[41] https://lifepod.com/

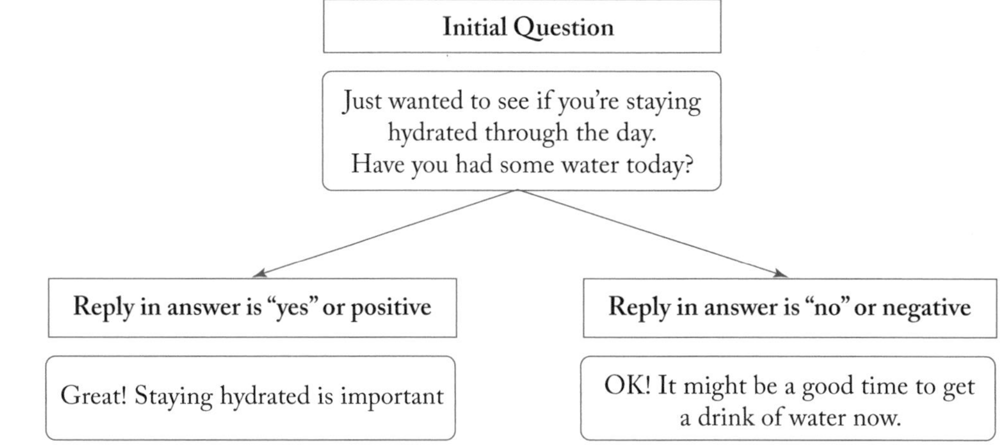

Figure 1.3: Template for a hydration reminder. Based on description in Patterson [2020, p. 125].

in a recipe hands-free by speaking step-by-step instructions, accompanied by video instructions in the case of smart speakers with displays. Two types of user input are typically supported[42]:

1. commands to navigate the recipe, e.g., *next step*, *previous step*, *what is step 5?*, and commands and queries about ingredients, e.g., *next ingredient*, *how much butter?*, etc.; and

2. general questions about cooking, e.g., *can I replace soda with baking powder?*, *how much is that in grams?*, etc.

Amazon Alexa supports similar skills, see, for example, the BBC Food Alexa Skill,[43] and the Allrecipes skill.[44]

Slot-Filling Dialogues

Slot-filling dialogues are similar to form-filling on the web. The system asks a series of questions to collect slot values for **destination**, **departure_date**, **departure_time**, and so on that are required in order to complete a task such as booking a flight, as in Example 1.12:

Example 1.12

U1: I want to book a flight.
S1: where do you want to fly to?
U2: Boston.
S2: what date do you wish to depart?

[42] Example taken from the Google Assistant app: https://support.google.com/googlenest/answer/7309433.
[43] https://www.bbcgoodfood.com/howto/guide/how-use-bbc-good-food-alexa-skill
[44] https://www.allrecipes.com/article/introducing-allrecipes-on-amazon-alexa/

S3-N: (System continues to ask questions until all the slots are filled).

One advantage of the slot-filling approach is that it provides some flexibility in the dialogue. The user can simply state their requirements without specifying any required values, as in the previous example, or they can specify several of the slots in a single utterance (this is known as *over-answering*), as in Example 1.13:

Example 1.13

U: I want to fly from London to Boston on Friday.

In this case the slots for **departure_city**, **destination**, and **departure_date** have been filled, so the system only needs to ask about any remaining unfilled slots, such as **departure_time**. This type of interaction is supported in VoiceXML and other tools that are reviewed in Chapter 2, Section 2.3.

A possible deviation from the happy path of a slot-filling dialogue is where the user requests repetition or clarification, as in 1.14:

Example 1.14

S: What kind of food would you like?
U: What are my choices?

Interpreting and responding to clarification requests from the user are usually handcrafted into slot-filling dialogues in current systems as special cases that have been predicted at design time.

1.4.3 MULTI-TURN OPEN-DOMAIN DIALOGUE

Multi-turn open-domain dialogue is more like conversations between humans in which the user and the system can engage in an extended interaction, where both participants can take the initiative and the dialogue is not restricted to a particular domain. Open-domain conversational systems have become a hot topic in Conversational AI. As Guo et al. [2018] write:

> *Achieving sustained, coherent and engaging dialog is the next frontier for Conversational AI, …*

Similarly, Adiwardana et al. [2020] state that

> *The ability to converse freely in natural language is one of the hallmarks of human intelligence, and is likely a requirement for true artificial intelligence.*

The following are some recent approaches to multi-turn open-domain dialogue.

Table 1.1: Open Request Pattern and Example. Source: Moore and Arar [2019, p. 93].

Open Request Pattern	Open Request Example
U1: FULL REQUEST	U1: Can you recommend a nearby Mexican restaurant?
S1: GRANT	S1: Mario's is located at Beach and Main.
U2: SEQUENCE CLOSER	U2: Thanks.
S2: RECEIPT	S2: You're welcome!

The Natural Conversation Framework

The Natural Conversation Framework (NCF) [Moore and Arar, 2019] is a design framework for dialogue systems based on patterns of conversational interaction that have been identified and documented in the Conversation Analysis (CA) literature [Schegloff, 2007]. One hundred patterns are documented that cover different types of conversational interactions, such as Inquiry (User), Open Request, and Extended Telling. There are also patterns for sequence-level management, such as different types of repair, and patterns for conversation-level management, such as openings and closings.

Table 1.1 shows the basic Open Request pattern along with an example. Note that in contrast to the one-shot exchanges typical of user-initiated interactions with smart speakers the pattern specifies two additional turns beyond the initial exchange in which the user closes the sequence by saying "thanks" and the system acknowledges. This expansion of the basic one-shot exchange enables the user to demonstrate that they have understood the system's response and are satisfied with it and it also allows the system to accept the user's acknowledgement and close the exchange. In this way mutual understanding between the conversational partners is achieved and acknowledged. Achieving mutual understanding is an important objective in conversational interaction and motivates conversational turns that are not part of the informational and transactional elements of a conversation. This principle has been adopted recently by some current dialogue systems that respond appropriately to user follow-ups such as *thanks*, *goodbye*, or *see you later* by saying something like *don't mention it* or *it's my pleasure*.

Sequences can be expanded if the system or the user requests more detail or asks for repetitions or paraphrases. Table 1.2 shows how a variation on the pattern in Table 1.1 is expanded by the system asking for more detail.

Example 1.15 shows how a basic exchange can be expanded in many ways with requests for further detail and paraphrases.

Example 1.15

U1: Do you know about restaurants?
S1: I know a few places.
U2: A few what?

Table 1.2: Open Request Detail Request Pattern and Example. Source: Moore and Arar [2019, p. 96].

Open Request Agent Detail Request Pattern	Open Request Agent Detail Request Example
U1: PARTIAL REQUEST	U1: Can you recommend a Mexican restaurant?
S1: DETAIL REQUEST	S1: Walking distance or car ride?
U2: DETAIL	U2: Walking distance.
S2: GRANT	S2: Mario's is located at Beach and Main.
U3: SEQUENCE CLOSER	U3: Thanks.
S3: RECEIPT	S3: You're welcome!

S2: Places.
U3: Can you recommend one close by?
S3: What kind of food do you want?
U4: Well, what are my choices?
S4: Around here Mexican, Japanese or Indian.
U5: Mexican.
S5: Okay. Mario's is on Beach and Main.
U6: What do you mean?.
S6: Mario's is a Mexican restaurant just a couple of blocks west on Chester Street.
U7: Oh ok, thanks
S7: You're welcome! Anything else?

U1 is a preliminary expansion that checks on the conditions required for the agent to be able to answer the upcoming query in U3. There are several inserted expansions: U2 is a user-initiated request for clarification or additional information, as is U4, while S3 is a system-initiated request for additional information, similar to a slot-filling question. Note that in addition to bringing the dialogue to a potential close in S7, the system asks if the user wants anything else, a question typically asked by agents at the end of service encounters that opens up the possibility of further interaction.

Sequence expansions enable conversational systems to adapt to the particular user on a local, turn-by-turn basis. One user may be able to complete the sequence without any sequence expansions, while another user may require many. In this way sequences cannot be pre-determined but evolve on a turn-by-turn basis as a result of the interactional work by the participants in the conversation as they aim to achieve their goals and demonstrate mutual understanding. The NCF provides patterns that enable the flexibility required in multi-turn open-domain dialogues. The many examples presented in Moore and Arar [2019] are taken from a conversational agent Alma that was implemented using NCF on the IBM Watson Assistant service and could in principle be implemented on other platforms.

The Amazon Alexa Prize

The Alexa Prize was set up by Amazon in 2016 as a challenge to student teams from universities to create a *socialbot* that could converse with members of the general public on a wide range of topics. The first challenge was held in 2017 [Khatri et al., 2018b] and the second in 2018 [Khatri et al., 2018a]. The third challenge was launched in 2019 and the finals were held in 2020.[45] The technologies developed by the teams in the Alexa Prize 2020 are reviewed in Chapter 5, Section 5.6.

The idea behind socialbots is that, like chatbots, they should be able to handle chit-chat but in addition they should also be able to talk with users about recent news and other topics of interest. Like traditional chatbots they should be reactive to the user's questions, but they should also be also proactive, for example, by introducing new topics into the conversation. In other words, they should be able to engage in mixed-initiative, multi-turn, open-domain dialogue. The challenge for the teams is to create a socialbot that can converse coherently and engagingly with human judges for 20 minutes and obtain a rating of 4 or higher out of 5 from the human judges interacting with it. Example 1.16 is an extract from an interaction with the socialbot *Alana*, developed by a team from The Interaction Lab at Heriot-Watt University, Edinburgh, UK that achieved third place in the 2017 and 2018 challenges [Cercas Curry et al., 2018]. Alana has since been launched as a spin-out company in 2020[46]:

Example 1.16
Turn 5

ALANA: Welcome back then `username`. Since I remember that you like movies, I am looking forward to the new movie Jurassic world that was just released. What movie are you looking forward to watching?
USER: Vanilla Sky.

Turn 6

ALANA: Oh I heard something interesting about Vanilla Sky. In the cell, Carl Jung's book, Memories, Dreams, and Reflections can be seen on the table between David and McCabe. The book ...
USER: Interesting.

[45] https://developer.amazon.com/alexaprize/challenges/past-challenges/challenge3
[46] https://alanaai.com/

Turn 7

ALANA: I just think the world is full of strange and unexpected things like that. So, talking about movies, what famous actor or actress would you like to meet? I would love to meet **Will Smith**. **He**'s just so funny!
USER: Who is **he**?

Turn 8

ALANA: I guess you know that **Will Smith** is an American actor, film producer and rapper...So `username`, on the topic of movies, what's a movie that you like? ...
USER: I want to talk about music.

Turn 9

ALANA: So, talking about music. Who is a singer that you like?

Note the use of anaphoric reference across turns 7 and 8. Alana mentions *Will Smith* and uses *he* anaphorically within the same turn. The user continues the reference and then in turn 8 Alana uses the full reference *Will Smith*, which is a way of checking that they are both referring to the same person. Note also that Alana is trying in turn 8 to find out which movies the user likes, but is able to switch the topic to music on the user's request. In other turns Alana retrieves content from various knowledge sources, such as news, Wikipedia, and ontologies. Chapter 2 provides more detail on the technologies used by Alana and other socialbots in the Alexa prize, while Chapter 4 reviews the methods of evaluation that have been used to select the winners in the Alexa Prize and in other challenges and competitions.

Systems Using Neural Dialogue Technologies

Within the past few years neural dialogue technologies have been used to develop multi-turn open-domain dialogue systems. Example 1.17 shows a dialogue with Meena, an open-domain, end-to-end neural dialogue system developed by the Google Research Brain Team [Adiwardana et al., 2020].

Example 1.17

HUMAN: Hi!
MEENA: Hello! How are you?
HUMAN: I'm doing okay. How about you?
MEENA: I'm doing pretty good, thanks for asking!
HUMAN: What's your name?
MEENA: It's Kimberly! What's your name?
HUMAN: That's a nice name. My name is Paul.

MEENA: Nice to meet you Paul!
HUMAN: Nice to meet you as well Kimberly.
MEENA: So, what do you like to do?
HUMAN: I like going to the movies.
MEENA: Cool! What's your favorite movie?
HUMAN: Pulp Fiction.
MEENA: Nice! I love Reservoir Dogs.
HUMAN: Yes, that movie is good as well.
MEENA: Who's your favorite character in Reservoir Dogs?

Not all of the conversations with Meena were successful, however, and about one third of them degenerated into cross-turn repetitions in which turns are repeated, as shown in Example 1.18:

Example 1.18

HUMAN: Have you even been to India?
MEENA: No, but I'd love to go.
HUMAN: How about Japan?
MEENA: I'd love to go to Japan too.
HUMAN: How about Paris?
MEENA: I'd love to go to Paris too.
HUMAN: Are you lying to me?
MEENA: I'd love to go to Japan too.
HUMAN: i think you're lying to me, that makes me sad.
MEENA: I'd love to go to Japan, too.
HUMAN: You're blocking me out! You have to talk to me.
MEENA: I'd love to go to Japan.
HUMAN: Where else?
MEENA: I'd love to go to Japan, too!

The technologies behind Meena and other advanced neural systems will be reviewed in Chapter 5, Section 5.6.

1.5 DESIGNING AND DEVELOPING DIALOGUE SYSTEMS

There are three main approaches to the design and development of dialogue systems: *rule-based*, *statistical data-driven*, and *end-to-end neural*. In rule-based systems conversation flow and other aspects of the interface are handcrafted using best practice guidelines that have been developed over the past decades by voice user interface designers [Pearl, 2016], [Batish, 2018]. These include guidelines on elements of conversations, such as:

- how to design effective prompts;
- how to sound natural;
- how to act in a cooperative manner;
- how to offer help at any time;
- how to prevent errors; and
- how to recover from errors when they occur.

There are also higher-level guidelines, for example:

- how to promote engagement and retention;
- how to make the customer experience more personal and more pleasant; and
- the use of personas and branding.

Some of these guidelines address linguistic aspects of conversational interaction, such as maintaining the context in multi-turn conversations, asking follow-up questions, maintaining and changing topics, and error recovery. Others are more concerned with social competence, such as promoting engagement, displaying personality, and expressing and interpreting emotion. Finally, there are psychological aspects such as being able to recognize the beliefs and intentions of the other conversational participant, i.e., what is known as *theory of mind*. All of these aspects are important for a conversational agent to be effective as well as engaging for the user.

In the second and third approaches, dialogue strategies are learned from data. Statistical data-driven dialogue systems emerged in the late 1990s and end-to-end neural dialogue systems using deep learning began to appear around 2014. Rule-based systems are reviewed in Chapter 2, statistical data-driven systems in Chapter 3, and end-to-end neural dialogue systems in Chapter 5. Chapter 6 discusses recent developments in hybrid systems that combine rule-based with statistical and/or neural approaches.

SUMMARY

This chapter has introduced dialogue systems, looking first at what motivates developers to develop systems that can engage in conversations with human users and then reviewing the history of dialogue systems. Five different traditions were identified: text-based and spoken dialogue systems that were developed in academic and industrial research laboratories; voice user interfaces that were developed by companies and deployed in commercial environments; chatbots that aimed to simulate human conversation; embodied conversational agents that focused on multi-modal aspects of conversational interaction; and social robots and situated agents. Following this present-day dialogue systems were reviewed, looking in particular at the types of conversational interactions that can be supported on different platforms, and the situations and purposes for which the systems can be deployed. The final section identified three different approaches to the design and development of dialogue systems: a rule-based approach involving handcrafting, a statistical data-driven approach using machine learning, and an end-to-end neural approach using deep neural networks. The next chapter provides an overview of rule-based dialogue systems.

CHAPTER 2

Rule-Based Dialogue Systems: Architecture, Methods, and Tools

Until around 2000 dialogue systems developed in academic and industrial research laboratories were based on rules that determined the system's behavior. Consider Example 2.1 in which the system has to choose between three different possible responses to the user's utterance:

Example 2.1

U1: I want to book a flight to Boston.
S1.1: Sorry, please repeat that. (System cannot interpret U1).
S1.2: Did you say Boston? (System asks for confirmation).
S1.3: Ok, a flight to Boston. What date? (System confirms implicitly and asks for the value of the next slot).

In this example the system's choice of its next action could be determined by how confident it was in its interpretation of the user's utterance, based, for example, on the confidence score returned by the speech recognition component. In a rule-based system this decision would be anticipated by the system designer and included as a pre-scripted rule (see further discussion in Section 2.1.3). In an alternative approach, to be discussed in Chapter 3, decisions such as these are learned from data using technologies such as Reinforcement Learning (RL) (see Chapter 3, Section 3.3).

This chapter reviews the rule-based approach. The chapter is structured as follows. Section 2.1 presents a typical dialogue systems architecture and describes the workings of the different components of the architecture. Section 2.2 describes the development lifecycle for handcrafted dialogue systems, outlining the various stages in the lifecycle. Section 2.3 reviews some tools that have become available for developing dialogue systems while Section 2.3.3 shows how these tools can be used to implement the different types of dialogue introduced in Chapter 1. Finally, Section 2.4 reviews rule-based techniques that were used in some of the systems that have competed for the Alexa Prize in recent years.

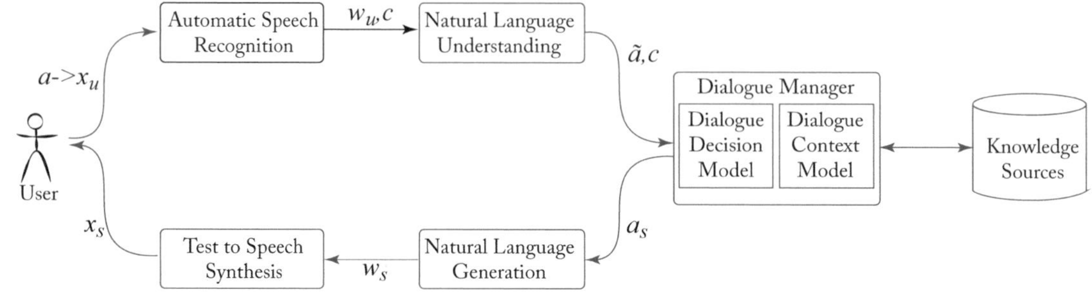

Figure 2.1: Typical dialogue systems architecture.

2.1 A TYPICAL DIALOGUE SYSTEMS ARCHITECTURE

Figure 2.1 shows a typical architecture for a dialogue system. The architecture applies to text-based as well as spoken dialogue systems. The main difference is that spoken dialogue systems have a speech recognition component to process the user's spoken input and a text-to-speech component to render the system's output as a spoken message. Text-based dialogue systems do not have these components. This architecture can be viewed as a pipeline architecture as the flow of interaction passes through the components as indicated by the directional arrows. The following is a typical flow.

1. The user produces a dialogue act a, such as a query, command, or response to a system prompt, which is rendered as an acoustic signal x_u.

2. x_u is input to the Automatic Speech Recognition component and recognized as a word string w_u with confidence score c.

3. The word string w_u (or possibly an N-best list or a word graph representing the speech recognition hypotheses) is input to the Natural Language Understanding component and interpreted as $\tilde{a}$ with confidence score c. $\tilde{a}$ is an estimate of a due to the possibility of recognition and understanding errors as it is often the case that $\tilde{a} \neq a$, i.e., what the system outputs as its representation of the user's input does not correspond to what the user actually intended.

4. The system's Dialogue Context Model, which contains information about the dialogue, is updated with ($\tilde{a}$,c).

5. Given the information in the Dialogue Context Model, the Dialogue Decision Model determines the next system action, which may involve producing a system dialogue act a_s.

6. The Dialogue Context Model is updated with a_s.

7. The Natural Language Generation component converts a_s into a word string w_s.

8. w_s is rendered by the Text to Speech Synthesis component as an acoustic signal x_s which may prompt the user for further input leading to another cycle through the process.

2.1.1 AUTOMATIC SPEECH RECOGNITION (ASR)

ASR involves taking the acoustic signal x_u that represents what the user said and outputting a string w consisting of one or more words that represent the system's estimate of the user's utterance. This process can be described in terms of the following conditional probability:

$$\hat{W} = \arg\max_{w} P(W|X) \tag{2.1}$$

which states that the estimate of the best word string W involves a search over all word strings w to find the maximum value of $P(W|X)$, which is the probability of the word string W given the acoustic input X. Applying Bayes rule this is transformed into:

$$\arg\max_{w} P(X|W)(W), \tag{2.2}$$

where $P(X|W)$—the probability of the acoustic signal x given the word string w—is known as the *observation likelihood* that is computed by the *acoustic model* that models the relationships between word strings and acoustic signals. The other component $P(W)$ is the *prior probability* that is computed by the *language model* which models the probability of sequences of words, often using N-gram language models but in some cases using finite state grammars. The acoustic and language models for ASR are trained on a large number of sample utterances so that the developer is only required to fine-tune the models, if this is supported on the ASR platform. Given these two probabilities, the most likely word string W can be computed for a given acoustic signal X using an appropriate search algorithm.

Until recently Hidden Markov Models (HMMs) were used for the acoustic modeling but from around 2010 DNNs have replaced HMM resulting in a dramatic increase in accuracy [Hinton et al., 2012], [Yu and Deng, 2016]. See Jurafsky and Martin [2020] for a comprehensive description of speech recognition, covering HMMs, language models, and deep neural network approaches.

ASR is a probabilistic process in which the output may be a set of word hypotheses, often ranked in an N-best list, or represented as a lattice that can encode multiple word sequence alternatives. In some dialogue systems the 1st-best hypothesis is chosen and passed on to the NLU component for further analysis. However, given that the 1st-best hypothesis may not be correct, there is merit in maintaining multiple recognition hypotheses so that alternatives can be considered at a later stage in the processing—for example, as a result of re-scoring based on information available from other components of the system.

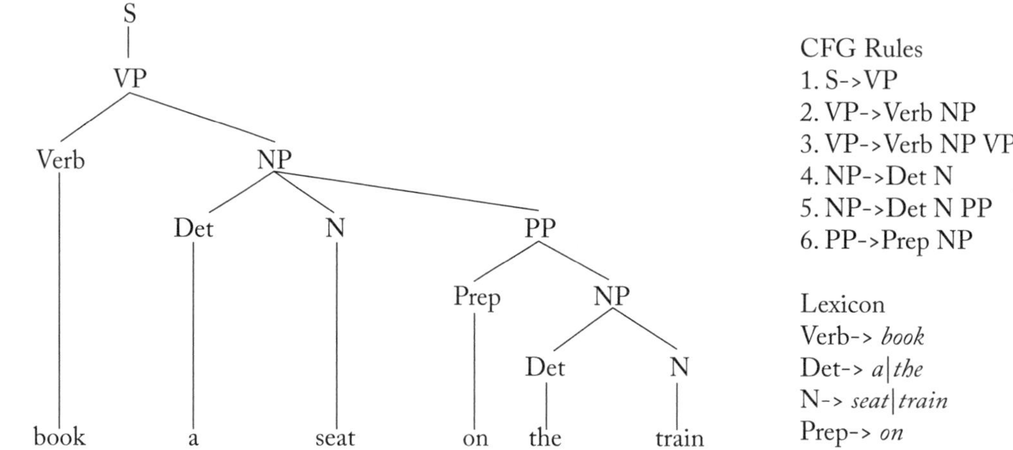

Figure 2.2: Context-free grammar and lexical rules with parse tree.

2.1.2 NATURAL LANGUAGE UNDERSTANDING (NLU)

Given a string of words W from ASR, the NLU component analyses the string to determine its meaning (or, in some systems, it outputs a dialogue act A that represents the function of the user's utterance W).

NLU can take several forms. In syntax-driven semantic analysis the input is first analyzed syntactically to determine how the words and phrases group together as constituents and then the meaning is derived using semantic rules attached to the constituents. Logic is often used to represent the meaning of the string, with the advantage that this allows the application of standard mechanisms for inference to provide a deeper level of understanding. Figure 2.2 shows an example of a small Context-Free Grammar (CFG) consisting of grammar and lexical rules, along with a parse tree of the sentence *book a seat on the train*.

An alternative approach that was used in early dialogue systems was to derive the meaning of the user's input utterance directly from the recognized string W using a *semantic grammar*. A semantic grammar uses grammar rules in the same way as a syntactic grammar, but the constituents in the semantic grammar are classified in terms of their function or meaning rather than in terms of syntactic categories. Generally, semantic grammars for spoken dialogue systems and other NLU systems are domain-specific. So, for example, a system involving flights will have categories relevant to the flight domain, such as **flight**, **destination**, and **departure_date**, whereas a system involving banking will have categories such as **account**, **balance**, and **transfer**. Table 2.1 shows an example of some semantic grammar rules for the sentence *book a flight to London on Friday* in which the bar | indicates alternatives and the symbols in caps are non-terminal categories that are expanded in further rules.

Table 2.1: Semantic grammar rules

FLIGHT_BOOKING	->	book | I would like | …
FLIGHT	->	a flight | flights
DESTINATION	->	to CITY
CITY	->	London | Paris | New York | …
DEPARTURE_DATE	->	on DAY
DAY	->	Monday | Tuesday | …

The application of these rules to the input *book a flight to London on Friday* would produce the following output:

```
FLIGHT_BOOKING:
    FLIGHT:
        DESTINATION: London
        DEPARTURE_DATE: Friday
```

Semantic grammars are more robust to the sorts of ungrammatical input and recognition errors that occur in spontaneous speech. The Phoenix Parser [Ward and Issar, 1994] is a good example of a semantic parser that was used to provide robust parsing in a number of spoken dialogue systems. Semantic grammars are used in VoiceXML applications for semantic interpretation of the user's input.[1]

Handcrafted grammars can capture fine-grained distinctions in the input but the main disadvantage is that they require separate rules for every possible input, so that small variations require additional rules in order to be accepted by the grammar. For example, the following sentences that have the same meaning would require separate rules:

book a flight to London from Belfast
book a flight to Belfast from London

Thus, the number of rules can quickly accumulate, resulting potentially in conflicts and overlaps between rules and leading to problems with maintaining the grammar.

The toolkits that are widely used to create present-day dialogue systems, as described below in Section 2.3.3, do not make use of rule-based grammars—instead they use machine-learning methods to classify utterances and extract from them the user's *intent* and the *entities* that are contained in the utterance. Intents represent what the user wants to achieve, e.g., **book a flight**, **find a restaurant**, **book a taxi**, etc., while entities are the parameters required to fulfill an intent, e.g., **destination location**, **time**, **cuisine**, etc.; see Chapter 3, Section 3.2.1.

[1] https://www.w3.org/TR/semantic-interpretation/

Applications created with most current toolkits are generally domain-specific, so that it is not necessary to identify which domain the user's utterance is addressing. However, in open-domain interactions, for example, involving personal digital assistants such as Siri, Google Assistant, or Amazon Alexa, an interaction may switch across several different domains. For example, an initial question may be about **weather** in some location and the next question may be about **open-air concerts** in that location. Identifying the domain can often help to reduce ambiguity in the interpretation of utterances. Recent approaches to domain classification in dialogue systems are reviewed in Robichaud et al. [2014] and Xu and Sarikaya [2014].

As mentioned earlier, the output of the NLU component may take the form of a *dialogue act*. Dialogue acts, also known as *speech acts*, *conversational acts*, and *dialogue (or conversational) moves*, represent the function of the user's utterance—for example, whether it was intended as a question, command, promise, or threat. There are several classifications of dialogue acts. The Dialog Markup in Several Layers (DAMSL) [Allen and Core, 1997] has been used widely to annotate corpora of dialogues and as a basis for implementing the process of dialogue act recognition. DAMSL provides a generic level of description in which each utterance is tagged according to two main functions.

- *Forward-looking acts*: for example, acts such as statements, action-directives, and information-requests that expect a response.

- *Backward-looking acts*: for example, acts such as agreement, accept, and acknowledge that respond to a forward-looking act.

Bunt et al. [2017] have built on a number of annotation schemes including DAMSL and have developed an ISO standard that provides a comprehensive, application-independent annotation scheme for dialogue acts. The interpretation of dialogue acts is mainly modeled as a process of supervised classification in which classifiers are trained on a corpus of dialogues where each utterance is labeled with a dialogue act (see, for example, Stolcke et al. [2000]).

This description of the ASR and NLU components of a spoken dialogue system suggests a serial model in which the result(s) of the ASR stage are passed on to NLU for the next stage of analysis. However, there are a number of alternative approaches, one of which is to apply a stage of post-processing of the results from the ASR stage before proceeding to NLU. Ringger and Allen [1996] use a noisy channel model of ASR errors for this task, while López-Cózar and Callejas [2008] use statistical models of words and contextual information to determine the corrections. It is also possible to use evidence from later stages in the interpretation process. For example, Purver et al. [2006] and Lemon and Gruenstein [2004] use combinations of features at various levels, including ASR and NLU probabilities as well as semantic and contextual features to re-order the N-best hypotheses from the ASR stage.

2.1.3 DIALOGUE MANAGEMENT

The Dialogue Manager (DM) is the central component of a spoken dialogue system, accepting interpreted input from the ASR and NLU components, interacting with external knowledge sources, producing messages to be output to the user, and generally controlling the dialogue flow [Lee et al., 2010], [López-Cózar et al., 2014], [Traum, 2017], [Wilks et al., 2011]. For example, given the user's query *I want to book a flight from Belfast to Malaga*, DM takes the interpretation from NLU and checks to see what additional information is required, such as the departure date, before it can look up the flights database and provide a list of suitable flights. DM might decide to confirm the flight details at the same time as asking for the departure date, so that the output of DM might be an action such as:

```
Action:
    Query_and_Confirm_FlightDetails:
        Query: Departure_Date
        Confirm:
            Departure_Location: Belfast
            Destination_Location: Malaga
```

DM consists of two components:

- The *Dialogue Context Model* (known in statistical dialogue systems as *Dialogue State Tracking* or *Belief State Tracking*).
- The *Dialogue Decision Model* (known in statistical dialogue systems as the *Dialogue Policy Model*).

The Dialogue Context Model keeps track of information relevant to the dialogue in order to support the process of dialogue management. This may include information about what has been said so far in the dialogue and the extent to which this information is grounded, i.e., shared between the system and the user. A Dialogue Context Model may include knowledge sources such as the following.

- *Dialogue History*: A record of the dialogue so far in terms of the propositions that have been discussed and the entities that have been mentioned.
- *Task Record*: A representation of the information to be gathered in the dialogue. This record, often referred to as a form, frame, template, or status graph, is used to determine what information has been acquired by the system and what information still has to be acquired. This information is often encoded in a data structure known as the *agenda*.
- *Domain Model*: This contains specific information about the domain in question, for example, flight information. Often this information is encoded in a database from which relevant information is retrieved by the dialogue system. In recent work domain information is often represented in a *knowledge graph* or *ontology*.

- *Model of Conversational Competence*: This includes generic knowledge of the principles of conversational turn-taking and discourse obligations—for example, that an appropriate response to a request for information is to supply the information or provide a reason for not supplying it.

- *User Preference Model*: This model may contain relatively stable information about the user that may be relevant to the dialogue—such as the user's age, gender, and preferences—as well as information that changes over the course of the dialogue, such as the user's goals, beliefs, and intentions.

The Dialogue Decision Model determines the next system action given the user's input utterance and the information in the Dialogue Context Model. Decisions may include prompting the user for more input, clarifying or grounding the user's previous input, or outputting some information to the user. In rule-based systems these decisions are pre-scripted, with choices based on factors such as the confidence levels associated with the user's input. For example, if the confidence levels are above a certain threshold, the system can assume that it has correctly interpreted the input and can proceed to its next action, whereas if the levels are low it may first try to verify that it has interpreted the input correctly or even ask the user to repeat their utterance. Decisions such as these can be anticipated at design time and hard-coded into the Dialogue Decision Model.

Dialogue decisions can also be taken dynamically, based, for example, on reasoning about the current dialogue state and using evidence from a combination of different domain and dialogue knowledge sources. Thus, in addition to confidence scores from the ASR and NLU components, DM may also take other factors into account such as the relative importance of the information that has been elicited, what needs to be achieved in the task at hand, the user's needs and preferences, and the history of the dialogue so far. There may also be mechanisms to enable the system to adapt its output and style of interaction to different users, as well as sophisticated ways of detecting and handling errors. In each case the designer creates rules to handle these situations. However, as the number of rules increases, it becomes more difficult to maintain the Dialogue Decision Model and avoid duplication and conflict between the rules. Porting to other domains is also problematic as the rules often have to be re-written for each new domain. Alternative methods for handling dialogue decision making are discussed in Chapter 3.

2.1.4 NATURAL LANGUAGE GENERATION (NLG)

The Natural Language Generation (NLG) component is responsible for the text to be output to the user, based on the output of the dialogue manager. As shown in Figure 2.1, NLG involves converting the output a_s from DM into words w_s. For example, given the output from the Dialogue Manager in the previous section, NLG would output a string of words such as: *What date do you wish to fly from Belfast to Malaga?*

Note that sometimes the term *Response Generation* is used to refer to the NLG component. However, this is confusing as in neural network dialogue systems *response generation* is used to cover the combined output from both the DM and the NLG components (see further Chapter 5).

Generally, NLG has received less attention in the research literature in comparison with the effort devoted to the interpretation of the user's input by the NLU component. In commercial systems NLG is often a fairly trivial task involving either canned text or the insertion of items retrieved from a database or from the previous dialogue into a pre-defined response template. The following is an example of a template in which the values for the variables $origin, $destination, and $day are extracted from earlier utterances in the dialogue:

so you want to travel from $origin to $destination on $day?

A more advanced approach to NLG views generation as a series of stages of processing in a pipeline model, consisting of: Document Planning, Microplanning, and Realization [Reiter and Dale, 2000]. Document Planning involves issues such as how to determine what to say by selecting and ranking options from the content to be expressed; planning the use of discourse relations, such as comparison and contrast, in order to present the information in a meaningful way; and adapting the information to the user's perceived needs and preferences. Microplanning is concerned with creating the sentences to convey the information, involving tasks such as dealing with referring expressions and how to refer to entities within a particular context. Finally, Realization is concerned with how to express the content in terms of grouping different propositions into clauses and sentences, generating appropriate referring expressions, and using appropriate discourse cues. Statistical approaches for NLG in Spoken Dialogue Systems have been developed by Oh and Rudnicky [2002], Lemon [2012], Lemon [2011], Rieser et al. [2010], and Rieser et al. [2014], as discussed further in Chapter 3. The most recent NLG systems that have been developed and evaluated in the end-to-end neural dialogue approach treat NLG as a decoding problem in which the text is generated word-by-word from a hidden state [Dušek et al., 2020]. See further discussion in Chapter 5.

2.1.5 TEXT-TO-SPEECH SYNTHESIS (TTS)

Once the output from NLG w_s has been determined, the next step is to transform it into a spoken utterance x_s. Commercial systems often use pre-recorded prompts in cases where the output can be predicted at the design stage. This involves the use of *voice talents*, i.e., professional voice actors who record the system's outputs. However, although this results in high quality output, it is an expensive option and is only suitable for outputs that do not change over time. The alternative is to use Text to Speech Synthesis (TTS) in which the text to be spoken is synthesized. TTS is required for messages that are dynamically constructed and that cannot be predicted in advance, such as delivering up to the minute news and weather reports or reading emails aloud. The quality of TTS engines has improved considerably over the past decade so that output using TTS is not only easy to comprehend but also pleasant for the listener. If the text to be synthesized is known in advance, or if it is in the form of a template with values to be inserted at run-time, it can be marked up for prosody and other relevant features using the Speech Synthesis Markup

Table 2.2: Examples of SSML supported in Google Assistant

Type	Example
Insert pause	Welcome. <break time="200 ms"> How can I help you?
Speak as date, e.g., "the tenth of September"	<say-as interpret-as="date" format=>10-9</say-as>
Speak as characters, e.g., "I B M"	<say-as interpret-as="characters">IBM</say-as>
Speak as ordinal, e.g., "First"	<say-as interpret-as="ordinal">1</say-as>
Speak abbreviation, e.g., "Dr"	_{Dr.}
Prosody, e.g., speak slowly at 2 semitones lower than normal	<prosody rate="slow" pitch="-2st"> Can you hear me now?</prosody>

Language (SSML).[2] SSML was developed originally by the Voice Browser Working Group to enhance the spoken output of VoiceXML applications (see Section 2.3.2). SSML is now available on many voice-enabled platforms such as Amazon Alexa,[3] Microsoft Cortana,[4] and IBM Watson,[5] among others. Table 2.2 shows some examples of SSML tags that are supported on Google Assistant.[6]

There are two stages in traditional TTS: Text Analysis and Waveform Synthesis. In Text Analysis the text to be spoken is transformed into a representation consisting of phonemes and prosodic information. Before this the text is normalized, which involves transforming abbreviations, acronyms, and other nonstandard words into normal text. In the second stage, Waveform Synthesis, the internal representation is converted to a waveform that can be output as spoken text. Until recently the most popular method for waveform synthesis has been *concatenative synthesis* in which segments of recorded speech are concatenated.

Within the past few years end-to-end TTS systems have been developed using Deep Neural Networks (DNNs), showing promising results. For example, the WaveNet deep neural network developed by DeepMind outperformed the best existing TTS systems for U.S. English and Mandarin Chinese in 2016 [Oord et al., 2016]. However, there are still problems to be resolved, for example, with rendering emotion and with aspects of prosody such as the correct use of stress for contrastive emphasis.

[2]https://www.w3.org/TR/speech-synthesis11/

[3]https://developer.amazon.com/en-US/docs/alexa/custom-skills/speech-synthesis-markup-language-ssml-reference.html

[4]https://docs.microsoft.com/en-us/cortana/skills/speech-synthesis-markup-language

[5]https://cloud.ibm.com/docs/text-to-speech?topic=text-to-speech-ssml

[6]https://cloud.google.com/text-to-speech/docs/ssml

2.2 DESIGNING A DIALOGUE SYSTEM

Designing a dialogue system is in many ways similar to developing any other software system. The main difference lies in determining the interactional requirements and the conversational user interface of the dialogue system. The following are the main steps to be taken in designing a dialogue system[7]:

- Requirements analysis.
    1. Determine if conversation is the right approach for the application, e.g., identify typical use cases where conversation provides added value over alternative types of interface, for example, booking a hotel room, providing information or instructions, engaging in chit-chat.
    2. Analyze the users, e.g., teenagers, adults, elderly users, to determine their goals and how they will use the system.
    3. Decide on a persona for the system, e.g., professional, casual, friendly, etc.
- Technology analysis: consider the technical requirements for the application and review the limitations of different platforms and preferred devices for the application.
- High-level design.
    1. Create sample dialogues (like movie scripts) and enact them with one participant playing the role of the user and the other the system. This could involve the Wizard of Oz method in which the person playing the role of the system (the wizard) is concealed from the human users who are not aware that the wizard is a human and not a dialogue system [Fraser and Gilbert, 1991]. The interactions should be recorded and transcribed for analysis in order to determine the function, vocabulary, and structure of the responses provided by the user, including questions that are answered inappropriately and other areas of conversational breakdown. Alternatively, transcripts and/or recordings of human-human conversations could be used to provide examples of typical interactions.
    2. Create high-level flows, beginning with *happy paths* in which the user behaves as expected, and then develop *edge cases* to handle possible errors and cases where the user deviates from the predicted happy paths.
    3. Prototype the high-level flows using one of the many visual editing tools for creating a conversation flow (see Section 2.3.1).
    4. Test and iterate.

[7]Based on design guidelines for Actions on Google: https://designguidelines.withgoogle.com/conversation/

A more detailed description with many examples can be found at the Actions on Google website. Similar sets of design guidelines are available from other providers and on numerous blogs on the internet. See also [Pearl, 2016] and [Shevat, 2017].

2.3 TOOLS FOR DEVELOPING DIALOGUE SYSTEMS

Over the past few years a large number of tools and frameworks have appeared that help developers create dialogue systems. Lukianets [2019] lists more than 50, but in fact there are many more. These tools can be divided roughly into the following types:

- tools for designing and prototyping dialogue systems using a visual interface with a drag-and-drop editor;
- scripting tools for specifying and handcrafting dialogue systems;
- advanced toolkits and frameworks that use AI technology to implement some elements of the dialogue system; and
- toolkits for conducting state-of-the-art research in dialogue systems.

2.3.1 VISUAL DESIGN TOOLS

Visual design tools make it easy for developers who do not have a background in programming to map out the conversation flow visually and prototype it in an emulator. In many cases the designed system can be integrated with more advanced development tools such as Dialogflow, Google Assistant, Alexa Skills Kit, and RASA (see Section 2.3.3). There are many visual design tools available, each with varying levels of functionality. Figure 2.3 shows an example of how to visually design a conversation flow by creating a Conversation Flow Project on Botmock. [8] The Block Selector (not shown in Figure 2.3) allows the designer to insert actions and conversation blocks in the flow such as User says, Bot says, Image, Quick replies, Buttons, API Block, Jump Block, etc. Once designed the flow can be tested using the Interactive Simulator and by typing or speaking to the bot. Figure 2.4 shows an example of a dialogue produced from the conversation flow shown in Figure 2.3.[9]

2.3.2 SCRIPTING TOOLS FOR HANDCRAFTING DIALOGUE SYSTEMS

As an alternative to visual design tools there are several tools that enable developers to script the dialogue flow and specify other aspects of a dialogue system. Two widely used scripting tools are VoiceXML, which supports system-directed dialogues in which the system controls

[8]Source: http://help.botmock.com/en/articles/2635479-getting-started-working-with-intents-variables-and-entities-within-your-flow-project.

[9]Source: http://help.botmock.com/en/articles/2635479-getting-started-working-with-intents-variables-and-entities-within-your-flow-project.

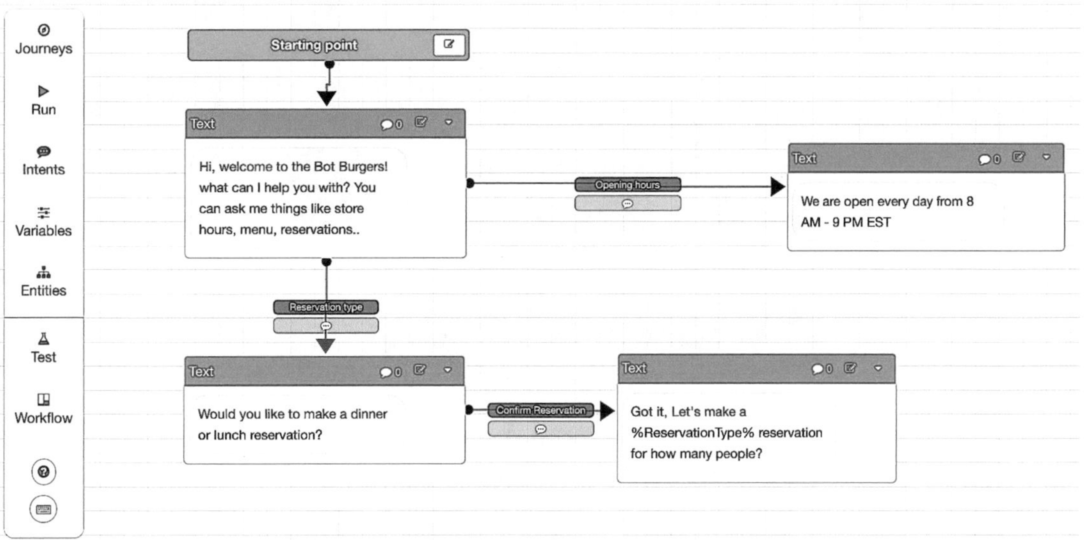

Figure 2.3: Conversation flow design using Botmock's Conversation Flow Design tool. Used with permission.

the interaction, and AIML, which supports user-initiated dialogues in which the interaction is controlled by the user.

VoiceXML

Voice Extensible Markup Language (VoiceXML) is a markup language based on XML (Extensible Markup Language). VoiceXML was developed by the Voice Browser Working Group[10] of the World Wide Web Consortium (W3C). VoiceXML is designed for creating system-directed spoken dialogue systems that users connect to over the Public Services Telephone Network (PSTN).[11] VoiceXML 1.0 was launched in 2000 and substantially updated in 2004 by VoiceXML 2.0. VoiceXML 2.1 appeared in 2007 with some additional updates. The complete VoiceXML package includes several additional markup languages: SRGS (Speech Recognition Grammar Specification), SSML (Speech Synthesis Markup Language), SISR (Semantic Interpretation for Speech Recognition), and CCXML (Call Control Extensible Markup Language).

In VoiceXML applications once the user has called the system, the system takes control and directs the dialogue The basic element of interaction in VoiceXML is the *form* which contains a number of fields to be filled using spoken interaction. The system elicits values for one or more fields in the form and the user responds to the system's prompts. The fields contain grammars that specify the set of permissible inputs for each field. The following is an example

[10]https://www.w3.org/Voice/
[11]https://voicexml.org/

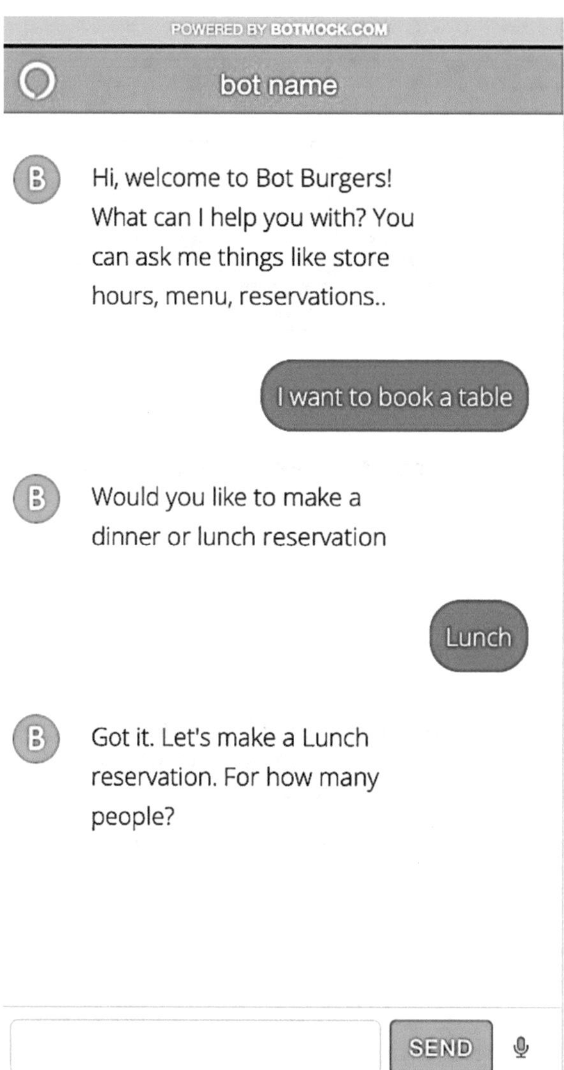

Figure 2.4: Dialogue produced using Botmock's Interactive Simulator. Used with permission.

of a form containing a single field consisting of a system prompt and a grammar specifying the user's input.

```
<?xml version="1.0" encoding="UTF-8"?>
<vxml version="2.0">
<form id="transfer">
    <field name="dest-acc">
    <prompt>
    Which account do you want to transfer funds to?
    </prompt>

    <grammar mode="voice" xml:lang="en-US" version="1.0"
         root="account">
        <rule id = "account"
            <one-of>
            <item> checking </item>
            <item> savings </item>
            <item> business </item>
            </one-of>
        </rule>
    </grammar>

    </field>
</form>
</vxml>
```

A form such as this is a declarative specification of a system-directed dialogue. The form is processed by the Form Interpretation Algorithm (FIA) which progresses sequentially through each field in the form, executing the prompts and processing the user input. The required values are extracted from the user's responses to the system's prompts and are assigned to field variables. Thus, in the example form above, if the user says *savings* in response to the prompt *Which account do you want to transfer funds to?*, the value "savings" is assigned to the field variable **dest-acc**. VoiceXML also supports a limited form of mixed-initiative dialogue that allows for greater flexibility in the user's input but potentially at the cost of more errors in ASR and NLU. For more detail and examples, see the VoiceXML specification document.[12]

VoiceXML is used widely by companies that provide automated customer self-service over the telephone.

[12]https://www.w3.org/TR/voicexml20/

AIML

Artificial Intelligence Markup Language (AIML) is an XML-based scripting language that was developed by Dr. Richard Wallace as a language for specifying conversations with chatbots. AIML is hosted on the Pandorabots platform.[13] Wallace used AIML to create the ALICE chatbot that won the Loebner Prize in 2000, 2001, and 2004, and subsequently a number of award-winning chatbots have been created using AIML, most notably Mitsuku, introduced in Chapter 1, a five-times winner of the prize. Currently, more than 300,000 chatbots have been built on the Pandorabots platform. AIML has also been used in socialbots such as Alana to provide chit-chat interactions (see Section 2.3.5). In contrast to VoiceXML, AIML supports user-initiated dialogues in which the user says something and the system responds. The dialogue can extend over multiple turns as long as the user continues to make inputs in contrast to other user-initiated dialogues that take the form of one-shot exchanges, as described in Chapter 1, Section 1.3.1.

Authoring a chatbot in AIML involves creating a large number of categories that at the basic level consist of a pattern that is matched against the user's input and a template that specifies the chatbot's response. The following is a simple example of a category:

```
<category>
<pattern> what is type 2 diabetes? </pattern>
<template> type 2 diabetes is a metabolic disorder that is characterized by high blood
glucose in the context of insulin resistance and relative insulin deficiency </template>
</category>
```

If the user's input is matched against the text in the pattern, the contents of the template are executed. Matching in AIML is done by the Graphmaster, which stores all the patterns in a graph [Wallace, 2004], [Wallace, 2009]. The graph is traversed until a pattern is found that matches the input. If no pattern is found, the *Ultimate default category* is invoked that outputs a response such as *tell me more* to try to keep the conversation going.

AIML contains some mechanisms to match inputs that are similar, thus avoiding an unnecessary proliferation of rules. For example, synonymous inputs can be mapped on to a single canonical pattern using the <srai> tag. Given the category shown above for the input *what is type 2 diabetes*, synonymous inputs can be created as follows:

```
<category>
<pattern> tell me about type 2 diabetes? </pattern>
<template>
<srai> what is type 2 diabetes? </srai>
</template>
</category>
```

[13] https://home.pandorabots.com/home.html

Here the chatbot's response is retrieved recursively by finding it in the category that contains the pattern of the canonical pattern. Other uses of <srai> are described here.[14]

The use of wildcards is a another way to deal with a range of inputs. On its own, the wildcard * captures any input for which there is no matching category and triggers the Ultimate default category described above. In other cases the wildcard * may match one or more words in the input, allowing similar patterns to be treated as variants of the same pattern:

What are the main symptoms of type 2 diabetes?
What are the * symptoms of type 2 diabetes?
What are the * symptoms *?

A further use of wildcards is to allow the words captured by the wildcard to be repeated back in the template by using the <star/> tag. For example, in response to a question about symptoms, the user might say *I feel tired*, to which the chatbot might reply *what do you think makes you feel tired?*. This is achieved by using the following pattern and template to cover any input beginning with *I feel*:

```
<category>
<pattern> I feel * </pattern>
<template> What do you think makes you feel * </template>
</category>
```

More examples of the use of wildcards are described in [Worswick, 2018c].

Other mechanisms available in AIML include dealing with conversational context by enabling the system to remember the last sentence it has said; setting a topic to cover a longer stretch of dialogue, where only those patterns within the scope of the topic will be matched; the ability to learn from information provided by the user; and the facility to create a knowledge base containing general knowledge about objects. For example, Mitsuku's knowledge base contains over 3000 objects that enable it to correctly handle queries that violate common sense such as *can you eat a chair?* [Worswick, 2018a].

Although AIML was originally used to create chatbots that engage in chit-chat, its use has now been extended to give it the functionality of a personal digital assistant, e.g., supporting commands to the device such as setting alarms and directing queries to Web services. The Call-Mom app is an example of a personal digital assistant created in AIML.[15] More generally, the Pandorabots platform is now being used to develop solutions for top global brands and larger enterprises to provide automated customer service and also for developers creating entertainment solutions.

As with other handcrafted solutions scaling up to a complex system in AIML leads to a proliferation of rules (or categories) with the potential for overlap and conflict. Mitsuku, for

[14] https://medium.com/pandorabots-blog/aiml-tutorial-the-srai-tag-5bb1f9d08169
[15] http://callmom.pandorabots.com/static/callmom/

example, contains over 300,000 categories and has been in development for more than 15 years with new categories being added regularly to keep the chatbot's knowledge topical. Other popular scripting tools include Chatscript[16] and the Facebook Messenger Developers Kit.[17]

2.3.3 ADVANCED TOOLKITS AND FRAMEWORKS

There are a number of toolkits and frameworks that support the development of more advanced dialogue systems. In these toolkits machine learning is used in the NLU component to classify the user's utterances as intents, while in most of the toolkits DM and NLG are developed using handcrafted rules. A list of the main advanced toolkits is provided in the Appendix. The next subsections provide some examples of how the various types of conversational interaction described in Chapter 1, 1.4 are handled in these systems.

User-Initiated Dialogue

In user-initiated dialogue the system designer cannot easily control what the user says, so there is a requirement for NLU to be able to handle a wide range of user inputs. A second issue is that on receiving a system response, the user might wish to continue with a follow-up utterance that the NLU component would have to be able to handle.

Interpreting the user's inputs Generally, some form of NLU is required to interpret the user's utterances. AIML is an exception as here the user's inputs are matched against a large set of predesigned patterns, using the techniques described earlier to handle utterances that are similar. If an input cannot be matched, the Ultimate default category is invoked to output a non-committal response and to try to keep the conversation going. The advantage of this approach is that there is no requirement for an advanced NLU component. The disadvantage is that the developer has to anticipate everything a user might say to the system. Using the Ultimate default category may work fine for chit-chat dialogues but would not be acceptable in more serious dialogues, such as business encounters or healthcare support.

The advanced tools use machine learning algorithms in the NLU component to identify intents and extract entities from the user's utterances. The developer supplies sample utterances that are typical of what a user might say in a particular application and the system uses machine learning to identify the intents behind the user's utterances and extract the entities in the utterances (see Chapter 3, Section 3.2.1). Most tools have libraries of system intents and system entities and the developer only needs to create those are specific to the domain of the application. For example, Dialogflow[18] supports more than 40 system-entities such as: date, time, number, duration, temperature, address, zip-code, and geo-state.[19]

[16] https://sourceforge.net/projects/chatscript/
[17] https://developers.facebook.com/docs/messenger-platform/
[18] https://cloud.google.com/dialogflow/
[19] https://cloud.google.com/dialogflow/es/docs/reference/system-entities

Table 2.3: Follow-up intents in Dialogflow

Intent	Utterance	Context
Parent	What's the weather forecast for London?	Output context: weather
Child	What about Belfast?	Input context: weather

Teneo from Artificial Solutions[20] offers a hybrid approach to NLU in which machine learning and linguistic models are combined. The motivation for the use of linguistic models is that they provide greater precision, i.e., more accurate interpretation, particularly for utterances that could be classed as similar with a machine learning algorithm but that might have different meanings. For example, in a dialogue system for a shopping application a user might say something like *I bought a pair of trousers, how do I return them?* Rather than classifying this utterance along with other utterances mentioning purchases as an intent to make a purchase, this utterance should be treated as a different use case. To do this, the developer specifies a special rule to capture this use case and an alternative dialogue flow is generated to handle it.[21] Note that handcrafted linguistic rules such as these are applicable to specific business domains and that Teneo is intended for such applications and not for open-domain conversations where it would not be realistic to predict and specify a complete set of alternative interpretations in this way.

Handling follow-up utterances Recall from Chapter 1, Section 1.4.1 that users can follow-up an utterance with a related query or command. For the follow-up utterance to be successfully interpreted, the system needs to be able to preserve the context of the initial query. This can be done in different ways.

In Dialogflow follow-up queries are handled by setting an output context for the initial intent (known as the *parent*) and a matching input context for its *child intent*. This means that the interpreter will prioritize subsequent utterances that have a matching input context. Table 2.3 shows a simple example.

Without these context settings, the utterance *what about Belfast?* would be treated as a new query, with a response such as *Belfast is the capital and largest city of Northern Ireland and the second largest on the island of Ireland.*[22]

[20] https://www.teneo.ai/

[21] See https://www.brighttalk.com/webcast/17594/408812/demo-using-hybrid-nlu-to-rapidly-build-conversational-ai-solutions.

[22] This was the response to a follow-up question on a smart speaker in 2018. More recently that system has been able to handle follow-up questions correctly.

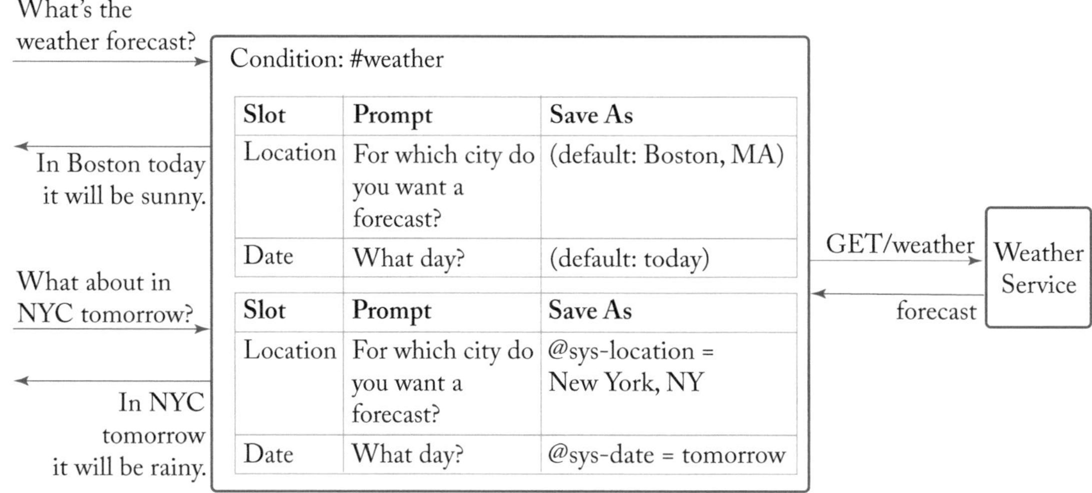

Figure 2.5: Follow-up utterances in the IBM Watson Assistant. Based on https://cloud.ibm.com/docs/assistant?topic=assistant-dialog-slots.

In the IBM Watson Assistant[23] and the Amazon Alexa Skills Kit[24] each query has associated slots. As shown in Figure 2.5 this technique supports system clarification requests and follow-up questions by the users.[25]

For example, a weather forecast query has slots for **location** and **date**. If either of these are missing in the user's utterance, the system prompts for them and then saves the responses as default values. If the user asks a follow-up question, slot replacement is used. For example, the question *what about in NYC tomorrow?* results in the **location** slot being set to "New York" and the **date** being set to "tomorrow". This method also supports correction of a value by the user. The main drawback with this approach is that the designer has to specify the slots that are required for any potential user query. This is only possible with domain-specific dialogues, particularly those involving a specific business use case.

In some implementations of the slot-based approach queries and their slots are associated with a particular domain. For example, in the previous examples the query *what's the weather in Boston?* would be associated with the **weather** domain. However, in a multi-domain dialogue the follow-up query might be mapped to a different domain with different slot names so that it cannot be handled using simple slot replacement. The example in Table 2.4 illustrates.

In this example the name of the slot for "San Francisco" changes across the three utterances due to the fact that each domain has its own schema for the representation of slots and intents.

[23] https://www.ibm.com/cloud/watson-assistant/

[24] https://developer.amazon.com/en-US/alexa/alexa-skills-kit/

[25] Source: https://cloud.ibm.com/docs/assistant?topic=assistant-dialog-slots.

Table 2.4: Slot carry-over in multi-domain dialogue. Based on Naik et al. [2016].

Utterance	Domain	Slot
What's the weather in San Francisco?	Weather	WeatherLocation: San Francisco
Are there any restaurants nearby?	LocalSearch	City: San Francisco
Send directions to my phone	Traffic	Town: San Francisco

Because of this it is difficult to maintain contextual relations across domain boundaries [Naik et al., 2016].

System-Directed Dialogue

In system-directed dialogue the system prompts the user for input so that the user's utterances are generally more constrained than in user-initiated dialogues. The system also controls the flow of the dialogue.

In Section 2.3.2 it was shown how VoiceXML implements slot-filling dialogues by specifying the slots in a form that is then processed by the Form Interpretation Algorithm. Various similar techniques are used in the advanced tools.

Dialogflow uses a parameter table to specify slots that are required to be filled in the dialogue. The system executes the prompts for each slot and extracts the required values from the user's responses. IBM Watson Assistant uses a similar parameter table. Figure 2.6 shows an example of a parameter table in Dialogflow for a restaurant reservation system where the required slots are **number**, **date**, and **time**. If the boxes in the Required column are ticked, the system will elicit the values for those slots. Examples of prompts to elicit the slot values are shown in the Prompts column.

In Amazon Alexa a Dialog Model is created in which required and optional slots are specified along with prompts to elicit and confirm the values. The Dialog Interface manages the slot-filling using the **dialogState** property to determine if additional steps are required in the dialogue or if all steps have been completed.

Microsoft Bot Builder[26] provides two different approaches to slot-filling. In the Bot Builder SDK (Software Developer Kit) for .NET, the developer creates a FormFlow—a C# class or JSON (JavaScript Object Notation) schema—that is used to collect information from the user. The dialogue is automatically generated based on the form. As an alternative the Bot Builder SDK for Node.js makes use of a Waterfall dialogue model in which a sequence of steps is specified for completing an action or prompting the user for information. The waterfall is implemented as an array of functions where the results of the first function are passed as input to the next function.

[26] https://dev.botframework.com/

REQUIRED	PARAMETER NAME	ENTITY	VALUE	IS LIST	PROMPTS
✓	number	@sys.number	$sys.number	☐	Sure. For how many people?
✓	date	@sys.date	$sys.date	☐	And on what day?
✓	time	@sys.time	$sys.time	☐	What time would you prefer?
☐	Enter name	Enter entity	Enter value	☐	—

+ New parameter

Figure 2.6: Parameter table in Dialogflow.

Multi-Turn Open-Domain Dialogue

The simplest approach to multi-turn dialogues is to map out the complete predicted conversation flow, as described in Section 2.3.1. However, as mentioned earlier, this approach is only possible with simple dialogues and quickly becomes unmanageable when more choices and branchings are added. For example, Meyer [2020] states that a pizza ordering skill with seven topping combinations could require more than 5,000 dialogue paths.

In order to address the intricacies of multi-turn open-domain dialogue, it is also necessary to include mechanisms for dealing with various conversational phenomena, such as:

- cohesion, e.g., dealing with anaphoric reference, as in Example 2.2.

  Example 2.2

  ALANA: I would love to meet **Will Smith**. **He**'s so funny.
  USER: Who is **he**?

- Coherence, e.g., dealing with topic maintenance, shifts in topics, and returns to previous topics. This requires the ability to handle discourse markers such as *As I was saying …*, *To go back to your previous point, …, etc.*

- Ellipsis resolution, e.g., resolving elliptical or fragmentary utterances to full sentences to facilitate natural language understanding and discourse processing. For example, the user's elliptical utterance *I do* as a response to the system's question *Do you like wine?* would be resolved to *I like wine*.

Table 2.5: Interactive learning in RASA

User	System
search_concerts	0.72 action_search_concerts
compare_reviews	**System choices** 0.53 action_show_venue_reviews 0.46 action_show_concert_reviews
The bot wants to run "action_show_venue_reviews", is this correct?	

These phenomena have been discussed extensively in computational approaches to discourse and dialogue [Brady and Berwick, 1983], [Grosz and Sidner, 1986], [Webber, 2001], [Moore and Wiemer-Hastings, 2003], but they have barely been addressed in current dialogue systems. See, however, some attempts to address discourse phenomena in the systems participating in the Alexa Prize (Sections 1.4.3 and 2.4).

Optimizing Dialogue Management One of the main tasks for DM is to decide on the next system action. In rule-based DM dialogue decisions are hand-crafted, as in most of the tools discussed in this section. Two exceptions are RASA[27] and Alexa Conversations.[28]

In RASA machine learning is used to optimize the dialogue management component using interactive learning. In the interactive learning mode the developer runs dialogues in test mode and provides step-by-step feedback on every step in the dialogue. If the system chooses the wrong action, the developer tells it what the correct action should have been and the dialogue model is updated. In this way an optimal dialogue policy (see Section 3.3.4 can be learned within a fairly small number of training dialogues. Table 2.5 shows a simple example, adapted from the tutorial on interactive learning in Rasa in which the numbers represent action probabilities.[29]

The user's first utterance is classified as the intent **search_concerts** and the system selects **action_search_concerts** as its next action. The user's next utterance is classified as the intent **compare_reviews**. There are two possible next system actions: **0.53 action_show_venue_reviews** and **0.46 action_show_concert_reviews**. The system suggests **action_show_venue_reviews** as the one with the higher probability. The user can reject this suggestion and choose **action_show_concert_reviews** as the correct system action.

Alexa Conversations is an AI-driven dialogue manager that addresses the issue of creating a large number of dialogue paths in goal-oriented dialogues. The developer provides sample annotated dialogues along with system prompts and expected system actions, and the system uses a dialogue simulation engine to automatically generate synthetic training data [Meyer, 2020].

[27] https://rasa.com/
[28] https://developer.amazon.com/en-US/docs/alexa/conversations/about-alexa-conversations.html
[29] https://rasa.com/docs/rasa/core/interactive-learning/

In this way DM is able to learn the large number of paths that the dialogue might take and can predict the optimal next system action in the dialogue.

2.3.4 RESEARCH-BASED TOOLKITS

In addition to the commercial toolkits discussed in the previous sections, there are many research-based toolkits that have been developed in university and industry research laboratories (see Appendix A). This section presents a brief overview of one of these research-based toolkits—the Plato Research Dialogue System—developed at Uber AI [Papangelis et al., 2020].

Plato is a platform for building, training and deploying Conversational AI agents, enabling researchers to conduct state of the art research in Conversational AI, create prototypes, and collect conversational data. A range of different conversational architectures is supported, including rule-based, statistical, and end-to-end. The system can interact with human users, simulated users, and other conversational agents and can be trained online (through interactions) or offline (using data).

In a recent paper, Papangelis et al. [2019] described how the Plato platform was used to train two conversational agents to talk to each other where one of the agents had to ask for restaurant information and the other provided the information. The interaction was modeled as a stochastic collaborative game in which each agent had to learn to operate optimally in an environment with multiple sources of uncertainty (its own NLU and NLG, the other agent's NLU, Dialogue policy, and NLG). Over time the conversations became more and more natural, while in an evaluation study it was found that the stochastic-game agents outperformed deep learning-based supervised baselines.

2.3.5 WHICH IS THE BEST TOOLKIT?

With so many toolkits to choose from, we might ask which is the best for developing a dialogue system. This is not a simple question to answer, as it depends on a number of different factors.

The original motivation behind visual design tools was to help designers and developers create dialogue systems without needing to code. Many simple systems have been created in this way. However, as providers began to add more functionalities to their tools, visual tools have come to be seen more as a way to quickly specify and test all the possible flows in a dialogue system before moving on to the next stage where more advanced functionalities are coded, usually in one of the advanced toolkits. Visual flows are best suited for dialogue systems with few branchings, otherwise the flows quickly become unmanageable. Indeed, conversation flows for some commercial systems can run to hundreds of pages [Paek and Pieraccini, 2008].

One advantage of VoiceXML is that the developer can specify dialogue behaviors declaratively without having to think about how the code is interpreted. To take a simple example, a **noinput** event, where the system does not detect any input from the user, can be specified declaratively as follows:

```
<noinput count="1"> Sorry I didn't hear anything <reprompt/> </noinput>
```

<noinput count="2"> I still can't hear you. Please speak louder or move closer to the microphone. </noinput>

The FIA keeps count of the number of times the event fires and executes the required prompts. In other systems such as Dialogflow these behaviors would have to be coded in a language such as Node.js.

One downside, however, is that in some cases it can be difficult to easily predict the behavior of the FIA without a detailed understanding of the algorithm [Akolkar, 2010]. Indeed, as Rojas-Barahona and Giorgino [2009] conclude, VoiceXML provided a single dialogue formalism at a time when there were many incompatible approaches but at the cost of adding more complexity and requiring considerable engineering effort to implement.

Another issue with VoiceXML is that it was designed primarily for voice-based interactions on standard landline phones and was not able to take advantage of the multimodal capabilities of smart phones and other devices with visual displays. The World Wide Web Consortium (W3C) produced a document in 2008 describing the W3C Multimodal Architecture that included various W3C markup languages, including SCXML, CCXML, VoiceXML 2.1, and HTML.[30] These recommendations have not been adopted in current dialogue toolkits and platforms and as a result conflicting terms and approaches are often used when referring to the same phenomena. The Voice Interaction Community Group within the W3C is an attempt to address this issue;[31] see also Dahl [2017].

AIML is a popular scripting language for chatbot developers and more than 300,000 chatbots have been created using AIML on the Pandorabots platform.[32] The advantage of AIML is that it is easy to learn and does not require a background in programming. However, authoring a chatbot in AIML requires a good appreciation of how conversation works in order to predict and specify user inputs as patterns and determine appropriate system responses. Moreover, in order to handle more complex dialogues, new mechanisms have to be devised. See, for example, Worswick's solutions in AIML for dealing with situations where the user's input is off topic and how to bring the conversation back on track [Worswick, 2019].

The advanced toolkits listed in Appendix A offer a wider range of features, particularly for intent recognition in the NLU component. There are numerous blogs comparing tools in terms of factors such as ease of use, integration with platforms such as Google Assistant and Facebook, languages supported, NLU accuracy, quality of documentation, and costs. Dialogflow is often seen as being the easiest tool for developers with less coding experience who wish to create fairly basic applications. Creating a more advanced Dialogflow application, however, requires an ability to code. See, for example, tutorials in the Google Codelabs.[33] Amazon Lex assumes that developers have a solid grounding in machine learning and conversational systems development, while IBM Watson Assistant and Microsoft Bot Framework are targeted more toward corpo-

[30] https://www.w3.org/TR/mmi-auth/
[31] https://w3c.github.io/voiceinteraction/voice%20interaction%20drafts/paArchitecture-1-1.htm
[32] https://www.pandorabots.com/docs/
[33] https://codelabs.developers.google.com/

rations and enterprises. Rasa has an advantage for some developers in that it is open-source. All of the platforms offer extensive documentation, often with lively videos.

In summary, there is no easy answer to the question "which is the best tool" as it depends on a number of factors: what sort of system is to be developed, the developer's level of expertise, the availability of the toolkit, e.g., whether it is open-source, subject to a license, etc., the performance of its components, e.g., how accurately the NLU can classify user intents, how well the system is documented, what resources are provided, e.g., datasets for training, pre-trained models, etc.

The tools and techniques described in this chapter are intended to support designers and developers who follow the traditional approach of handcrafting dialogue systems. Chapters 3 and 5 will review alternative approaches in which handcrafting is avoided in favor of the use of machine learning algorithms to optimize the various aspects of dialogue systems. However, some of the most advanced dialogue systems have used a combination of rule-based and machine-learning-based methods. Hybrid dialogue systems will be discussed in more detail in Chapter 6. The next section describes some of the rule-based techniques that have been used in systems participating in the Amazon Alexa prize.

2.4 RULE-BASED TECHNIQUES IN DIALOGUE SYSTEMS PARTICIPATING IN THE ALEXA PRIZE

As mentioned in Chapter 1, the Alexa Prize was set up by Amazon in 2016 as a challenge to student teams from universities to create a socialbot that could converse with Alexa on a wide range of topics. Most teams used a combination of handcrafted (rule-based) and machine learning-based approaches. In this section we will describe some of the rule-based methods used in the 2018 competition by the top three teams, Gunrock [Yu et al., 2018], which came first, Alquist [Pichl et al., 2018], which came second, and Alana [Cercas Curry et al., 2018], which came third.

Gunrock [Yu et al., 2018] took an interesting approach to dealing with potential speech recognition problems by creating an ASR Correction module that consulted a special knowledge base if the word confidence score was below a certain threshold. The knowledge base contained lists of homophones and the system would query the knowledge base for the domain of the current conversation to retrieve substitute noun phrases in the user's utterance using homophone information.

For NLU the systems used pipelines of various complexity that performed several operations on the recognized input. Gunrock used a sentence segmentation strategy to break down longer inputs into multiple sentences that were easier for the NLU to process. Alana's NLU pipeline consisted of nine components, including a Contextual Preprocessor for transforming elliptical responses using contextual information, a Named entity Recognizer ensemble, Sentiment Analyzer, Entity Linker, and Entity Topic Classifier. The Entity Linker was used to map a given surface form in the user's utterance to an entity in the related knowledge base in order to identify additional information about an entity that may have been referenced by a different surface form in the knowledge base. An interactive clarification module was used to identify ambiguous entities produced during entity linking. The module generated a clarification question, analyzed the user's response and then resumed the dialogue, as shown in Example 2.3:

Example 2.3

ALANA: Oh I know Tom Hardy. Do you mean Tom Hardy the English actor, screenwriter and producer or Thomas Hardy the English novelist and poet?
USER: I mean the novelist.

Response generation used a mixture of rule-based as well as machine learning-based techniques. Two of the bots in Alana's bot ensemble—Persona and ELIZA—were handcrafted using AIML rules, while the rest were retrieval-based and used machine-learning techniques (see Chapter 5, Section 5.4). The Persona bot was used to respond to specific user questions about Alana's personality, e.g., *How old are you? Do you like dancing?*, while the ELIZA bot, which is an extension of the AIML-based ROSIE chatbot, provided basic chit-chat. Interestingly, the Alana team performed a series of ablation studies in which a bot would be removed and then the quality of the conversations without that bot was assessed. It was found that removal of the ELIZA bot had the largest negative impact on the quality ratings [Cercas Curry et al., 2018]. A deep learning method was developed for selecting the best bot response in context from the priority bot list [Shalyminov et al., 2018].

For text-to-speech output the socialbots used the Alexa TTS services. However, in the case of Gunrock the prosodic aspects of the output were marked up using SSML. Users evaluating the version of the system using SSML reported that it sounded more natural.

Several handcrafted techniques were used to improve the conversational performance of the socialbots. Each of the teams used a hierarchical dialogue management structure in which an overall Dialogue Manager controlled a set of smaller components that handled different tasks, such as conversations about different topics. Various techniques were used to select the best bot for a particular task, such as topic identification and selection. Alana used a Priority Bot List that determined which bot should handle the current turn, where the priorities were based on probabilistic decisions with handcrafted weights.

Dialogue Management in Alquist was implemented using Hybrid Code Networks (HCNs) [Williams et al., 2017] that combined a Recurrent Neural Network (RNN) (see Chapter 5, Section 5.3.2) with domain-specific knowledge encoded as software and system action templates. When a new sub-dialogue was to be created, its content and inner decision logic were handcrafted using a graphical dialogue editor. The finished dialogue was then converted to training examples for the HCN by generating all possible transitions through the dialogue.

Remaining on topic and continuing the conversation is an important element of a multi-turn conversation. For this Alana used the Coherence Bot that makes use of a simple model of the user's preferences, as shown in Example 2.4:

Example 2.4

ALANA: Welcome back then `username`. Since I remember that you like movies, I am looking forward to the new movie Jurassic world that was just released. What movie are you looking forward to watching?

...

ALANA: Since I know you like books, what have you read recently?

Alana is also able to accept the user's requests to change the topic, as in Example 2.5:

Example 2.5

ALANA: I think Chewbacca is my favorite character.
USER: I want to talk about music.
ALANA: So, talking about music ...

The socialbots were all able to engage in mixed-initiative dialogue. For example, Alana could switch topic if the conversation demanded it, i.e., if it looked like the conversation was coming to a halt. Similarly, if Gunrock detected that the user did not have a clear intent or actionable request, the system would propose a new topic or ask a relevant question.

SUMMARY

This chapter has reviewed the rule-based approach that has been the traditional way to develop a dialogue system. In this approach the behaviors of the various components of the system, and in particular the Dialogue Manager, are handcrafted and the processing follows a typical pipeline architecture. The various stages involved in developing a dialogue system were described: initial use case definitions, requirements analysis, preliminary exploration, using methods such as simulation and Wizard of Oz, scripting, and design. A range of tools for developing dialogue systems was presented, including authoring tools with a visual interface for designing conversation flows, code-based scripting tools, more advanced toolkits using some AI, and research-based toolkits.

Creating multi-turn open-domain dialogues remains a challenge for dialogue system developers, especially when the conversation flow becomes more complex and cannot be easily specified in advance using visual or other tools. Some solutions using a mixture of handcrafting and machine learning have been provided by teams competing in the Alexa Prize, where the aim is to develop a system that can converse in a coherent and engaging way for up to 20 minutes.

While the rule-based approach is less fashionable nowadays in research environments, it is still the preferred method of implementation for many commercially deployed systems. One reason is that the development team can feel assured that they have full control over the operation of their system. Nevertheless, machine learning-based approaches now dominate the field of dialogue systems and Chapters 3 and 5 will review developments in this area.

CHAPTER 3

Statistical Data-Driven Dialogue Systems

While rule-based dialogue systems as described in Chapter 2 are still widely used, particularly in commercially deployed dialogue systems, an alternative approach involving machine learning from data has come to dominate current dialogue systems research and is also being increasingly applied in commercial systems. As Serban et al. [2015] write:

> There is strong evidence that over the next few years dialogue research will quickly move toward large-scale data-driven model approaches, in particular in the form of end-to-end trainable systems.

There have been two main phases in the history of statistical data-driven dialogue systems. In the first phase, beginning around the late 1990s, systems continued to be developed using the modular architecture presented in Chapter 2 but efforts were directed toward the use of machine-learning techniques to optimize the components of the architecture, in particular the Natural Language Understanding (NLU), Dialogue Manager (DM), and Natural Language Generation (NLG) components.

In the second phase, a different approach known as *end-to-end neural dialogue systems* emerged. In this approach Deep Neural Networks (DNNs) are used within a Sequence to Sequence (Seq2Seq) architecture to map input utterances directly to output responses without requiring any processing by the modules of the traditional modular architecture. End-to-end dialogue systems will be covered in Chapter 5.

This chapter presents an overview of statistical data-driven dialogue systems based on a modular pipelined architecture. The chapter is structured as follows. Section 3.1 provides a brief motivation for the statistical data-driven approach, while Section 3.2 shows how statistical data-driven methods have been applied to the various components of the traditional dialogue systems architecture. Section 3.3 reviews a new approach to DM in which Reinforcement Learning (RL) is used to train and optimize the Dialogue policy of DM.

3.1 MOTIVATING THE STATISTICAL DATA-DRIVEN APPROACH

Proponents of the statistical data-driven approach argue that rule-based dialogue systems are costly to develop, cannot be easily adapted to new domains, require advanced skills to engineer, and are difficult to maintain [Young, 2000], [Rieser and Lemon, 2011b], [Lemon, 2012]. It is also argued that rule-based systems are not robust to errors and cannot easily handle problems such as misunderstandings or unexpected input. As far as dialogue management is concerned, a rule-based dialogue strategy is designed according to best practice guidelines but cannot be guaranteed to be optimal. Furthermore, the dialogue strategy is essentially static unless manually updated, whereas a dialogue strategy that is learned from data can be updated automatically.

In a statistical data-driven dialogue system the processes involved in the various components of the system are modeled probabilistically. For example, the system's dialogue strategy is based on uncertain information that has been derived from the output of the ASR and NLU components. As a result, the system's belief state, i.e., its beliefs about the current state of the dialogue, in particular its beliefs about what the user has said, are uncertain and DM has to maintain a distribution over multiple hypotheses of the dialogue state. Learning in a statistical data-driven dialogue system is data-driven. The data can take various forms. On the one hand, it can be data from previous dialogues that are similar in domain to that of the current system. Systems that learn from data in this way are referred to as *corpus-based* or *example-based* (see further Section 3.2.2). Another type of data derives from interactions with the system using either real or simulated users, where the data is used to optimize the system's dialogue strategy (known in this approach as its *Dialogue policy*, see Section 3.3.4). This approach uses the techniques of *Reinforcement Learning* (see further Section 3.3). The following sections describe how the statistical data-driven approach has been applied to the various components of the traditional modular dialogue systems architecture.

3.2 DIALOGUE COMPONENTS IN THE STATISTICAL DATA-DRIVEN APPROACH

In Chapter 2, a typical modular pipelined architecture for spoken dialogue systems was presented in Figure 2.1. The architecture is shown here for convenience in Figure 3.1 with one modification: in the sub-components of the DM component *Dialogue policy* has replaced *Dialogue Control*, and *Dialogue state tracking* has replaced *Dialogue Context Model*. These changes reflect the terminology used currently in the literature, particularly with reference to Reinforcement Learning-based dialogue systems (see further Section 3.3).

3.2.1 NATURAL LANGUAGE UNDERSTANDING

The NLU module takes the output from the ASR module and produces a representation of the meaning of the user's utterance. In spoken dialogue systems the NLU module is often called *Spoken Language Understanding (SLU)* and the term *Conversational Language Understanding* has also been used to emphasize that the nature of the language involved differs from that of more formal written text [Tur et al., 2018]. In this book the more neutral term *Natural Language Understanding* is used.

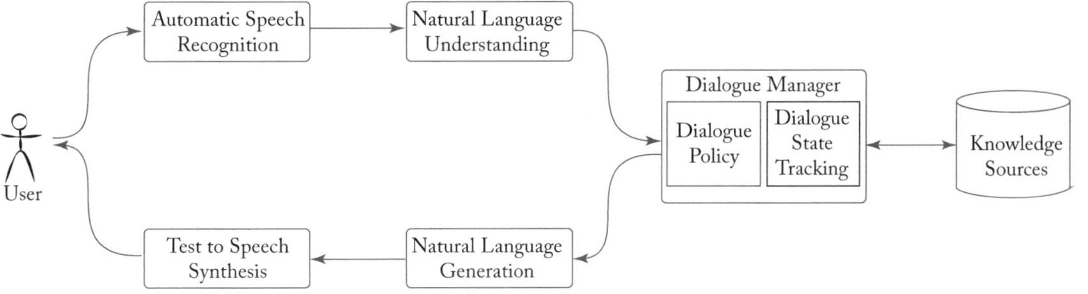

Figure 3.1: Spoken dialogue systems architecture.

The traditional approach to NLU as described in Chapter 2 involved handcrafting grammars containing all the rules required to cover all anticipated inputs, and then building a parser to apply the rules to the inputs. One problem is that it is impossible to guarantee that all possible inputs have been covered by the rules. Another problem is that in this approach the input has to match the rules exactly or else it cannot be parsed, so that small variations in the input require additional rules in order to be accepted by the grammar. These variations can take the form of synonymous strings that should result in the same meaning representation. For example: the string *I want to travel from Belfast to London on Friday* should have the same meaning representation as *I want to travel to London from Belfast on Friday* and *I want to travel on Friday from Belfast to London*, even though they are syntactically different. Catering for these syntactic variations in a handcrafted grammar would quickly lead to an explosion in the number of rules required. A further problem is that spoken input often includes disfluencies and other phenomena such as self-corrections, for example, *I want to travel from Belfast to London um let me think on Friday no not Friday Thursday*. It would be difficult, if not impossible, to capture phenomena such as these in a traditional rule-based grammar.

Another problem is when a string is ambiguous, i.e., it has more than one syntactic analysis giving rise to more than one semantic reading. Prepositional phrase attachment is a common cause of syntactic ambiguity. A simple parse tree was shown in Figure 2.2 in Chapter 2. However, as shown in Figure 3.2 there are actually two possible parse trees for the string *book a seat on the train* given the CFG rules listed in the figure.

In this CFG there are two Verb Phrase (VP) rules and two Noun Phrase (NP) rules. Taking VP rule 2 and NP rule 5 produces Parse 1, in which the object of *book* is derived from NP rule 5, i.e., *a seat on the train*, giving the meaning that the seat being booked is on the train. Within NP rule 5 there is an application of NP rule 4 to parse the phrase *the train*. Parse 2 results from the application of VP rule 3, in which the object of *book* is derived from NP rule 4, i.e., *a seat*, with the phrase *on the train* analyzed as a PP (Prepositional Phrase) attached to the verb *book*, giving rise to a reading in which the booking of the seat is being done on the train, but it is not necessarily a seat on the train—for example, in a context where someone plans to book a

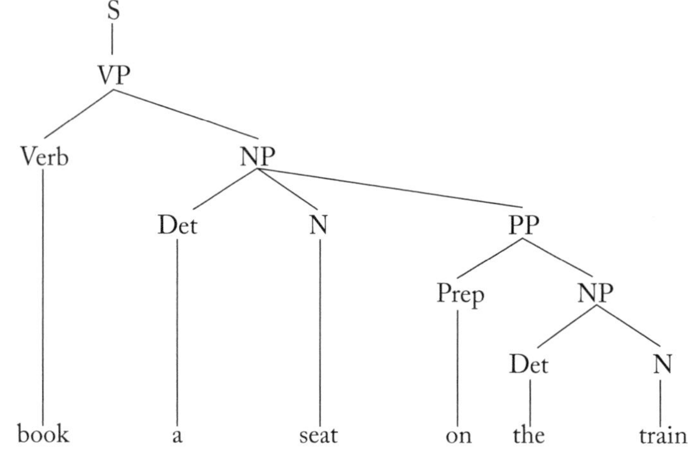

CFG Rules
1. S->VP
2. VP->Verb NP
3. VP->Verb NP VP
4. NP->Det N
5. NP->Det N PP
6. PP->Prep NP

Lexicon
Verb-> *book*
Det-> *a*|*the*
N-> *seat*|*train*
Prep-> *on*

Parse 1: book (a seat on the train)

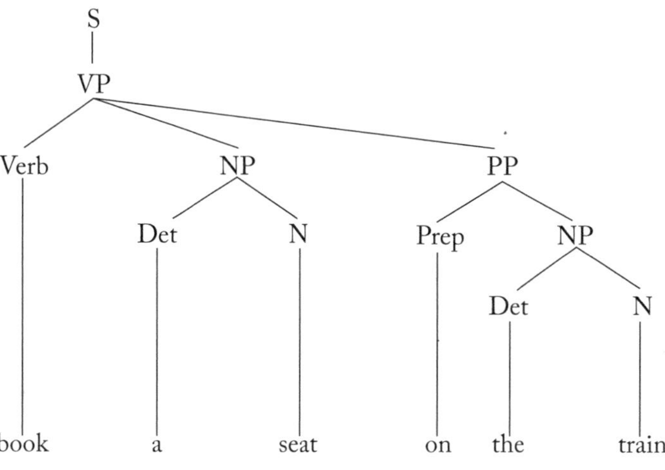

Parse 2: book (a seat) (on the train)

Figure 3.2: Two parse trees for the string *book a seat on the train*.

seat at the theatre and should do it once they have boarded the train. The first reading is more likely in most contexts but it is not possible to determine this using only syntactic information. The alternative parses would have to be passed to another component of the system that could determine which is the correct (or more probable) interpretation. This may not be a problem with simple examples such as this, but the number of ambiguities can expand exponentially if more prepositional phrases are added (see an example and discussion in Jurafsky and Martin [2020], Chapter 11).

Probabilistic grammars and parsers offer a solution to the problem of ambiguity by ranking the probabilities of multiple parses so that the most probable parse can be selected. The probabilities can be passed on to DM, enabling it to make decisions about the best action to take given the level of uncertainty in the interpretation of the user's input.

Probabilistic context-free grammars (PCFGs) are the most frequently used type of probabilistic grammar. In a PCFG each rule of the grammar is associated with a probability. The probabilities for the rules can be learned from a corpus of parsed sentences, e.g., a treebank such as the Penn Treebank [Marcus et al., 1993]. Probabilistic parsers have been developed as extensions of standard parsing algorithms. The Stanford parser is a widely used example of a probabilistic parser. For a comprehensive discussion of probabilistic grammars and parsers, see Jurafsky and Martin [2020], Chapter 14.

In handcrafted as well as in probabilistic NLU the aim is to parse the complete input utterance in order to produce a representation of its meaning. This approach is known as *deep parsing*. More recently the emphasis has been on shallower parsing that aims to extract from the input those elements that are relevant to the current task. As described in Chapter 2 (Section 2.1.2), typically three elements are extracted: the *domain* to which the utterance relates (for example, flight reservations), the user's *intent* (for example, to book a flight), and the *entities* that are required to make the reservation (for example, destination, date of travel, etc). This information is sometimes called a *semantic frame*.

Training the NLU module requires a corpus of utterances taken from the domain of the specific dialogue system. Alternatively, in the commercial toolkits described in Chapter 2 such as Dialogflow, Amazon Lex, and RASA, developers create a list of the intents that will be used in a particular dialogue system and supply a list of training utterances for each intent. Entities in each training utterance are labeled and their synonyms are identified. These training utterances and entities are then combined with the training utterances and entities in the toolkit's corpus.

Identification of an utterance as a particular intent can be seen as a classification problem for which machine learning technologies such as the Support Vector Machine (SVM) have been widely used [Schuurmans and Frasincar, 2019], [Larson et al., 2019]. Extracting the entities is treated as a sequence classification problem using techniques such as conditional random fields [Tur and De Mori, 2011]. This approach to the identification of intents is more robust than handcrafted grammar rules as utterances can be mapped on to intents even when the wording is not exactly the same as in the original training examples. Moreover, given additional data obtained from interactions with the application, the model can be re-trained to provide even greater accuracy and wider coverage. Hahn et al. [2010] present a comprehensive evaluation of different models for data-driven NLU. See also Henderson and Jurčíček [2012], Tur and De Mori [2011]), Tur et al. [2018], and Wang et al. [2011].

Recently deep learning methods have been applied in NLU and have been shown to outperform other machine learning-based approaches. Hinton et al. [2006] and Sarikaya et al. [2014] applied Deep Belief Networks (DBNs) to utterance classification and intent determination. Tur et al. [2012] used Deep Convex Nets (DCNs) to address the issues of accuracy, efficiency, and scalability associated with DBNs. Convolutional Neural Networks (CNNs) have become widely used for utterance classification [Collobert and Weston, 2008], often combined with or replaced by Recurrent Neural Network (RNN) (see Chapter 5, Section 5.3.2 and [Socher et al., 2011]). Different variants of RNNs have also been used widely for slot filling [Mesnil et al., 2013], [Mesnil et al., 2014]. Hakkani-Tür et al. [2016] used a bi-directional Recurrent Neural Network (RNN) to jointly classify intents and extract entities, while Vanzo and Lemon [2019] presented a new neural architecture for frame semantic parsing that jointly extracted intents and entities and that out-performed state-of-the-art tools such as RASA, Dialogflow, LUIS,[1] and IBM Watson Assistant.[2] For more detail on deep learning in NLU, see Tur et al. [2018].

3.2.2 DIALOGUE MANAGEMENT

The main task of DM is to decide what action to take next given the user's input and the current state of the dialogue. Traditionally, dialogue management has involved using rules handcrafted by a dialogue designer to implement predetermined design decisions. For example, handling potential ASR misrecognitions might involve considerations as to whether and when to confirm the user's input and whether to use information such as ASR confidence scores. These design decisions, which are generally based on experience and best practice guidelines, are applied in an iterative process of design and testing until the optimal system is produced.

However, designing all the rules that are required to cover all potential interactions of a dialogue system soon becomes a difficult, if not impossible task, particularly when taking into account the uncertainties that pervade every level of dialogue, from the recognition of what words were spoken to understanding the intentions behind the words. For this reason statistical data-driven methods have been proposed as a method for determining and optimizing the decision processes of DM.

There are two main approaches to data-driven statistical dialogue management. The first approach, which will be discussed in this section, involves learning the parameters of the statistical dialogue model from a corpus of dialogues. This approach is known as *corpus-based dialogue management* [Griol et al., 2008], [Griol et al., 2014]. The second approach involves the use of *Partially Observable Markov Decision Processes (POMDPs)* and Reinforcement Learning. This is the most widespread approach to statistical dialogue management and will be discussed in Section 3.3. Other approaches include: example-based dialogue management [Lee et al., 2009], which is similar to the corpus-based approach; modeling using Hidden Markov Models [Cuayáhuitl et al., 2005]; and modeling using Bayesian networks [Paek and Horvitz, 2000], [Meng et al., 2003].

In the corpus-based approach a dialogue is seen as a sequence of states where each state consists of a system turn (A) and a user turn (U). The task of DM is to find the best system act

[1] https://www.luis.ai/

[2] https://www.ibm.com/cloud/watson-assistant/

Ai at each time i, taking into account the preceding states of the dialogue. More formally:

$$\hat{A}_i = \underset{A_i \in A}{\arg\max} P(A_i | S_1, \ldots, S_{i-1}). \tag{3.1}$$

However, taking into account all the preceding states of the dialogue is likely to lead to combinatorial explosion. For this reason Griol et al. [2008] proposed that the state space could be partitioned though the use of a Dialogue Register (DR) that is similar in function to Dialogue state tracking as used in the RL approach (see Section 3.3.3). DR contains information about the concepts and attributes provided by the user over the previous states of the dialogue. The information in the DR is coded taking only into account whether the user had provided a value for the concept or attribute along with its confidence score rather than representing the actual value. A further simplification is that different sequences of state spaces that lead to the same DR are considered equivalent. In this way the state space can be reduced at a possible cost of the loss of the chronological sequence of events, although this is not considered significant, as the main requirement is to elicit values for a number of data items but not in any particular order. Given the DR, the problem of finding the best system act can then be specified as:

$$\hat{A}_i = \underset{A_i \in A}{\arg\max} P(A_i | DR_{i-1}, S_{i-1}). \tag{3.2}$$

The corpus-based DM was developed in the DIHANA project that provided information about train services, schedules, and fares in the Spanish railway system [Griol et al., 2008]. A corpus of dialogues was collected using the Wizard of Oz technique and a user simulator was used to extend the corpus automatically. Two different dialogue situations were investigated: in the first all of the data in the DR had confidence scores higher than a fixed threshold (safe state), while in the second situation one or more of the data had values lower than the threshold (uncertain state). These different situations each had a set of recommendation rules for the dialogue strategy. For example, in the safe state the system could use an implicit confirmation strategy while in the uncertain state an explicit confirmation strategy was used.

One problem faced by the corpus-based approach is when a pair (DR, S) is encountered that is unseen, i.e., is not in the training corpus. Example 3.1 based on Hurtado et al. [2005] illustrates:

Example 3.1

S1: Welcome to the railway information system. How can I help you?
U1: I want to go to Barcelona
S2: Do you want to know the timetables?
U2: Yes, for the Euromed train
S3: Tell me the departure date.
U3: Tomorrow

At U2 an unseen sequence has occurred as there is no (DR, S) in the corpus addressing the attribute **Train-Type (Euromed)**, so the system selects the nearest (DR', S') which asks about the **Departure-Date** and ignores the fact that the user asked about the type of train (Euromed). Different solutions have been evaluated for selecting the closest pair. In Hurtado et al. [2005] a distance measure was used. In an evaluation of this approach, although more than 25% of the dialogues contained unseen situations, the overall dialogue success rate was 85%. In another solution the coverage problem was treated as a classification issue, in which all pairs (DR, S) that provide the same system response in the training corpus are assigned to a class. During a new dialogue each unseen pair is then classified into one of the available classes, i.e., possible system answers. Hurtado et al. [2006] extended the use of this classification to manage both seen and unseen situations, using a multilayer perceptron (MLP) for the classification process.

Building on this earlier work, Griol et al. [2014] presented a corpus-based methodology for the development of statistical dialogue managers and the optimization of dialogue strategies. The statistical model was estimated from training data obtained from dialogues with a user simulator and automatically labeled. Task-independent information was separated from the model in order to make it domain-independent. The model was validated using four spoken dialogue systems of different levels of complexity (domains ranging from transaction to problem-solving tasks) and in three different languages (English, Spanish, and Italian). The evaluation results showed that the use of this framework allowed the rapid development of different dialogue managers for the various domains.

Recent work on corpus-based methods for dialogue management has benefited from the availability of large datasets. The MultiWOZ (Multi-Domain Wizard-of-Oz) dataset is a fully labeled collection of 10K human-human written conversations covering multiple domains and topics [Budzianowski et al., 2018], [Eric et al., 2020]. MetaLWOz (Meta-Learning Wizard-of-Oz)[3] is a dataset designed to help develop models capable of predicting user responses in unseen domains with the aim of reducing the amount of data required to train domain-specific dialogues [Shalyminov et al., 2020a], and Eric et al. [2017] describe a corpus of 3,031 multi-turn dialogues covering 3 domains to support the development of task-oriented dialogue systems; see Chapter 5, Section 5.8.1 for further discussion of datasets for dialogue systems development.

In some cases there is insufficient data to train a dialogue system. To address this issue Shalyminov et al. [2019] applied a *few-shot learning* setup in which they leveraged background knowledge from the MetaLWOz dataset, achieving state-of-the-art results; see further discussion of this work in Chapter 6.

3.2.3 NATURAL LANGUAGE GENERATION

As shown in Figures 2.1 and 3.1, NLG takes the output from DM and converts it into text. For example, DM's output might be a Communicative Act such as inform(number=10, cui-

[3]https://www.microsoft.com/en-us/research/project/metalwoz/

sine=Indian, price=cheap) which could be realized as *There are ten restaurants that serve Indian food and are in the cheap price range* [Lemon, 2012].

NLG is important since the quality of the system's output can affect the user's perceptions of the usability of the overall system. In Chapter 2, handcrafted methods using templates and rules were described. This section reviews some data-driven statistical methods.

Corpus-based methods have been used to optimize the output of NLG. Using a corpus of suitable data, such as the utterances of a domain expert, has the advantage that the generated text will be of good quality. In this approach, known as *over-generation and re-ranking*, a number of candidate outputs are generated and the best one is selected based on a re-ranking algorithm.

Oh and Rudnicky [2002] focused on the tasks of content selection, sentence planning, and realization. For the sentence planning phase output utterances were modeled by bigrams and appropriate outputs were chosen using bigram statistics. For the surface realization phase the corpus utterances were modeled by N-grams of varying length and new utterances were generated stochastically. With this approach it was possible to generate high quality output without the need for complex handcrafted grammar rules. Experiments showed that the stochastic system performed as well as a baseline template-based system.

Mairesse and Young [2014] is another example of a corpus-based approach. The authors developed a data-driven natural language system (BAGEL) in which generation involved searching for the most likely sequence of semantic concepts and realization phrases from data generated through crowdsourcing. The evaluation showed, among other things, that the BAGEL system was able to learn to generate utterances over a large, real-world domain and that human judges did not perceive them to be less natural than the outputs of a highly tuned handcrafted system.

While the corpus-based studies focus primarily on the generation of text at the level of realization, other work has been concerned with optimization of the decisions involved in content selection, known here as Information Presentation (IP) [Lemon, 2012], [Rieser et al., 2010], [Lemon, 2011], [Rieser et al., 2014]. In this work, NLG is seen as a process of planning under uncertainty, where the dialogue policy of the NLG component can be optimized using Reinforcement Learning (RL). In IP the problem for NLG is how to present information that takes the form of a set of search results, taking into account trade-offs between utterance length, the amount of information to be conveyed, and the current state of the user, e.g., cognitive load. The text for a set of search results can be generated in different ways, for example, as a summary, by comparing items, or by recommending one particular item, and the NLG policy can be optimized automatically using RL. Table 3.1 shows some examples of IP strategies in which a user model (UM) was used in some cases to take account of the user's preferences, in this case `price=cheap`.

The following is an example of a strategy learned by the RL policy.

```
If the initial number of items returned from the database is high, start
with a summary.
    If the user selects an item, stop generating.
```

Table 3.1: Example realizations generated from the user input cuisine=Indian. Source: Lemon [2012, Table 6.1].

Strategy	Example Utterance
SUMMARY no UM	I found 26 restaurants, which have Indian cuisine. Eleven of the restaurants are in the expensive price range. Furthermore, ten of the restaurants are in the cheap price range and five of the restaurants are in the moderate price range.
SUMMARY UM	Twenty-six restaurants meet your query. There are ten restaurants which serve Indian food and are in the cheap price range. There are also 16 others which are more expensive.
COMPARE by item	The restaurant called Kebab Mahal is an Indian restaurant. It is in the cheap price range. And the restaurant called Saffrani, which is also an Indian restaurant, is in the moderate price range.
COMPARE by attribute	The restaurant called Kebab Mahal and the restaurant called Saffrani are both Indian restaurants. However, Kebab Mahal is in the cheap price range while Saffrani is moderately priced.
RECOMMEND	The restaurant called Kebab Mahal has the best overall quality among the matching restaurants. It is an Indian restaurant, and it is in the cheap price range.

```
    Otherwise, continue with a recommend.
If the number of database items is low, start with a compare and then
continue with a recommend, unless the user selects an item.
```

In experimental studies the policy generated using reinforcement learning was compared to several baselines and was found to significantly outperform the baselines in most scenarios. Furthermore, as described in Rieser et al. [2014], the trained policy improved task success for real users with an increase in task success of up to 8.2%.

Recently, researchers have been exploring the use of neural approaches to NLG. Wen et al. [2015] describe a system that is based on a semantically controlled Long Short-term Memory (LSTM) Recurrent Neural Network (RNN). The system learns from unaligned data by jointly optimizing the sentence planning and surface realization components. Experiments involved a spoken dialogue system that provided information about hotels and restaurants in San Francisco. The generator outperformed several baseline systems using objective metrics and was also shown to produce high quality and more natural output in a subjective evaluation. Wen et al.

[2016] extended this work to multi-domain dialogues in which models were adapted across four different dialogue domains, enabling good performance to be achieved with less training data.

In contrast to these findings, Castro Ferreira et al. [2019] compared the use of neural pipeline and end-to-end data-to-text approaches in NLG, reporting that the pipelined approach produced better results. Both approaches were implemented using state-of-the-art deep learning methods (Gated-Recurrent Units and Transformer) and were evaluated in automated and human evaluations. It was found that the pipeline-based approach produced better texts and was able to generalize better to unseen inputs.

In the first shared task on end-to-end NLG 21 systems were evaluated covering a range of different architectures: template-based, rule-based, data-driven, and Sequence to Sequence (Seq2Seq) [Dušek et al., 2020]. Seq2Seq systems performed better than other architectures on some metrics, in particular, word overlap and human ratings, but they required a strong semantic control mechanism. None of the systems in the challenge matched texts produced by humans in terms of diversity of the response. See Chapter 5 for a discussion of Seq2Seq architectures.

3.3 REINFORCEMENT LEARNING (RL)

RL has been widely used as a means of optimizing dialogue strategies. RL operates as follows. An agent explores an environment consisting of a set of states with transitions between the states. At each time step the agent is in a particular state, chooses an action from a number of options available in that state and moves to another state, receiving a reward. The exploration continues until a final state is reached, resulting in a final reward. The aim is to find an optimal path (or policy) that maximizes the expected rewards. This exploration can be modeled mathematically as an Markov Decision Process (MDP) and the search for the optimal solution can be found using RL.

Dialogue can be viewed as a sequence of user and system turns and this allows it to be modeled within the RL framework as a sequential process of moving through a state space to reach some desired outcome (for example, the completion of a task such as booking a flight). At each time step the system decides on an action to take based on its internal state, i.e., what it believes has been said so far in the dialogue and the current state of the task to be solved. An optimal path (or policy) through the state space involves choosing the best action at each state in the dialogue in order to achieve a given success metric, such as a successful and efficient completion of the dialogue, or some measure of user satisfaction.

3.3.1 REPRESENTING DIALOGUE AS A MARKOV DECISION PROCESS

In the first applications of RL to spoken dialogue systems dialogue was represented as an MDP [Levin et al., 2000]. An MDP can be defined as a tuple $\langle S, A_s, T, R, \lambda \rangle$ where S is a set of system states; A_s is a set of actions that the system can take; T is a set of transition probabilities $P_T(s_t|s_{t-1}, a_{t-1})$, i.e., the probability of the next state given the previous state and the previous system action; R is an immediate reward that is associated with taking a particular action in a given state; and λ is a geometric discount factor $0 \leq \lambda \leq 1$ that makes more distant rewards worth less than more immediate rewards.

The state space represents the state of the dialogue system at a certain point in time s_t. The set of actions describe what the system can do at s_t. The dialogue policy π, which is a mapping between the state space and the action set, prescribes for any given state what should be the next action to perform. Thus, transition from state s_t to state s_{t+1} is determined by the DM's choice of action a_t at s_t given the user's action and the ASR and NLU results. For example, in a flight information system, DM starts in an initial state where it does not know the values of the parameters that form the basis of the user's information request, such as the destination, origin, date, and time of the flight. Over the course of the dialogue DM elicits values for these parameters and eventually arrives at a state in which it can access a database and offer one or more flights that satisfy the user's requirements. DM may have a choice of actions at a given state s_t. For example, DM might ask the user questions about the values of unknown attributes, ask questions to confirm known attributes, clarify some misunderstanding, or access a database. To behave optimally, DM must select an action in each state that leads to the maximum reward, where the choice of action is based on the information that DM has available to itself in its current state.

Given such an MDP, learning the best dialogue strategy is a matter of computing an optimal policy π for choosing actions in the MDP that maximize the expected sum of the rewards received over the transaction (known as the *return*). With multiple action choices at each state, RL is used to explore the choices systematically and to compute the best policy for action selection based on rewards associated with each state transition, using empirical data such as interactions of real or simulated users with the system. Since RL algorithms typically take many thousands of dialogues to learn an optimal strategy, they will explore other strategies along the way, some of which may be spurious. As a result, learning often starts using a simulated user since real users would typically not tolerate thousands of dialogues with nonsensical behaviors.

The reward captures the immediate consequences of executing an action in a state. For example, each user interaction may incur a small negative reward, while successfully concluding the dialogue may result in a large positive reward. Other rewards may include the number of corrections, the number of accesses to a database, speech recognition errors, dialogue duration, and user satisfaction measures. In some studies (for example, Walker et al. [2002]), the performance function is a combination of a number of these measures, as in the PARAdigm for Dialogue System Evaluation (PARADISE) dialogue evaluation methodology [Walker et al., 1997], which combines measures of task efficiency and user satisfaction (see Chapter 4, Section 4.4.1).

The NJFun system, which helps people choose recreational activities in New Jersey, is an example of how RL can be applied to decision-making in dialogue management using an MDP [Singh et al., 2002]. In this system the relevant dialogue decisions involved choices of dialogue initiative, system prompt, grammar type, and confirmation strategy. However, early systems such as NJFun usually had very small state spaces and action sets in order to aid tractability so that decisions made by RL were limited to specific points for optimization rather than learning the whole dialogue policy.

3.3.2 FROM MDPS TO POMDPS

One of the main problems with using MDPs to model dialogue is that in an MDP it is assumed that the contents of the system state are fully observable. However, given the various uncertainties inherent in dialogue interactions, it cannot be assumed that the system's belief state is correct. For example, the system cannot be certain that it has correctly interpreted the user's intentions given the uncertainties associated with speech recognition and natural language understanding. There may also be ambiguities and uncertainties related more generally to the user's goals and intentions, even when speech recognition and natural language understanding are perfect. For these reasons a Partially Observable Markov Decision Process (POMDP) is preferred over the standard MDP model since it can represent a probability distribution over all the different states that the system might be in, albeit with much larger state spaces and resulting in problems of tractability.

A POMDP can be defined as a tuple $\langle S, A_s, T, R, O, Z, \lambda, b_0 \rangle$, where S, A_s T, R, and λ are as defined above for an MDP; O is a set of possible observations that the system can receive from the world; Z is the probability of a particular observation given the state and the machine action $P(o'|s'a)$; and b_0 is an initial belief state $b_{0(s)}$ where b represents a summary of the complete dialogue [Williams and Young, 2007], [Young et al., 2013]. The operations of the POMDP are similar to those described above for MDPs except that the states of the POMDP are unobserved and the system's belief state is a distribution over possible states. So for the POMDP at each time step the system is in an unobserved state s_t with belief state b_t, where $b_{t(st)}$ represents the probability of being in the state s_t. Based on a noisy observation o_t (the user's utterance) and b_t (the system's current belief state) the system selects an action a_t, receives a reward r_t, and transitions to another state s_{t+1}. The belief state is updated (b_{t+1}). The system's choice of actions is determined by a policy π and the system continues to the end of the dialogue and receives a final accumulated reward R, which is maximized by the policy π, as measured by the *Q-function*, which represents how good it is for an agent to be in a particular state in terms of an expected total reward.

Formulating the belief state b as a distribution over states provides a principled mathematical framework for dealing with the uncertainties associated with the ASR and SLU components. Whereas in an MDP the output from these components is treated as a single interpretation, in a POMDP the N-best lists from ASR and SLU can be maintained as multiple hypotheses, enabling the system to proceed even if confidence in the ASR/SLU is low. The user model provides a probability for each user act given each possible dialogue hypothesis and if a misunderstanding is detected the system does not necessarily need to backtrack. Each time a new observation is received, such as a new user input, the belief distribution is re-calculated. This process is known as *belief monitoring*. Figure 3.3 shows an example in which a POMDP

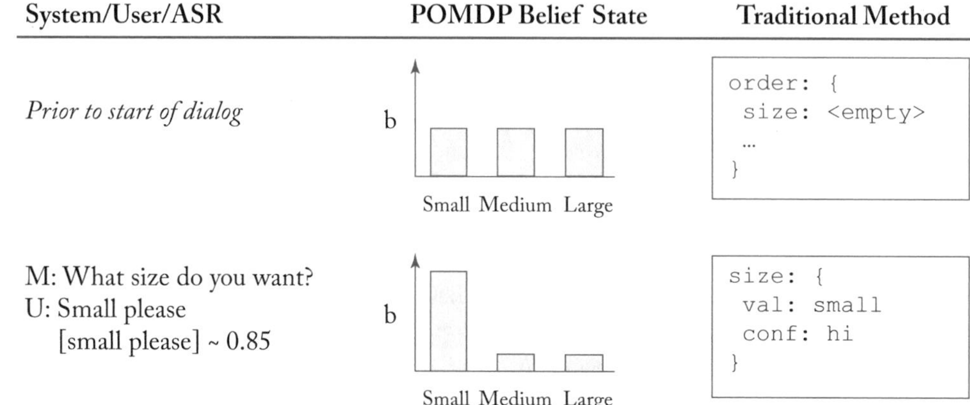

Figure 3.3: Example of a conversation with a spoken dialogue system illustrating a high confidence score. Based on Williams and Young [2007].

belief state represents the degree of magnitude of the scores in a high confidence recognition compared with the traditional method where the values are quantized, e.g., as [reject, low, hi[4]]. Figure 3.4 shows an example where the confidence scores are low but the POMDP is able to maintain a cumulative score whereas a traditional system would simply reject the input.

RL with MDPs and POMDPs has mainly been applied to information inquiry dialogues involving slot filling, for example, tourist information [Singh et al., 2002], [Thomson and Young, 2010], [Young et al., 2010], and appointment scheduling [Janarthanam et al., 2011]. The more complex domain of troubleshooting has also been modeled [Williams, 2007], and Williams [2011] demonstrated a POMDP system in the "Let's Go" challenge in which the spoken dialogue systems provided bus information to casual callers using a variety of mobile phones in noisy environments [Black et al., 2011]. The POMDP system achieved a word error rate that outperformed the baseline system used in the challenge.

3.3.3 DIALOGUE STATE TRACKING

As shown in Figure 3.1, dialogue management consists of two sub-components: Dialogue state tracking and Dialogue Policy. The Dialogue state tracking sub-component interprets the user's utterances and updates the dialogue state accordingly, while the Dialogue Policy sub-component determines the next system action on the basis of the current dialogue state.

The Dialogue State, also known as the Belief State, contains information about the dialogue from the viewpoint of the system. In slot-filling dialogues the dialogue state contains information about the slots, whether they have been filled, which slots still have to be filled, and possibly the system's level of confidence about the filled slots. In a POMDP system this infor-

[4]In the figure the value "hi" = "high".

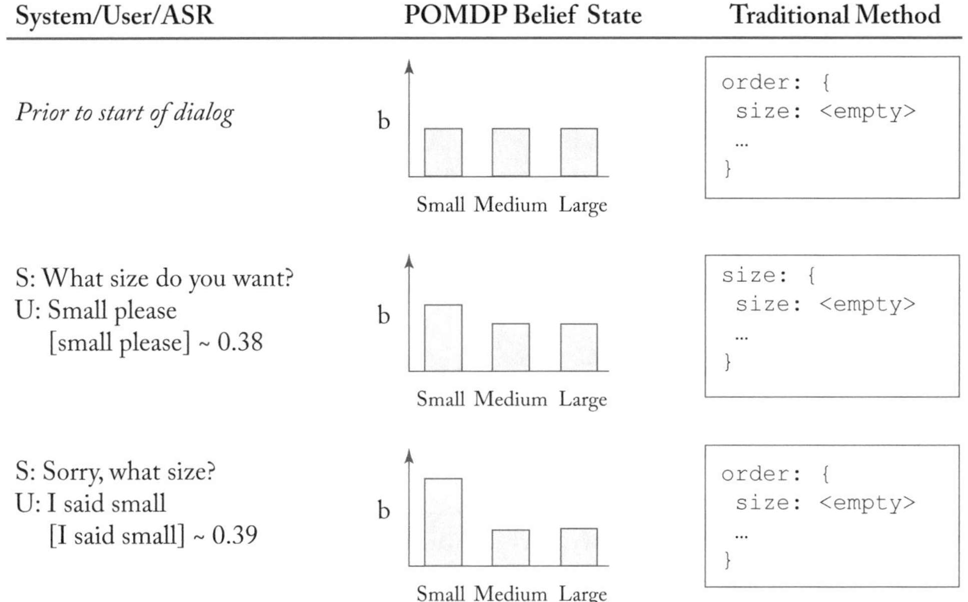

Figure 3.4: Conversation with a spoken dialogue system illustrating two successive low confidence recognitions. Based on Williams and Young [2007].

mation is represented probabilistically because information about the user (what the user has said, what the user believes, what the user wants to achieve) is uncertain due to the fact that the outputs from ASR and NLU are probabilistic. More complex information about the dialogue state has been represented in frameworks such as the *Information State Update Theory* [Larsson and Traum, 2000]. Heeman [2007] showed how handcrafted Information State Update rules could be combined with RL.

Given an appropriate representation of the information in the Dialogue State, the problem is how to update this information as the dialogue progresses. In Information State Theory the update rules were handcrafted. In statistical approaches they can be learned from data using statistical learning algorithms [Henderson, 2015], while more recently neural network approaches have been used [Henderson et al., 2013], [Mrkšić et al., 2015], [Mrkšić et al., 2016]. For example, Mrkšić et al. [2015] built a Belief Tracker using RNN (see Chapter 5, Section 5.3.2) that was able to operate across multiple dialogue domains and that outperformed each of the domain specific models, while Mrkšić et al. [2016] presented the Neural Belief Tracker (NBT) which takes three items as input: the last system utterance, the last user utterance, and any slot-value pair that is being currently tracked. The items are mapped to an intermediate vector representation (see further Chapter 5, Section 5.3.1) and these representations (or embeddings) are used to determine which intents have been expressed by the user in the conversation. This process

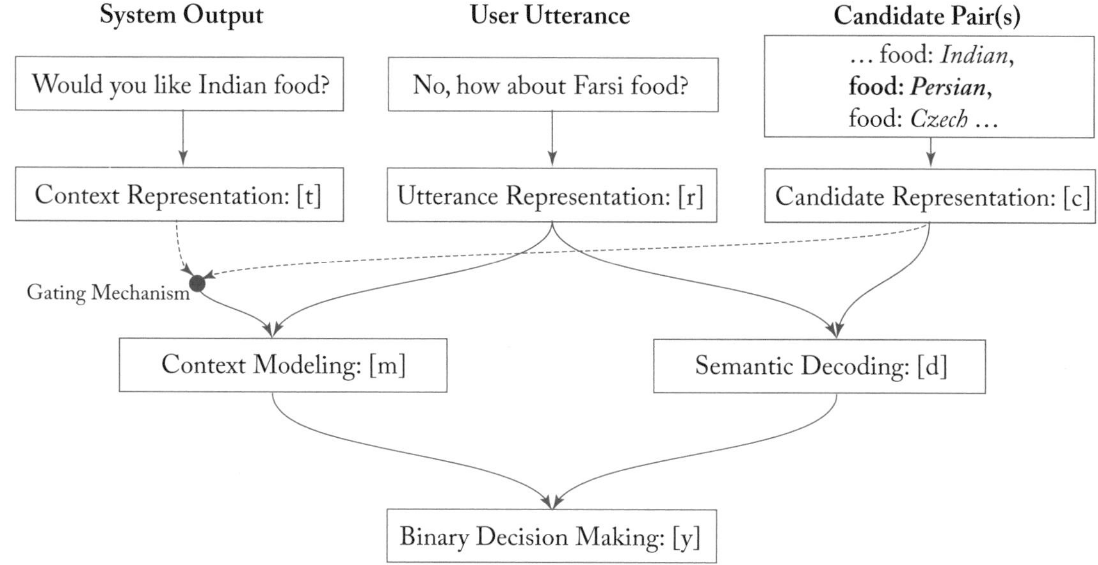

Figure 3.5: The Neural Belief Tracker. Based on Mrkšić et al. [2016].

is shown in Figure 3.5. NBT has the advantage of coupling NLU and Dialogue state tracking without requiring handcrafted semantic lexicons. An evaluation on two datasets showed that the NBT approach matched the performance of state-of-the-art models containing handcrafted semantic lexicons and surpassed them when the lexicons were not provided.

Dialogue state tracking has been explored extensively in the Dialogue State Tracking Challenge (DSTC) where multiple belief tracking approaches are compared on a shared task [Henderson et al., 2014a], [Henderson et al., 2014b], [Williams, 2012], [Williams et al., 2013]. For more detail on the Dialogue State Tracking Challenge, see Chapter 5, Section 5.8.2.

3.3.4 DIALOGUE POLICY

Given the representation of the dialogue state space as an MDP or POMDP, the task of RL is to find the optimal path through the state space that maximizes an objective function. The optimal path is known as a policy π. The policy determines the system's next action in the current state, i.e., it maps states to actions ($\pi: S \mapsto A$). However, while in the current state the system cannot be sure whether the action it plans to take is good, as it can only estimate its long-term value. For example, taking an action such as seeking an explicit confirmation will result in a longer dialogue but might be preferable to allowing a misunderstanding to persist. The system will only know if the action chosen was optimal when it reaches the end of the dialogue. In this way RL performs within an environment with a delayed final reward (or return).

Finding an optimal policy involves selecting those actions that lead to the highest final reward. This is performed using a process of exploration, for example, by using a large number of sample dialogues with real or simulated users to explore sequences of state-action pairs. RL uses a value function that calculates how desirable it is to take an action in the current state while considering all the states that are likely to follow until the end of the dialogue, i.e., by calculating how much reward can be expected from that state by taking the action and following a particular policy. This process is known as the Q-function as it operates by adjusting the Q-values, which are the values of each state-action pair.

There are many different algorithms in RL that can be used to find the optimal policy. Two of the more common are the SARSA (State-Action-Reward-State-Action) algorithm and Q-learning. The Deep Q-Networks (DQNs) algorithm [Mnih et al., 2013], [Cuayáhuitl et al., 2015] uses neural networks to estimate Q-values, however DQNs can only handle discrete, low-dimensional action spaces. This issue is addressed by the Deep Deterministic Policy Gradient (DDPG) algorithm that learns policies in high-dimensional, continuous action spaces. For a comprehensive discussion of RL algorithms and their application to dialogue systems, see Rieser and Lemon [2011b].

3.3.5 PROBLEMS AND ISSUES WITH REINFORCEMENT LEARNING AND POMDPS

The application of POMDPs as a statistical model for spoken dialogue systems is problematic due to factors such as scalability. Increasing the number of user goals leads to a very large space of possible belief states, making exact belief state updating intractable. Various solutions have been proposed to address this problem.

In the Summary POMDP method a summary space is created in which the probability mass of the highest-ranking value is represented along with the combined mass of other hypotheses but the value itself is disregarded [Williams and Young, 2005]. This allows scaling up to a larger number of slots in a slot-filling dialogue. Another solution, the Hidden Information State model, involves partitioning the state space so that partition beliefs are computed instead of state beliefs and the master state space is reduced into a summary space [Young et al., 2010]. The Hidden Information State addresses the dialogue-modeling problem of how to track multiple hypotheses efficiently while the summary space addresses the problem of how to keep the learning of the optimal dialogue policy tractable.

Thomson and Young [2010] addressed the problem of making belief updating tractable using a framework for Bayesian updates of dialogue state (BUDS) based on the loopy belief propagation (LBP) algorithm that treats all the items of information in the belief state as independent. The framework was evaluated using simulations as well as a user trial against a system with a handcrafted dialogue policy and two MDP systems. The results showed that the BUDS approach outperformed the various alternatives.

In another approach, Gašić and Young [2013] proposed modeling the Q-function as a Gaussian Process (GP) that exploits similarities between different parts of the belief space. Experiments using a system based on the BUDS dialogue manager showed that the GP dialogue policy is able to learn faster than other methods and that it is possible to train systems efficiently in interaction with real users as opposed to user simulators. A further advantage was that basing the dialogue policy directly on the full belief space could reduce designer effort rather than requiring handcrafted modeling of a summary space. Other approaches to the issue of tractability include Linear Function Approximation [Henderson et al., 2008] and Hierarchical RL [Lemon et al., 2006]. With these methods it has been possible to use more complex state representations and to learn policies for larger sets of dialogue actions [Lemon and Pietquin, 2007].

There are several issues that need to be addressed when applying reinforcement learning to dialogue systems that are intended for commercial deployment [Paek and Pieraccini, 2008]. The objective function that determines the optimal dialogue policy is generally based on maximization of the expected cumulative reward or on post-hoc measures of usability. However, it is not clear whether every dialogue can be seen in terms of such an optimization problem. Moreover, it is likely that most developers would not have the required experience with optimization to choose or adapt an objective function. The local reward, which contributes to the expected cumulative reward, is also problematic. The normal procedure is to penalize the system for additional turns in the interests of dialogue efficiency. However, in some dialogues, where the user wishes to explore different possibilities, it may be preferable to increase the reward for longer dialogues.

Another problem concerns the Dialogue policy that is learned by a DM using RL, as the reasons for the decisions taken by DM are unlikely to be clear to users or system designers. Given the obligation in commercially deployed systems to satisfy customers and to be able to fix design problems, designers would expect to be able to exert more control over the design of their systems. Furthermore they are unlikely to be able to remedy problems arising from learned dialogue policies without a deep knowledge of reinforcement learning [Williams, 2007].

One solution to this issue is to integrate principles of conventional design involving business rules and design knowledge with POMDPs in order to produce more efficient systems in which the conventional DM nominates a set of one or more actions and the POMDP DM chooses the optimal one [Williams, 2007], [Williams et al., 2017]. Using this method spurious action choices that would have been explored by the POMDP DM are pruned so that optimization can run faster and more reliably than in a POMDP system that does not take account of such designer knowledge.

Optimizing a dialogue system usually involves interaction with users to create the large number of dialogues required to train an optimal dialogue policy. However, it is often not possible to recruit sufficient users to engage with the system for this purpose. For this reason user simulators trained on corpora have been used to replicate user behavior [Schatzmann et al., 2006]. The user simulator is combined with an error simulator model to match the characteristics of the ASR and NLU components, i.e., capturing potential recognition and understanding errors by using a full distribution of ASR and NLU hypotheses at each user turn [Schatzmann et al., 2007]. One problem is that, while it is possible to obtain high performance when training and testing on the simulators, performance in field trials may not be comparable [Schatzmann et al., 2005]. Rieser and Lemon [2011b] propose a different solution in which they show how it is possible to train a dialogue policy with a limited data set.

RL offers a principled mathematical framework for handling uncertainty in spoken dialogue systems, enabling an optimal dialogue policy to be learned rather than being designed manually. Recent results have demonstrated superior performance of RL systems compared to handcrafted baseline systems and there is some evidence that POMDPs can be scaled to handle real-world tasks. However, there are still many challenges facing the application of RL to dialogue systems in terms of issues of tractability and the availability of training data and also in terms of practical deployment.

SUMMARY

This chapter has looked at how statistical data-driven methods have been applied to the different components of the traditional pipelined architecture as an alternative to handcrafted rule-based approaches. In particular, the application of reinforcement learning to dialogue management was reviewed. Evaluations of the statistical methods have generally shown improvements over baseline rule-based methods.

Although evaluation has been mentioned several times in previous chapters we have not yet explained how evaluation of dialogue systems is carried out nor presented the metrics that have been used. In Chapter 4, different ways of evaluating dialogue systems will be discussed along with the wide range of metrics that have been used to evaluate both rule-based and machine learning-based dialogue systems.

Regarding the modularised architectures that have been used in rule-based as well as data-driven statistical dialogue systems, one problem is that attempting to optimize the individual components of a modular architecture can lead to the problem of knock-on effects on the other components in the architecture. To address this issue a new approach known as end-to-end neural dialogue learning has come to the forefront that will be reviewed in Chapter 5.

CHAPTER 4

Evaluating Dialogue Systems

Although dialogue systems go back a long way, it was not until the 1990s that competitions were set up to systematically compare the performance of different systems on specified tasks. An example in the U.S. was the DARPA Communicator Project that addressed the task of complex travel planning and included evaluations of systems developed in a number of research laboratories and companies across the U.S. and on several affiliated partner sites in Europe [Walker et al., 2000b]. Various comprehensive evaluation frameworks were developed for use within the scientific community in Europe by the Expert Advisory Group on Language Engineering Standards (EAGLES), providing guidelines on how to carry out evaluations and how to make the results available in such a way that they could be easily interpreted and compared.[1] More recently, evaluation has benefited from very large datasets collected in various projects and competitions (see Chapter 5) and from the application of machine learning to the analysis of the data. For comprehensive surveys of dialogue system evaluation, see Deriu et al. [2020] and Hastie [2012].

Evaluation is important for a number of reasons:

1. for developers it is important to determine whether the system performs as expected;

2. for users it is important to determine whether the system meet s the user's needs—whether it understands their utterances, whether in the case of task-oriented systems it helps them achieve their goals efficiently, and, in the case of non-task-oriented systems, whether it gives them an enjoyable experience; and

3. for researchers it is important to establish whether the aims of the research have been met, for example, to validate a new research technique or to investigate whether the system shows improvement on various evaluation metrics against a baseline state-of-the-art system.

Note that evaluation is typically a black box function and so the discussion in this chapter applies to all dialogues irrespective of the underlying technologies.

One of the main goals of current approaches to evaluation is to have a procedure that is automatic and repeatable, and that correlates highly with human judgements [Deriu et al., 2020]. Automatic evaluation is desirable due to the considerable costs and time required to recruit human users for the evaluations. Automated metrics are also useful as they can provide a training objective during the initial training of dialogue models [Dinan et al., 2019a]. Another

[1] http://www.ilc.cnr.it/EAGLES/home.html

issue is that it is difficult to maintain consistency when human users are involved as judgements can vary considerably across users and even within the same user on different occasions.

This chapter is structured as follows. Section 4.1 looks at the question of how to conduct the evaluation of a dialogue system, whether in the laboratory or "in the wild"; what sorts of users to involve and how to recruit them; the use of user simulations for evaluation; and the use of crowdsourcing. Task-oriented and non-task-oriented dialogue systems differ in what users wish to achieve in the interaction and not surprisingly different evaluation metrics have been proposed for these different types of dialogue system. Section 4.2 reviews quantitative and qualitative metrics that have been used to evaluate task-oriented systems, looking first at metrics that evaluate the overall performance of a system followed by metrics that evaluate the performance of individual components of systems with modularised architectures. Section 4.3 discusses metrics that are used to evaluate non-task-oriented open-domain dialogue systems and that have been applied in challenges and competitions such as the Amazon Alexa Prize. Section 4.4 reviews some widely used evaluation frameworks. Finally, Section 4.5 looks at whether there is a single technique or set of techniques that could be used to evaluate dialogue systems.

4.1 HOW TO CONDUCT THE EVALUATION

There are several ways to conduct evaluations of dialogue systems. Traditionally, the choice has been between evaluations conducted in a laboratory setting and evaluations conducted "in the wild". User simulations and crowdsourcing are increasingly being used to address the issues involved in recruiting users to perform the evaluations.

4.1.1 LABORATORY STUDIES VS. EVALUATIONS IN THE WILD

For laboratory evaluations users are recruited from available resources, for example, in the case of academic research laboratories the users may be college students who have volunteered to take part, while in industrial laboratories there may be a panel of users who have agreed to take part in tests and evaluations. Users interact with the dialogue system in pre-defined scenarios and complete a questionnaire at the end of the session. In this way the evaluation is tightly controlled and a range of different scenarios can be investigated, ensuring within-test and between-test reliability and allowing more extensive data and feedback to be collected. However, a problem with evaluations in the laboratory is that they may not reflect real-life usage so that the validity of the measurements is negatively affected.

Evaluations in the wild involve recording users interacting with a real dialogue system to accomplish a real task. For example, users interacted with the Let's Go! system that was developed at Carnegie Mellon University (CMU) and made available for public use. The users interacted with the system to obtain bus schedule information in Pittsburgh. At the end of the conversation they were asked to provide feedback on their experience [Black et al., 2011].

The value of using the ratings of users has been questioned on several grounds. According to Evanini et al. [2008] the judgements of users can vary considerably and are unreliable, while Gašić et al. [2011] found that users in a laboratory-based evaluation tended to forget the instructions and so were unable to correctly assess the task success metric. Schmitt and Ultes [2015] focused on the cognitive demands placed on users if they have to evaluate the dialogue at the level of the exchange, i.e., following each pair of turns by the system and the user. This is a method that is used if a more fine-grained measure of quality is desired as opposed to a single rating at the end of the dialogue.

For these reasons Ultes et al. [2013] distinguish between user raters and expert raters. User raters engage in an interaction with a dialogue system and rate it either during the interaction or (more commonly) at the end of the interaction. Expert raters, on the other hand, listen to recorded interactions and rate them as though they had been the actual users. Ultes et al. [2013] investigated differences and similarities between expert and user raters finding a high correlation between the two groups. This finding led to the conclusion that expert raters could replace user raters, resulting in savings in the time and costs involved when using real users as raters. The implications of this finding are discussed further below in relation to obtaining judgements of quality at the exchange level (see Section 4.3.1).

Differences between evaluations in the laboratory and in the wild have been investigated in several studies. Ai et al. [2007] compared corpora of dialogues collected from recruited subjects in a laboratory setting with corpora of real users in the wild when interacting with the Let's Go! spoken dialogue system. It was found that dialogues involving recruited subjects were longer and contained more caller actions compared to the dialogues of real users in the wild. This is possibly because laboratory users may be prepared to engage longer in order to complete their assigned tasks, while real users may give up more quickly if the system does not work satisfactorily for them. Another difference was that there were fewer barge-ins in the laboratory studies and the subjects tended to speak faster. The reason for this may be that while the laboratory setting provides a quiet environment that facilitates spoken interaction with a dialogue system, interactions in the wild are often conducted in a noisy environment that is detrimental for speech recognition. The different style of interaction may also have been due to the fact that users in the wild experience a higher cognitive load as they are engaging with the system in a noisy street environment and need information quickly as otherwise they might miss the next bus, whereas subjects in the laboratory setting do not have these pressures.

In another study with the same dialogue system, Black et al. [2011] found that there was considerable variation between laboratory users and real users, with the laboratory users producing a lower word error rate, a higher task completion rate, and longer dialogue duration. Similar findings were reported in a study in Finland where it was also found that the proportion of dialogues with repeat requests was much lower during real usage [Turunen et al., 2006].

In summary, it is important to be aware of the effects of different environments and types of user on the results that can be obtained in evaluations. While laboratory settings provide a greater degree of experimental control, they do not necessarily reflect how users in real settings interact with the dialogue system. Another problem is how to recruit sufficient users for the evaluation, as it can be costly to set up user studies. These problem have been addressed using user simulators and crowdsourcing.

User Simulators

User simulators are one way to address the issue of the costs of recruiting real users and conducting user studies. The idea of a user simulator is that it should interact with a dialogue system as if it were a real user. User simulators enable the collection of large amounts of training data, which is a necessary requirement for statistical, data-driven dialogue systems. They also support the exploration of dialogue strategies that may be difficult to obtain using real users and that may not be represented in existing dialogue corpora [Eckert et al., 1997], [Schatzmann et al., 2006].

One of the earliest user simulators for dialogue system evaluation used handcrafted rules and a range of user profiles to generate a wide variety of user utterances [López-Cózar et al., 2003]. In more recent approaches probabilistic user simulators learn to produce possible user responses from corpora of dialogues [Keizer et al., 2012]. One way to launch a dialogue simulation is to provide the dialogue manager with a user goal. In the agenda-based approach, as described in Schatzmann and Young [2009], the user goal consists of *inform slots* and *request slots*. To illustrate from the movie ticket domain, inform slots represent information that the user should provide, such as **number_ of_tickets**, **date**, and **movie_name**, while request slots are information that is to be provided by the system such as **ticket_details**, **theatre_name**, and **start_time**. Based on these slots an agenda is constructed that determines the dialogue flow. El Asri et al. [2016] developed a similar approach in which a user model produced the next user action based on contexts collected during the dialogue, such as the system's previous action, inconsistency between the system's information, and the user's goals.

Möller et al. [2006] introduced the MeMo workbench as a tool for automatic usability evaluations, focusing on simulations of user errors derived from empirical observations. The MeMo workbench is an interactive tool that allows the developer to create models of the system and the user, run simulations, and evaluate the results [Engelbrecht et al., 2008]. The types of error investigated included system-driven errors—for example, due to poor speech recognition,—as well as user-driven errors due to the user's misconceptions—for example, errors arising from discrepancies between the user's expectations of the system and the system's actual behavior.

For reasons of efficiency many user simulators model the user's utterances at the level of intentions, i.e., as dialogue acts, rather than as actual spoken text. However, modeling at this level does not allow the performance of the ASR and NLU components to be investigated. To address this issue, López-Cózar et al. [2006] employed a corpus of possible user utterances for each semantic representation that was input to the speech recognizer, thus enabling the evaluation of the whole interaction cycle. See also Jung et al. [2009].

An important consideration is whether user simulators re-produce realistic user behaviors. Schatzmann et al. [2006] investigated this question by:

1. comparing simulated user responses with real user responses in an unseen test set in order to assess the extent to which the response of the user simulator was realistic; and
2. comparing corpora of simulated dialogues with corpora of real dialogues to evaluate how well the behaviors in the simulated dialogues cover the variety of behaviors in the training data.

Several approaches to stochastic user simulation were investigated in this survey. While it was shown that some of the approaches led to improvements in the quality of user simulations, it was also found that it was possible to distinguish simulated datasets from real datasets, raising the question of the validity of evaluation data obtained from user simulations.

The MeMo workbench was evaluated in a detailed study in which different user characteristics, such as familiarity with technology, anxiety, and problem solving strategies were associated with behavioral rules that specified user actions. Two different user groups (young and old) and two system versions were compared. It was found that using the user simulation data it was possible to predict which version of the system was rated better by which group of users [Engelbrecht et al., 2009]. Other studies evaluating the benefits of user simulators include Ai and Litman [2008] and Pietquin and Hastie [2013]. User simulators were provided in an experimental platform for entrants at the Microsoft Dialogue Challenge[2] which was held at the 2018 IEEE Workshop on Spoken Language Technology [Li et al., 2018b].

Crowdsourcing

The availability of crowdsourcing websites such as Amazon Mechanical Turk (AMT) has made it easier to recruit large numbers of users for evaluation studies. Crowdsourcing allows developers to devise clearly defined tasks and to recruit users who fit a specified profile. The benefits of crowdsourcing as well as the issues to consider are discussed in [Eskenazi et al., 2013].

Jurčíček et al. [2011] assessed the reliability of AMT workers interacting with a dialogue system, comparing results with those collected from users in a controlled setting. No differences were found between the groups in terms of task performance and ranking. However, the use of AMT workers was found to be more efficient in terms of recruitment and costs. Nowadays, most research in open-domain dialogue systems rely on crowdsourcing for human evaluations (see, for example, Ramanarayanan et al. [2017], Serban et al. [2017a], Yang et al. [2010], and [Wen et al., 2017]). Crowdsourcing is also used in competitions such as the Alexa Prize; see Section 4.3.4.

4.2 EVALUATING TASK-ORIENTED DIALOGUE SYSTEMS

Dialogue systems developed in research laboratories and for commercial deployment have traditionally been task-oriented and so evaluation metrics are used that measure the performance

[2] https://github.com/xiul-msr/e2e_dialog_challenge

of the system in the task, for example, *task completion*, *dialogue duration*, and *user satisfaction*. Task-oriented dialogue systems can be viewed as *supervised* systems since they incorporate an objective metric for the evaluation whereas non-task-oriented dialogue systems are *unsupervised* as they do not have such an objective evaluation metric [Lowe et al., 2016].

Metrics for the evaluation of task-oriented dialogue systems can be either quantitative (objective) or qualitative (subjective). Furthermore, the metrics can be applied to the evaluation of the overall dialogue system or to the sub-components of the system.

4.2.1 QUANTITATIVE METRICS FOR OVERALL DIALOGUE SYSTEM EVALUATION

Quantitative metrics are computed from the logs of interactions with users. Some metrics can be retrieved automatically while others have to be calculated by annotators of the logs. The following are popular quantitative metrics for overall system evaluation:

- task success;
- task duration;
- number of system turns;
- number of user turns;
- number of barge-ins;
- number of repair utterances;
- number of timeouts;
- word error rate; and
- response latency.

Some additional metrics have been introduced in commercial dialogue systems, particularly those deployed in contact centers, where the objective is to address the sometimes competing goals of minimizing costs (by reducing staff through automation) and ensuring user satisfaction [Larson, 2005]. The following are some commonly used metrics.

- *Time-to-task*: measures the amount of time that it takes to start engaging in a task after any instructions and other messages provided by the system.
- *Correct transfer rate*: measures whether the customers are correctly redirected to the appropriate human agent.
- *Containment rate*: measures the percentage of calls not transferred to human agents and that are handled by the system. This metric is useful in determining how successfully the system has been able to reduce the costs of customer care through automation.

- *Abandonment rate*: this metric is the converse of the containment rate. It measures the percentage of callers who hang up before completing a task with an automated system.

4.2.2 QUANTITATIVE METRICS FOR THE EVALUATION OF THE SUB-COMPONENTS OF DIALOGUE SYSTEMS

As shown in Figure 2.1 in Chapter 2, dialogue systems have traditionally been viewed as consisting of a number of sub-components (or modules). These sub-components can be evaluated separately to measure their individual performance as well as to assess their contribution to the overall performance of the system. For example, the poor performance of the speech recognition component is likely to have a detrimental effect on the performance of the dialogue system as a whole, as was often the case with early spoken dialogue systems. The following sub-sections describe metrics used for each of the sub-components of spoken dialogue systems.

Automatic Speech Recognition (ASR)

The standard evaluation measure in speech recognition is the Word Error Rate (WER), which is calculated by comparing the recognized string against a reference string, such as a transcription by a human annotator. The following formula is used to calculate WER, where the error types in the recognized strings consist of insertions (I), deletions (D), and substitutions (S), and N represents the total number of words recognized:

$$WER = 100\frac{(S + D + I)}{N}\%. \tag{4.1}$$

One problem with using WER as an indication of the overall performance of a spoken dialogue system is that speech recognition errors may not always adversely affect the performance of the system as a whole as some of the errors might involve non-functional words that are less significant in the overall understanding of the input, so that even with a word error rate above a given threshold the user's intent may be successfully recognized and the user may be able to complete their task successfully.

Natural Language Understanding (NLU)

Evaluation of the NLU component involves comparing the component's output with a reference representation. Various metrics have been used, depending on how the output of the NLU component is represented. Formerly, the metric *sentence accuracy* was used where the output of the NLU component was a syntactic parse tree, or alternatively *concept accuracy* where the output was a semantic frame. In current SLU/NLU systems, as discussed in Chapter 2, Section 2.1.2, the output of NLU is the user's intent and the entities extracted from that intent.

Intent classification and entity extraction can be evaluated using a *confusion matrix* that shows how many items were correctly identified and how many were mistaken for other items.

Table 4.1 shows a confusion matrix for a hotel reservation system with 3 different intents: *book_room*, *cancel_booking*, and *change_booking* from a sample of 30 intent classifications. The

Table 4.1: Confusion matrix for hotel bookings

		Actual		
		book_room	cancel_booking	change_booking
	book_room	10	3	1
Predicted	cancel_booking	0	8	2
	change_booking	0	1	5

system classifies the input for *book_room* correctly 10 times, incorrectly as *cancel_booking* three times, and incorrectly as *change_booking* once. Based on a confusion matrix such as this, the *precision*, *recall*, and *F1* measures can be calculated. Precision is calculated as follows:

$$Precision = \frac{number\ of\ reference\ items\ correctly\ detected}{number\ of\ items\ detected}. \tag{4.2}$$

Recall is calculated as follows:

$$Recall = \frac{number\ of\ reference\ items\ correctly\ detected}{number\ of\ total\ \ reference\ items}. \tag{4.3}$$

F1 measures the balance between precision and recall, where adjusting one of the measures to improve it will often result in lowering the score for the other. For example, improving precision can result in a lower score for recall, and vice versa. F1 is calculated as follows:

$$F1 = \frac{2 \times (Precision \times Recall)}{Precision + Recall}. \tag{4.4}$$

Dialogue Management

The overall performance of a modularised dialogue system is a result of the combined performance of its various sub-components. For example, task success depends on the system being able to accurately recognize the user's spoken input (ASR), create a meaning representation from the recognized string (NLU), and engage in an appropriate dialogue to achieve the task, including where necessary requesting clarification when the user's input is unclear or underspecified (DM). The following are some items that can be associated more specifically with the performance of the dialogue management component:

- number of system turns;
- number of user turns;
- percentage of successful repairs (correction rate); and
- number of timeouts.

Different evaluation methods have been used for the sub-components of statistical dialogue managers, i.e., Dialogue state tracking and Dialogue policy. Dialogue state tracking has been evaluated in the various Dialogue State Tracking Challenge (DSTC) reviewed in Chapter 5, Section 5.8.2. Evaluation of state tracking typically involves comparisons of machine-learned and rule-based methods. In the DSTC2 evaluation two machine-learned methods were compared: discriminative and generative, and the metrics involved were *accuracy*, which measured the quality of the top hypothesis for each state and *L2*, which measured the accuracy of the whole distribution [Henderson, 2015]. It was found that the discriminative systems outperformed the rule-based and generative systems. Machine learning-based methods also produced the best performances in other evaluations, for example, DSTC1 and DSTC3.

The evaluation of methods for determining dialogue policy usually involves comparisons of an RL-based approach with a rule-based baseline. A study by Xu et al. [2018] is typical of this approach, where an RL dialogue policy was compared with a baseline rule-based policy using the DSTC2 and DSTC3 dialogue corpora and with three levels of SLU error rates (none, low, and high). The results showed that the rule-based approach achieved a 100% dialogue success rate when there was no SLU error, but even with a low SLU error rate the RL policy performed better. The RL policy also performed better on the dialogue completion metric by generating a policy that required fewer turns. Thus, the RL policy was shown to be more robust to SLU error and more flexible in terms of dialogue strategy.

Natural Language Generation

The NLG component takes the output from DM in the form of an abstract meaning representation and converts it into text. Traditionally, texts produced by NLG have been evaluated in several different ways [Reiter and Belz, 2009].

- *Task performance*: whether the text assists in the performance of a task. For example, Reiter et al. [2003] investigated whether text produced in the STOP system, which dealt with smoking cessation, actually managed to persuade people to stop smoking.
- *Human ratings*: Human judges compare and rate texts according to criteria such as quality, coherence, content, organization, writing style, and correctness.
- *Comparisons*: Texts produced by NLG are compared to human-authored texts.

In statistical approaches to NLG, evaluation typically takes the form of comparisons between a baseline rule-based system and a system trained using RL. For example, Rieser et al. [2014] describe a trained information presentation strategy that outperformed a baseline system in terms of task performance rate.

Due to the high costs of recruiting human evaluators, the current trend is toward automatic methods of evaluation that correlate highly with human judgements. However, this is still very much a work in progress. Novikova et al. [2017] investigated whether various automated metrics reflected human judgements in a comparison of texts produced by NLG systems with human ground-truth reference texts using metrics such as:

- word overlap,
- semantic similarity, and
- grammar-based metrics such as readability and grammaticality.

The human ranked measures were as follows.

- *Informativeness*: Does the utterance provide all the useful information from the meaning representation?
- *Naturalness*: Could the utterance have been produced by a native speaker?
- *Quality*: How do you judge the overall quality of the utterance in terms of its grammatical correctness and fluency?

It was found that the automated evaluation metrics did not sufficiently reflect human ratings, leading the authors to conclude that human evaluations were still required for NLG evaluation.

Building on this work, Dušek et al. [2020] report results from the first shared task on end-to-end NLG in which 21 systems were evaluated that had been developed using a range of different NLG approaches: template-based, rule-based, data-driven, and Seq2Seq (see Chapter 5 for a discussion of Seq2Seq architectures). The aim of the shared task was to assess whether end-to-end NLG systems are able to produce more complex outputs given a larger and richer training dataset. The evaluation involved a combination of automatic metrics and human evaluation. The automatic metrics were word-overlap and textual, i.e., measures of lexical richness and syntactic complexity. The human evaluation, which was conducted using crowdsourcing, used the *RankME method* [Novikova et al., 2018] in which the evaluators were presented with five randomly selected outputs of different systems and ranked them using continuous scales for quality and naturalness.

The overall winner was the SLUG system [Juraska et al., 2018], a Seq2Seq-based ensemble system that received the highest human ratings for naturalness and quality and also for automatic word-overlap metrics. An interesting finding was that handcrafted systems outperformed Seq2Seq models in terms of measures of overall quality and complexity, length and diversity of outputs. This suggests that there are still many challenges ahead for the use of Seq2Seq approaches in NLG.

Text-to-Speech Synthesis (TTS)

Assessing TTS systems has generally involved subjective measures such as intelligibility, naturalness, likeability, and human likeness. TTS has been evaluated annually in the Blizzard Challenge, which was launched in 2005 by Black and Tokuda [2005]. The general form of the challenge is that participants are given a speech database and they build a synthetic voice from the data.[3] The TTS systems then synthesize a prescribed set of test sentences and a panel of listeners evaluates the outputs. In 2019, the evaluation criteria were naturalness and similarity to the target speaker. One of the findings in 2019 was that neural approaches achieved superior naturalness compared with other approaches, although none of the systems was judged to have produced speech that sounded natural or was similar to the speech of the target speaker. Similar evaluations have been held at the ISCA ITRW Speech Synthesis Workshops that have taken place every 3 or 4 years since 1990.[4]

Wagner et al. [2019] discuss some of the issues and methods of TTS evaluation. One of the problems is that there is no gold standard for optimal speech quality as different situations require different types of output. For example, a car navigation TTS should be sufficiently loud, intelligible, and timely, while a virtual assistant should be clear and have a pleasant voice.

While most evaluations of TTS systems use subjective metrics, Wagner et al. [2019] describe some objective measures that use acoustic features to assess speech quality by comparing recorded natural speech as a reference against which the corresponding synthesized speech can be scored. Objective metrics could potentially provide a way to address the costs and time involved in conducting subjective evaluations, although, until recently, the results of these objective metrics have not correlated well with human perceptions of quality. However, new high-quality, probabilistic waveform-level synthesis models such as WaveNet can generate high-quality speech waveforms and also encode a lot of information about what a natural-sounding waveform looks like. As Wagner et al. [2019] suggest:

> It is entirely possible that the likelihood that a trained waveform-level synthesizer assigns to a given speech waveform could be a useful indicator of whether or not that waveform is "human-like" or not, without actual access to a comparable utterance from a human speaker.

The perceived quality of the TTS component of a dialogue system tends to be a primary factor in the user's acceptance of the overall system. Poor TTS quality can lead a user to judge the system as low on perceived intelligence, even if the system is able to perform its task successfully and efficiently.

Some Issues with the Evaluation of the Sub-Components of Dialogue Systems

The advantage of evaluating the sub-components of a modularised dialogue system is that it can help to pinpoint where a problem might lie. For example, the interaction may have been unsuccessful because of a high word error rate. Based on such information, the developer can address the problem by making adjustments elsewhere, for example, by employing more explicit confirmation requests in the dialogue management component.

Often, however, it is difficult to pinpoint an error. This is known as the *credit assignment problem*. For example, errors produced by ASR or NLU may be compensated for by DM without

[3] http://www.synsig.org/index.php/BlizzardChallenge
[4] https://synsig.org/index.php/Speech_Synthesis_Workshop_(SSW)

Table 4.2: Some items from SASSI

Scale	Item
System response accuracy	The system is accurate.
	The interaction with the system is consistent. The interaction with the system is efficient.
Likeability	The system is useful.
	I was able to recover easily from errors. I enjoyed using the system.
Cognitive demand	I felt confident using the system.
	The system was easy to use.
Annoyance	The interaction with the system is irritating.
	The system is too inflexible.
Habitability	I always knew what to say to the system.
	I was not always sure what the system was doing.
Speed	The interaction with the system is fast.
	The system responds too slowly.

affecting the quality of the overall system. Ratings from users are not reliable in this respect as a user may report that the system did not understand them a lot of the time, but this does not help to distinguish between ASR and NLU errors.

4.2.3 QUALITATIVE/SUBJECTIVE EVALUATION

Qualitative evaluation involves collecting data on the quality of a system in questionnaires where the users are asked to rate various statements on a Likert scale. Subjective Assessment of Speech System Interfaces (SASSI) is a widely used tool for the evaluation of spoken dialogue systems [Hone and Graham, 2000]. SASSI consists of 34 items distributed across six scales: System Response Accuracy, Likeability, Cognitive Demand, Annoyance, Habitability, and Speed. Seven-point Likert scales were used, labeled *strongly agree*, *agree*, *slightly agree*, *neutral*, *slightly disagree*, *disagree*, and *strongly disagree*. Some items from SASSI are shown in Table 4.2.

SASSI has been recommended for the evaluation of telephone-based spoken dialogue systems by the International Telecommunication Union. ITU-T Rec. P.851[5] provides a comprehensive overview of methods and procedures for the subjective evaluation of telephone services using spoken dialogue systems, describing how to set up experiments and devise questionnaires

[5]https://www.itu.int/rec/T-REC-P.851-200311-I/en

to quantify dimensions of quality and usability as perceived by users. In relation to questionnaires three different types are described.

1. Those that collect information about the user's background at the beginning of the evaluation, such as personal information (age, gender, etc.), task-related information, e.g., motivation, how often they have used such a system to perform some task, and system-related information, e.g., previous experience of spoken dialogue systems.

2. Those that collect information about the user's perceptions of their interactions with the system, e.g., information obtained from the system, perceived consistency and intelligibility, the system's interaction behavior, perceived system personality, perceived task success, and reliability of task results.

3. Those that collect information about the user's overall impression of the system, e.g., perceived usability, expected future use.

Many questionnaires have been developed for the evaluation of telephone-based spoken dialogue systems and voice user interfaces. Wei and Landay [2018] developed a set of 17 usability heuristics for the evaluation of smart speakers. The list of heuristics together with detailed descriptions and examples can be found here.[6] The heuristics were used by a group of usability experts to empirically evaluate Google Home, Amazon Echo, and Apple Siri on a set of 10 tasks. In addition to the evaluation of the smart speakers, usability problems were identified along with the most relevant heuristic for each problem. For example, one of the most frequently relevant heuristics was

S5: Pay attention to what the user said and respect the user's context.

The authors concluded that the set of heuristics was easy to understand and helped evaluators identify real usability problems as well as being useful as a set of design principles.

Questionnaires have also been used to evaluate User Experience (UX) with dialogue systems and chatbots. Kocaballi et al. [2018] created an assessment scheme to investigate the extent to which six widely used questionnaires including SASSI addressed UX dimensions such as: affect/emotion, enjoyment/fun, aesthetics/appeal, hedonic quality, engagement/flow, motivation, enchantment, frustration, and pragmatic quality. They found that SASSI covered most of the dimensions but concluded that the use of multiple questionnaires was recommended to obtain a more complete measurement of UX. The online tool *Chatbottest*[7] supports the design and evaluation of the following aspects of chatbots: personality, onboarding, understanding, answering, navigation, error management, and intelligence. Holmes et al. [2019] developed the Chatbot Usability Questionnaire (CUQ) based on these categories and demonstrated its applicability in the evaluation of three different chatbot systems.

[6] http://hci.stanford.edu/publications/2018/speech-he/sui-heuristics.html
[7] https://chatbottest.com/

There are many other standardized questionnaires for the evaluation of dialogue systems. Lewis [2016b] provides a review of a number of standardized questionnaires and assesses their reliability and validity.

Subjective evaluations provide useful feedback on how users experience interaction with a dialogue system. However, they have some limitations.

- The judgements of users are subjective and can vary widely across different users, so that it can be difficult to obtain a consistent perspective on usability and usefulness.
- Subjective evaluations typically take place after the users have interacted with the dialogue system and so the evaluations are liable to focus mainly on the user's overall experience with the system and not with issues that arose at particular points in the interaction. This problem is addressed in some evaluations where the evaluators (who are not the users who interacted with the system) explore and annotate logs of the interactions on a turn-by-turn basis [Schmitt et al., 2011]. See Section 4.3.1.

4.3 EVALUATING OPEN-DOMAIN DIALOGUE SYSTEMS

Recently, the focus of research in dialogue systems has shifted to open-domain dialogue systems. It is difficult to establish criteria for measuring the quality of an open-domain dialogue system since there is no clearly defined goal or task that can be measured using metrics such as task success or dialogue efficiency. Several different approaches are discussed in the following sections.

4.3.1 EVALUATION AT THE LEVEL OF THE EXCHANGE

Evaluation at the level of the exchange involves making a judgment about some aspect of the system's response to the user's utterance. This approach, which is known as *single-turn pairwise evaluation* [Li et al., 2019], has the advantage that it can provide a more fine-grained evaluation compared with a dialogue-level evaluation but there is also the disadvantage that issues that arise in the longer flow of the dialogue tend to be overlooked.

Using Metrics from Machine Translation

In Machine Translation (MT) using the Seq2Seq approach (see Chapter 5) an utterance in one language is encoded into a representation that is then decoded as an utterance in another language. This idea has been extended to dialogue in which the utterance that is encoded is from one of the dialogue participants, typically the user, and the decoded utterance is the response from the other participant, typically the system. Building on this dialogue researchers have investigated whether evaluation methods that have been used successfully in MT could be extend to the evaluation of dialogue.

Bilingual Evaluation Understudy (BLEU) is a widely used algorithm for evaluating the quality of translated text by comparing it to a good quality reference translation using a modified form of precision [Papineni et al., 2002]. BLEU also seems to correlate well with the judgements

Table 4.3: Example of an NUC question from the SubTle Corpus [Banchs, 2012]. Source: Lowe et al. [2016, Figure 1].

Speaker A: yo Speaker B: damone, it's mark		
	Best Answer	**Second Answer**
shut up, lemme me do it, red	☐	☐
tomorrow	☐	☐
well of course in my youth I was simply known as goldthwait	☐	☐
sorry that wasn't quite what I was looking for	☐	☐
mark, what happened to your date?	☐	☐

of human translators. Liu et al. [2016] performed a detailed analysis of the use of BLEU and other metrics from MT to evaluate conversations. Their main conclusion was that because the MT metrics measure word overlap between an input and a response, they are not valid for conversation where an appropriate response may have no overlap at all with the input yet still be highly appropriate. Moreover, there are often many appropriate responses to any given input in a dialogue so that the one-to-one mapping in MT is not applicable. Given these issues researchers have proposed alternative approaches to evaluation at the level of the exchange.

Next Utterance Classification (NUC)

Lowe et al. [2016] propose Next Utterance Classification (NUC) as a metric for evaluating the performance of a dialogue system. NUC involves selecting the best response to a previous utterance from a candidate list, as in retrieval-based response generation (see Chapter 5, Section 5.4). The advantage of NUC is that it is easy to compute automatically, however it is important to determine whether this automatic classification would correlate with the ratings of human evaluators.

To investigate these issues Lowe et al. [2016] conducted a series of experiments in which human evaluators with different levels of expertise were recruited on AMT and their performance on three datasets was compared with that of a state-of-the-art machine learning agent described in Lowe et al. [2015a]. Given the context of the conversation, the task was to select the most appropriate response from a list that included the actual next response of the conversation and other responses taken from elsewhere in the corpus. An example is shown in Table 4.3.

Although human evaluators outperformed the machine-learning agent, Lowe et al. [2016] maintain that NUC is a potentially useful approach to the automatic evaluation of dialogue systems and that NUC could be combined with other relevant metrics to more closely reflect the human evaluations.

Table 4.4: SSA scores for responses from GenericBot and Meena (base). Based on Adiwardana et al. [2020, Tables 4 and 8].

Sample Contexts	GenericBot	Meena (base)
A: You must have read a lot of books. B: Oh wow, how do you know? Do I look Nerdy?	B: I don't know. [*sensible: 1, specific: 0*]	A: I know because I've read a lot of books. [*sensible: 1, specific: 1*]
A: You know nothing, Jon Snow. B: You must be a fan of Game of Thrones.	A: OK [*sensible: 0, specific: 0*]	A: Yeah, I'm reading the books at the moment. [*sensible: 1, specific: 1*]

Sensibleness and Specificity Average

Sensibleness and Specificity Average (SSA) is a new metric for evaluating the system's response. SSA was first used to evaluate Google's open-domain chatbot Meena [Adiwardana et al., 2020], see Chapter 1, Section 1.3.1. SSA looks at two important aspects of the quality of a response.

- *Sensibleness*: whether the response makes sense.
- *Specificity*: whether it is specific.

For the first aspect, the evaluator judges whether a response is reasonable in context. For specificity, the judgment is whether the response is specific to the given context. For example, a response such as *that's nice* would be marked as "not specific" as it could be used in many different contexts. The sensibleness of a chatbot is the fraction of responses marked as "sensible" and specificity the fraction of responses marked as "specific". SSA is the average of the two scores. Table 4.4 shows some examples of the use of SSA to evaluate responses by GenericBot, a trivial bot that always replies to questions with *I don't know* and to statements with *ok*, and Meena (base), an end-to-end Meena model with the lowest perplexity.

SSA was used to evaluate and compare Meena with several other chatbots (see Chapter 5, Table 5.2). SSA, which is a metric based on human evaluation, was found to correlate strongly with *perplexity*, which is an automated metric that is available to any neural Seq2Seq model. Thus, measuring perplexity might provide a solution to the challenge of finding an automated metric that correlates strongly with human judgements.

4.3.2 EVALUATION AT THE LEVEL OF THE DIALOGUE

Evaluation at the level of the dialogue is less fine-grained than evaluation at the level of the exchange although it has the advantage that it can capture important aspects of the conversation

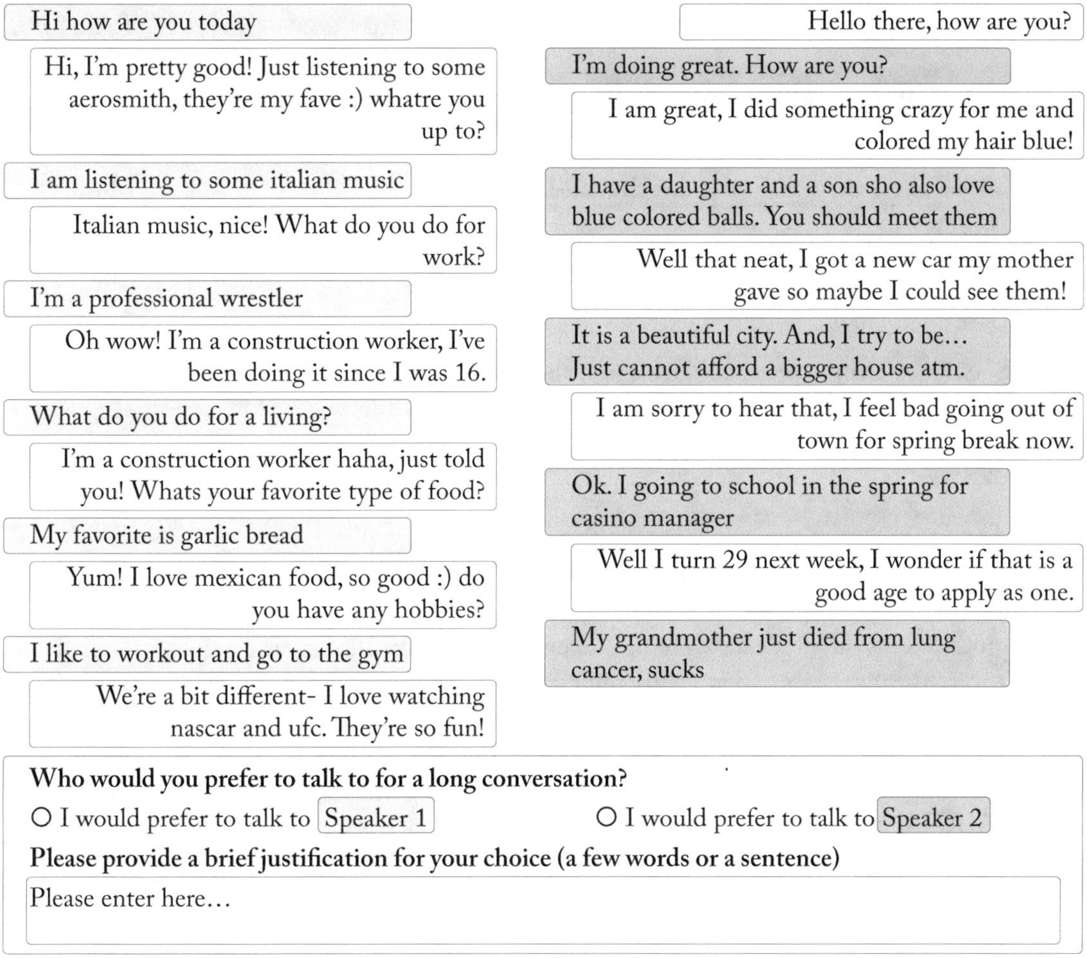

Hi how are you today

Hi, I'm pretty good! Just listening to some aerosmith, they're my fave :) whatre you up to?

I am listening to some italian music

Italian music, nice! What do you do for work?

I'm a professional wrestler

Oh wow! I'm a construction worker, I've been doing it since I was 16.

What do you do for a living?

I'm a construction worker haha, just told you! Whats your favorite type of food?

My favorite is garlic bread

Yum! I love mexican food, so good :) do you have any hobbies?

I like to workout and go to the gym

We're a bit different- I love watching nascar and ufc. They're so fun!

Hello there, how are you?

I'm doing great. How are you?

I am great, I did something crazy for me and colored my hair blue!

I have a daughter and a son sho also love blue colored balls. You should meet them

Well that neat, I got a new car my mother gave so maybe I could see them!

It is a beautiful city. And, I try to be... Just cannot afford a bigger house atm.

I am sorry to hear that, I feel bad going out of town for spring break now.

Ok. I going to school in the spring for casino manager

Well I turn 29 next week, I wonder if that is a good age to apply as one.

My grandmother just died from lung cancer, sucks

Who would you prefer to talk to for a long conversation?

O I would prefer to talk to Speaker 1 O I would prefer to talk to Speaker 2

Please provide a brief justification for your choice (a few words or a sentence)

Please enter here...

Figure 4.1: ACUTE-Eval: comparing two dialogues. Based on Li et al. [2019].

flow that occur in multi-turn dialogues and that otherwise would be missed in an exchange-based approach. The following are some approaches to dialogue-level evaluation.

Evaluation Based on Comparison of Dialogues

Following on from the work of See et al. [2019] in which human evaluators compared dialogue systems by answering questions about different aspects of conversational quality, Li et al. [2019] developed *ACUTE-EVAL* as a method for the systematic comparison of dialogues. ACUTE-EVAL aims to address the disadvantages of exchange-level and dialogue-level evaluations that are based on the use of Likert scales.

Table 4.5: Conversation turns and corresponding topics. Source: Guo et al. [2018, Table 2].

Turns	Utterances	Topics
1. User	Let's talk about music.	Music
1. Socialbot	Sure, what's your favorite musician?	Music
2. User	Bob Dylan.	Music
2. Socialbot	Bob Dylan is an American songwriter, singer, painter, and writer.	Music
3. User	Cool.	Phatic
3. Socialbot	Do you want to know more about Bob Dylan?	Music
4. User	No, let's talk about politics instead.	Politics
4. Socialbot	Sure, here are the latest updates about Donald Trump...	Politics

As shown in Figure 4.1, two dialogues are placed side by side and the evaluator has to compare them, focusing only on the utterances highlighted in gray and green, i.e., the utterances produced by the dialogue system. The evaluator is asked to answer a question related to the quality of the responses and to justify their choice. Questions used in the experiments focused on whether the responses being evaluated showed engagement or were interesting, knowledgeable, or human-like. The questions were optimized over a number of trials and the approach was benchmarked against several state-of-the-art response generation models. The main advantage of ACUTE-EVAL is that compared with other approaches it provides a more fine-grained and more sensitive evaluation of multi-turn dialogues while reducing effort and costs. ACUTE-Eval was used to evaluate Facebook's BlenderBot against Google's Meena (see Chapter 5, Section 5.6.3).

Topic-Based Evaluation

Topic-based evaluation assesses the extent to which an overall dialogue is coherent and, as a consequence, engaging and satisfying for users [Guo et al., 2018]. Thus, a dialogue agent should be able to talk coherently at length on a given topic (measured by the metric *topic depth*), and on a range of topics (measured by the metric *topic breadth*).

To investigate whether topic depth and topic breadth can be evaluated automatically and whether the evaluations correlate with those of human raters, Guo et al. [2018] trained a topic classifier to be able to identify coarse level topics such as *Sports* as well as fine-grained topic words such as *manchester_united*. Table 4.5 shows some examples of the topic annotations.

To measure topic depth the number of topic-specific turns in a sub-conversation was counted. For example, the topic **Music** has length 3 in Table 4.5, while the total number of topic-specific turns is 4. To measure topic breadth, the different topics in a conversation were identified using the topic classifier, which was an attention-based neural topic model that jointly learned a topic-word attention table along with the classification objective. In this way it was possible to identify the most likely topic for each utterance as well as salient topic-specific keywords. Good classification accuracy was obtained and comparisons were made with the ratings of users who evaluated their interactions with the Amazon Alexa socialbots. The measures of topic depth were found to correlate highly with the satisfaction ratings of the users.

Regarding topic breadth, it was found that the average topic breadth metrics correlated well with user ratings, suggesting that users evaluate the chatbot higher if they can chat with it on several different topics in the same conversation. Some of the topic breadth metrics, such as the ability of the chatbot to chat about topics in a balanced way as opposed to preferring certain topics, did not correlate as well with the user ratings. The authors suggest that this may be due to the fact that users are assigned randomly to the socialbots and may not experience the performance of a particular socialbot over several dialogues and thus would not be able to notice whether it was being repetitive across conversations. This behavior would be important to capture in the case of chatbots that interact frequently with the same user as repetitiveness could have a detrimental effect on user satisfaction.

Evaluation Using Multiple Metrics

Venkatesh et al. [2018] aimed to provide an automated metric that would correlate highly with the ratings of human users and that could be used to evaluate the conversational performance of the socialbots in the Alexa Prize. They began by developing a framework for evaluation that used multiple metrics including engagement, domain coverage, coherence, topical diversity, and conversational depth. These metrics provided a fine-grained analysis of dialogue systems and were shown to correlate well with human judgements based on validations against hundreds of thousands of conversations with the Alexa Prize socialbots.

In order to classify utterances into one of 26 predefined topical domains a topic classification model was trained on a dataset of Alexa conversations. The model was used to obtain a number of topic-based metrics. The metrics relating to conversational user experience were calculated as follows.

- *Engagement*: engagement indicates how interested the user was in the conversation and was measured by the number of dialogue turns and the total dialogue duration.

- *Coherence*: coherence is a measure of the relevance of the system's response. Coherence was measured using the metric Response Error Rate (RER) that was computed from annotations of incorrect, irrelevant and inappropriate responses taken from hundreds of thousands of randomly selected interactions.

- *Domain coverage*: domain coverage measures the distribution of topics covered in a conversation.

- *Conversational Depth*: conversational depth was measured by calculating the number of consecutive turns on the same topic.
- *Topical Diversity/Conversational Breadth*: this metric measures the diversity of topics in a conversation, covering coarse topic domains such as Politics and Sports as well as fine-grained topical keywords such as Merkel and Ronaldo.
- *Unification of evaluation metrics*: this measure aimed to provide a method for the ranking of the socialbots in the Alexa Prize in terms of total conversational quality.

The relevance of the individual metrics was determined by correlating each of them with user ratings. The unified metric correlated strongly with user ratings (0.66) which suggests that it could be used as a proxy for user ratings, thus providing an automated evaluation process for open-domain dialogue systems.

4.3.3 CHATEVAL: A TOOLKIT FOR CHATBOT EVALUATION

ChatEval[8] is a framework for the evaluation of open-domain Seq2Seq chatbots that aims to address the problem of the wide variety of evaluation procedures currently in use [Sedoc et al., 2019]. ChatEval provides an open-source codebase for automatic and human evaluations based on the dataset from the Dialogue Breakdown Detection Challenge (DBDC) [Higashinaka et al., 2017]. Model code, trained parameters, and evaluation results are provided. Automatic evaluation metrics provided in the ChatEval evaluation toolkit include: lexical diversity [Li et al., 2015], average cosine-similarity [Liu et al., 2016], sentence average BLEU-2 score [Liu et al., 2016], and response perplexity [Zhang et al., 2018]. Human evaluation involves A/B comparison tests in which the evaluator is shown a prompt and two possible responses from models that are being compared. The ChatEval evaluation toolkit is available on Github.[9]

4.3.4 EVALUATIONS IN CHALLENGES AND COMPETITIONS

There have been several challenges and competitions for open-domain dialogue systems for which a range of different evaluation metrics have been proposed.

Evaluation in the Loebner Prize

The Loebner Prize is an annual competition in which judges engage simultaneously in text-based interactions with a dialogue system (or chatbot) and a human interlocutor with the aim of determining which interlocutor is the human and which is the chatbot. As discussed in Chapter 1, Section 1.2.3, the Loebner Prize is intended as an implementation of the Turing test [Turing, 1950]. After interacting with the chatbots the judges rank them in terms of which is the most

[8]https://chateval.org/
[9]https://github.com/chateval/chateval

human-like chatbot [Loebner, 2009]. In many cases the chatbots have provided impressive performances. See, for example, logs of interactions with Mitsuku, the five times winner of the Loebner Prize.[10]

Comparing the performance of a chatbot with that of a human is not necessarily a good indicator of conversational ability. In the Loebner Prize the chatbots do not have access to the internet and so their ability to answer general knowledge questions depends completely on what has been hard-coded by their developers. In this case they will often fail on questions that are easy for a human but have not been predicted by the developer—for example, a recent item of news. In the more general case, however, a chatbot with access to the internet is able to answer questions that most humans would not be able to answer. Another issue is that in the Loebner Prize the judges simply provide a ranking and do not evaluate more fine-grained aspects of the conversational performance of the chatbots. Finally, as Venkatesh et al. [2018] point out, in competitions such as the Loebner prize chatbots can maintain a conversation by outputting minimal responses that add little content to the conversation. Responses such as these avoid the challenges that response generation and dialogue management face in Conversational AI where the aim is to build systems that can participate in engaging conversations with human users.

Evaluation in the Amazon Alexa Challenge

The main aim of the Amazon Alexa Challenge is to advance the current state-of-the-art in Conversational AI by inviting teams of researchers from universities to develop dialogue systems, known as socialbots, that users can interact with and evaluate. There are two different levels of evaluation:

1. user ratings to determine the finalists and ultimately the top three socialbots in the challenge and
2. evaluations to measure scientific progress in Conversational AI.

There are two stages in the collection of user ratings. In the first stage the socialbots are made available to the general public. Users initiate a conversation with a randomly selected participating socialbot and at the end of the conversation they are asked to rate the conversation on a scale ranging from 1 to 5. They are also asked to provide some short feedback on their experience. The ratings are used to decide which of the socialbots should proceed to the Alexa Prize finals. The feedback provides information that enables the team developing the socialbot to make improvements.

In the finals stage, specially selected judges interact with the socialbots. In each interaction one judge holds a conversation with the socialbot and three other judges evaluate the interaction in terms of coherence and engagement. The conversation is stopped if a majority of the judges determine that it is no longer coherent or engaging and the socialbot is rated by each of the judges on a scale of 1 to 5. The challenge for the teams is to achieve a composite score of 4.0

[10] http://www.square-bear.co.uk/mitsuku/home.htm

or higher and for two-thirds of the conversations with the socialbots to last for 20 minutes. To date, no socialbot has achieved this challenge. See Khatri et al. [2018b] and Khatri et al. [2018a] for more details of the 2017 and 2018 challenges.

While the user ratings are useful for evaluating the overall quality of the socialbots within the terms of the challenge, they do not provide more fine-grained information about the performance of the systems at the level of the turn. To address this, the following metrics have been defined to assess the responses generated by the systems [Khatri et al., 2018a].

- *Comprehensible*: whether the response makes sense.
- *On Topic or Relevant*: whether the response maintains the same topic as the user's utterance or is relevant to it.
- *Response Incorrectness*: whether the response is irrelevant or inappropriate.
- *Interesting*: whether the response provides new information.
- *Continue Conversation*: whether the response helps to continue the conversation.

A model was trained for the application of these metrics using features that can be extracted automatically from the conversation logs such as *past utterance*, *response context*, *dialogue act*, *entity*, *topic*, and *sentiment*. Some of these metrics provide assessments similar to the SSA metric for the Meena chatbot (see Section 4.3.1). In order to assess the scientific advancements made during the competition, each of the modules provided by the Alexa team to the competitors was assessed for improvements. For example, in 2017 there was an improvement in Word Error Rate (WER) of nearly 33% relative to the base model and in 2018 WER increased by 30% relative to the 2017 model. For further details of improvements in other modules, see Khatri et al. [2018b] and Khatri et al. [2018a].

Evaluation in the ConvAI Competitions

ConvAI is a competition that aims to measure the quality of open-domain dialogue systems [Dinan et al., 2019a]. The first ConvAI competition was held in 2017 and involved interactions between humans and dialogue systems about news articles.[11] The evaluations were performed by human assessors. Each system response was evaluated subjectively on a binary scale, although this part of the evaluation could be skipped. The dialogue as a whole was evaluated on a 1-10 point scale in terms of its breadth and engagement.

The second competition, which was held in 2018, focused on general chit-chat about people's interests [Dinan et al., 2019a]. The Persona-Chat training set [Zhang et al., 2018] was used to train the systems. The task involved engaging in a conversation to get to know someone, asking and answering questions, and maintaining a consistent persona that was assigned in advance of the conversation. Three types of metric were used.

[11] http://convai.io/2017/

1. Automated: *perplexity*, which measures how well a probability model predicts a sample, such as the next word or next response, *F1*, which measures the balance between precision and recall (see Section 4.2.2), and *hits@k*, which measures the accuracy of the next dialogue utterance when choosing between the gold response and distractors.

2. AMT: users (Turkers) interacted with the dialogue systems and scored them on a scale of 1-5 with three metrics: fluency, consistency, and engagingness. The ability of the system to maintain a consistent persona was also scored.

3. Live chat with volunteers in the wild. Volunteer users were solicited to interact with the systems through Facebook Messenger and Telegram. However, as many of the dialogues turned out to be senseless or offensive, the results from the evaluations in the wild were discarded.

Several other metrics were applied to the datasets of the dialogues.

- *Length statistics*: the average length of system and human responses.

- *Rare word statistics*: based on the idea that rare words might indicate that the response was more interesting.

- *Word and utterance repetition statistics*: measuring unigram, bigram, and trigram repeats in the system's responses, based on the idea that repetitiveness has a negative effect on judgements of quality.

- *Asking questions*: based on the idea that if the system asks too many questions, especially if the questions are not related to the previous conversation, then this has a negative effect on judgements of quality.

One of the aims of the evaluations was to find the best automatic evaluation metrics for dialogue that correlate with human evaluations. While there were some indications of correlations, there was insufficient data from the competition to measure correlations in depth. It was also noted that automatic evaluations fail to take into account important aspects of multi-turn conversation such as the balance in the number of questions asked and answered by the dialogue system and the human user, respectively.

4.4 EVALUATION FRAMEWORKS

In addition to the various metrics that have been used to evaluate dialogue systems, several larger-scale frameworks have been developed, including PARAdigm for Dialogue System Evaluation (PARADISE), Quality of Experience (QoE), and Interaction Quality (IQ).

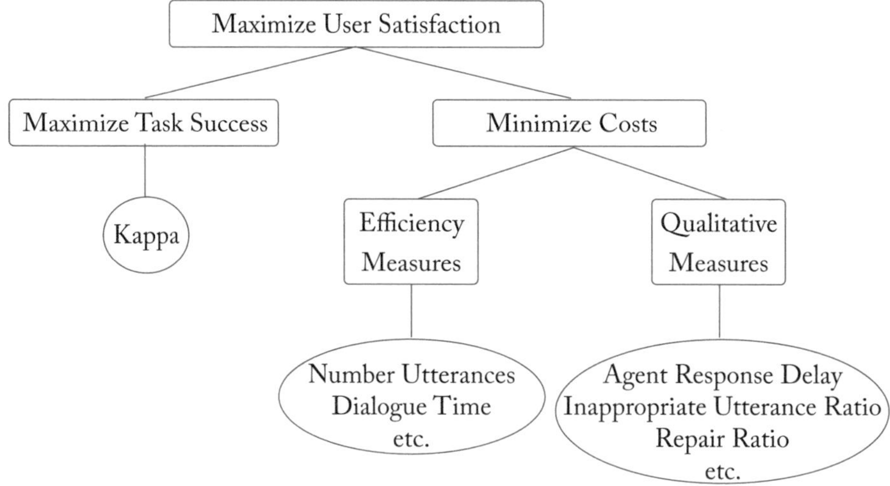

Figure 4.2: Maximizing User Satisfaction. Based on Walker et al. [1997].

4.4.1 PARADISE

PARAdigm for Dialogue System Evaluation (PARADISE) is a framework for evaluating task-oriented and multimodal dialogue systems [Walker et al., 1997], [Walker et al., 1998], [Beringer et al., 2002]. The starting point in PARADISE is that the overall goal for a dialogue system is to maximize User Satisfaction (US). This goal is subdivided into the sub-goals of maximizing task success and minimizing costs. The latter is in turn subdivided into efficiency measures and qualitative measures. The relationships between these goals are shown in Figure 4.2.

The main strength of the PARADISE framework is that US can be predicted automatically from the objective measures involved in maximizing task success along with the efficiency and qualitative measures involved in minimizing costs. US is modeled using multiple linear regression in which US is the dependent variable and the objective features are the independent variables. US is calculated using scores from the following questions [Walker et al., 2000a].

- Expected behavior: did the system work as expected?
- Future use: would you use this system again?
- Ease of use: was it easy to find the information you wanted?

The objective measures are calculated as follows. In a task-oriented dialogue such as a train timetable application, the various elements of the task, such as values for **departure city**, **arrival city**, and so on can be represented in an Attribute Value Matrix (AVM), as shown in Table 4.6.

Task success can be measured in terms of how well the information is elicited and conveyed and represented in a confusion matrix. Figure 4.3 is an example of a confusion matrix based on a

Table 4.6: Attribute Value Matrix for train timetable domain. Source: Walker et al. [1997, Table 1].

Attribute	Possible Values	Information Flow
Depart-city (DC)	Milano, Roma, Torino, Trento	To agent
Arrival-city (AC)	Milano, Roma, Torino, Trento	To agent
Depart-range (DR)	Morning, evening (DC)	To agent
Depart-time (DT)	6 am, 8 am, 6 pm, 8 pm	To user

	Key													
	Depart-City				Arrival-City				Depart-Range		Depart-Time			
Data	v1	v2	v3	v4	v5	v6	v7	v8	v9	v10	v11	v12	v13	v14
v1	**22**		1		3									
v2		**29**												
v3	4		**16**	4			1							
v4	1	1	5	**11**			1							
v5	3				**20**									
v6						**22**								
v7			2		1	1	**20**	5						
v8			1		1	2	8	**15**						
v9									**45**	10				
v10									5	**40**				
v11											**20**		2	
v12											1	**19**	2	4
v13											2		**18**	
v14											2	6	3	**21**
Sum	30	30	25	15	25	25	30	20	50	50	25	25	25	25

Figure 4.3: Confusion Matrix. Based on Walker et al. [1997].

dialogue reported in Danieli and Gerbino [1995] which shows the number of times the correct value was obtained and for incorrect values which value was substituted. Using this information the Kappa coefficient K is calculated.

The Kappa coefficient K is normally used to measure inter-observer reliability but in the PARADISE tool it is used to indicate how well the system performed a particular task within a given scenario. *P(A)* indicates how well the system recognized each of the slot values. For example, for **depart-city** the value *Milano* (v1) was correctly recognized 22 times, and the additional scores in the v1 column indicate misrecognitions, *Torino* (4 times) and *Trento* once. P(E) is the proportion of times that the AVMs for the dialogues and the keys were expected to agree by chance:

$$K = \frac{P(A) - P(E)}{1 - P(E)}. \tag{4.5}$$

Dialogue costs are measured in terms of efficiency measures such as the average time required to complete a task, the average number of turns per task, and the number of words correctly recognized per turn. Measures for evaluating the quality of the system include: the percentage of errors successfully corrected, the system's response time, the recognition rate, and the number of times the user requests repetition, requests help, and interrupts the system.

Given the US scores and the scores from the objective features US can be modeled using multiple regression analysis and the model can be used to predict subjective user ratings from the objective features and to discover trade-offs between different features of a system, for example[12]:

$$US = w_1 \times taskCompletion - W_2 \times dialogueLength, \tag{4.6}$$

where w_1 and w_2 are determined via a regression on the various scores. This idea is useful for optimization in RL as it can be used to discover a reward function [Rieser and Lemon, 2011a].

4.4.2 QUALITY OF EXPERIENCE (QOE)

Quality of Experience (QoE) has its origins in recommendations on the quality of speech communication services by the International Telecommunication Union (ITU-T SG12) and the Technical Committee Speech and multimedia Transmission Quality (STQ) of the European Telecommunications Standards Institute (ETSI) [Möller and Köster, 2017]. Originally, the recommendations focused on technical aspects of quality under the label Quality of Service (QoS), looking at measures of the performance of the system or its sub-components, such as word error rate or transaction success. More recently, the focus has shifted to QoE which describes the user's perceptions of quality in terms of aspects of usability such as effectiveness, efficiency, and user satisfaction [Möller et al., 2009]. User-perceived quality is a subjective measure of the user's perceptions of their interactions with the system in relation to what they expect or desire from the interactions. Much of the work on QoE has taken the form of developing taxonomies of aspects of perceived quality, as summarized in Figure 4.4, in which examples are given in the gray boxes and influences are indicated by arrows. The upper part of the figure shows factors of the system and of the context of its use that affect quality, for example, characteristics of the

[12] I am grateful to Oliver Lemon for this example and for pointing out the relevance to Reinforcement Learning.

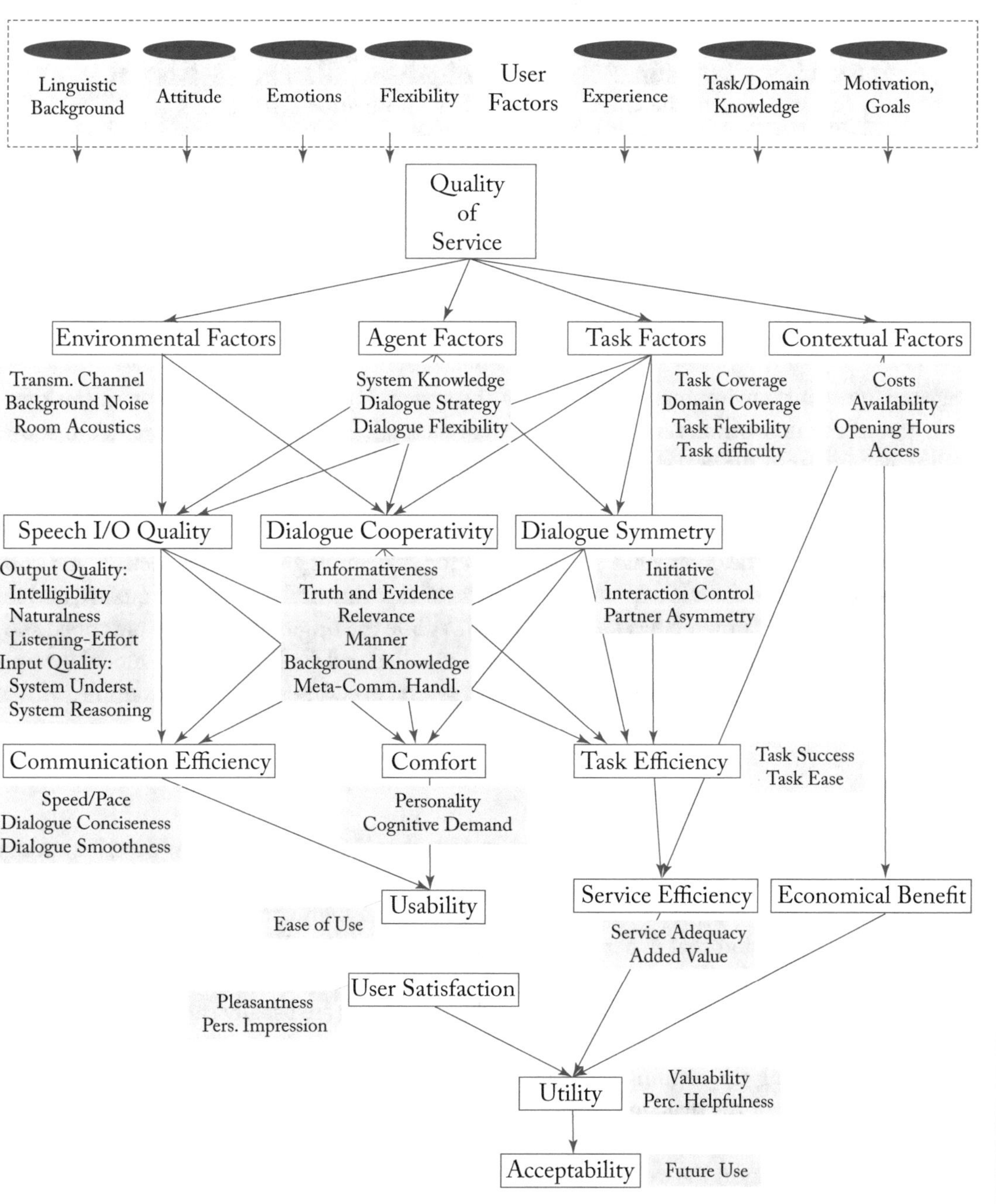

Figure 4.4: Taxonomy of quality aspects. Based on Möller [2004].

Table 4.7: Interaction Quality annotation 1. Source: Ultes et al. [2014, Figure 6].

	Utterance	
S:	Welcome to the CMU Let's Go! bus information system.	
U:	–	5
S:	What can I do for you?	
U:	Penn at Butler time is it the centre at Highland from runs …	5
S:	Leaving from Oakland. Is this correct?	
U:	Oakland	4

usage environment (environmental factors), of the system (agent factors), of the task (task factors), and of the non-physical context (contextual factors). The lower part of the figure shows quality features from the user's point of view such as speech input and output quality, dialogue cooperativity, communication and task efficiency, usability, and acceptability [Möller, 2004].

In addition to providing a classification of quality features and interaction parameters of dialogue systems, the taxonomy has proved useful for determining evaluation metrics and constructing questionnaires, for interpreting the results of experimental measures of quality, and for defining quality prediction models [Möller, 2004]. While the original taxonomy described spoken human-machine interaction, it has since been extended and applied to multi-modal interaction [Möller et al., 2009] and has been validated in several experiments (see, for example, Möller et al. [2007]).

4.4.3 INTERACTION QUALITY

The term *Interaction Quality (IQ)* was introduced by Schmitt et al. [2011] to describe ratings performed by experts as opposed to US, which is a measure of user ratings. As mentioned earlier, an investigation comparing expert and user ratings found a high correlation between the two, leading to the suggestion that expert ratings, which are easier and less costly to obtain, could replace user ratings in evaluations of dialogue systems [Ultes et al., 2013].

While evaluations of interactions with dialogue systems are usually carried out at the end of an interaction, the innovation in the IQ approach is that evaluation is carried out at the exchange level during the ongoing dialogue. Table 4.7 shows a dialogue annotation of extracts from the beginning of the dialogue when the dialogue is proceeding smoothly, while Table 4.8 shows an annotation at a point where the dialogue runs into difficulties.

Assessing quality at the exchange level enables a more fine-grained analysis of an interaction as problematic situations can be identified when they occur. Furthermore, if quality ratings can be estimated automatically during the ongoing dialogue, this information can be used by the DM to adapt the dialogue strategy dynamically. Schmitt and Ultes [2015] investigated how

Table 4.8: Interaction Quality annotation 2. Source: Ultes et al. [2014, Figure 6].

	Utterance	
S:	To ask about a new trip you can say, start a new query …	
U:	61A	2
S:	You can start a new query or goodbye.	
U:	5 Duquesne	1
S:	You can start a new query or goodbye.	
U:	Last the next	1

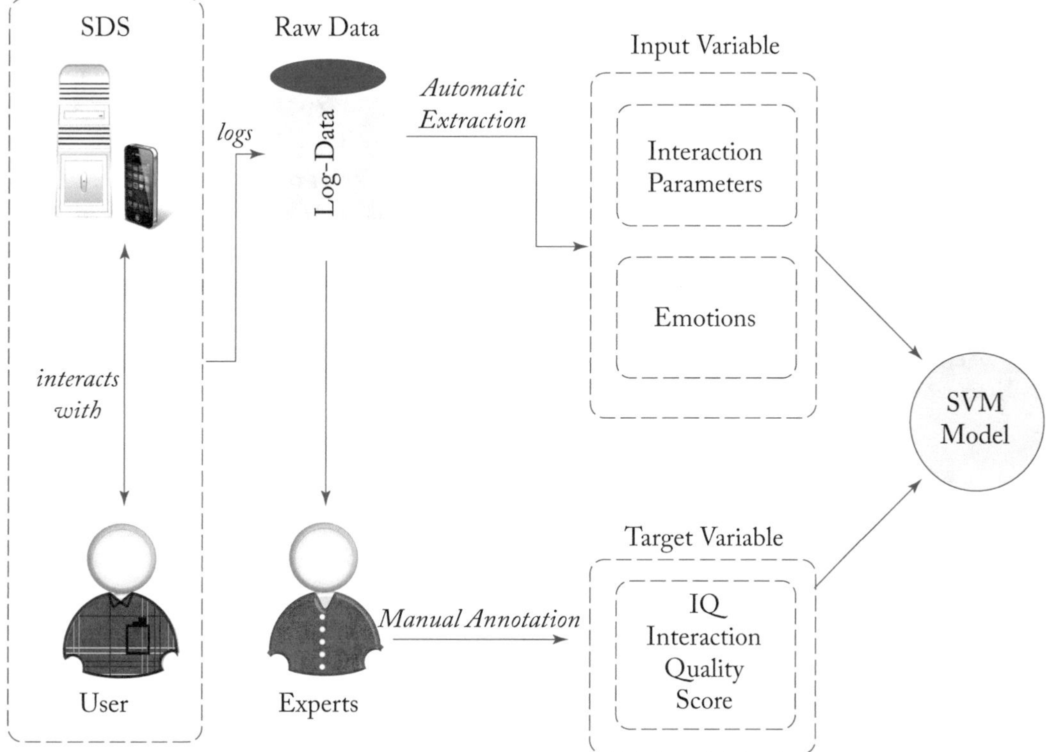

Figure 4.5: The IQ framework. Based on Schmitt and Ultes [2015].

IQ could be predicted automatically. Figure 4.5 provides an overview of the IQ process. Input parameters are defined for the automated IQ prediction. These include features related to speech recognition, spoken language understanding, dialogue management, dialogue act usage, emotional state, and factors such as the user's age, gender, and attitudes regarding spoken dialogue systems. These input parameters can be extracted automatically from the log data of the interactions. The target variables are provided through manual annotations by expert raters and a target variable is derived. The input variables and the target variable are fed into a statistical classification module—in this case an SVM model that is trained to estimate the IQ of the current exchange and in this way to automatically rate the dialogue at any point in time, as shown in Tables 4.5 and 4.6.

The next step is to determine if IQ could be used to adapt the dialogue strategy. To test this, Ultes et al. [2014] investigated how IQ could affect the choice of explicit or implicit confirmation prompts in a train booking dialogue system, where the value **2** represented a satisfied user and **1** a dissatisfied user. Slot values were confirmed implicitly if the user was satisfied and explicitly if dissatisfied. It was found that the adaptive strategy performed successfully and contributed to the overall user experience. Other approaches to dialogue strategy adaptation are described in Ultes et al. [2012], including the use of design patterns in a rule-based system and the incorporation of additional user state information in a POMDP-based dialogue manager. While estimating IQ can be carried out by performing the classification separately on each system-user exchange, Ultes and Minker [2014] found that classification of IQ was improved using Hybrid Hidden Markov Models to model the sequential characteristics of dialogue, incorporating the IQ from the previous exchange into an extended vector of the exchange being classified.

In summary, the IQ framework examines the quality of a dialogue at the level of the exchange using the ratings of expert raters who were shown to provide comparable ratings to real users. Expert raters are less costly and easier to recruit and manage. Given an IQ score the dialogue strategy can be adapted dynamically during the ongoing interaction, thus contributing to subsequent interaction quality.

4.5 WHAT IS THE BEST WAY TO EVALUATE DIALOGUE SYSTEMS?

A wide range of evaluation techniques have been reviewed in this chapter and it is appropriate to ask whether there is any one of these techniques or a collection of them that could be used to evaluate and improve dialogue systems. There is no simple answer to this question as a number of different factors are involved. We begin by summarizing the main issues to consider.

The primary aim of a dialogue system is that it should enable humans to engage in interactions with software agents. The system should be able to perform to the user's satisfaction, which is determined primarily by the user's perception of how well the system worked. Different types of system create different expectations. In task-oriented systems the user has clearly defined goals that can be measured objectively, such as completing a task successfully and efficiently. The user's perceptions of the usefulness of the system may be affected by features associated with the quality of the interaction, such as word error rate, number of corrections required, whether the system's persona is perceived as likeable, and so on. These factors could all impact on the user's level of satisfaction.[13]

With non-task-oriented systems user satisfaction is determined primarily by the quality of the interaction. This can be measured through questionnaires, although studies have found that users vary considerably in their assessments and so results can be unreliable. Evaluations of actual interactions with dialogue systems are an alternative. There are two types, each with strengths and weaknesses.

1. Overall assessment of dialogue quality. This can involve pairwise comparisons of dialogues, as in the ACUTE-Eval method or the use of dialogue level metrics such as *domain coverage*, *topic depth*, and *topic breadth*. These metrics indicate the extent to which the system can converse extensively on a topic and cover a range of topics. In many studies it has been shown that these metrics correlate strongly with indicators of user satisfaction in terms of whether the user finds the system to be *engaging*, *interesting*, and *human-like*. Overall dialogue assessment can also address issues that arise over the course of a multi-turn dialogue—for example, repetitive responses by the system that can have an adverse effect on judgements of dialogue quality.

2. Exchange-level assessment. Exchange-level assessment involves evaluating how the system responds to the user's utterances, looking at each utterance-response pair (or exchange) separately. Exchange-level evaluation can produce a fine-grained evaluation of dialogue quality, showing, for example, where the dialogue has broken down. Metrics have been developed for exchange-level evaluation, for example, SSA, discussed in Section 4.3.1. Exchange-level evaluation focuses mainly on metrics that evaluate the system's response in terms of whether it is *appropriate*, *relevant*, *coherent with the previous dialogue*, *specific* (adds new information), and *on topic*.

Finally, there are practical issues, such as whether evaluations should be conducted in research laboratories, where there is more control over the procedure but it may be less natural, or "in the wild", which is a more natural environment but over which there is less control. Another issue is the costs associated with the recruitment of users to interact with and evaluate the systems. The use of simulated users and crowdsourced evaluators has provided a way to overcome these issues.

A major focus of research has been to find automated metrics that correlate strongly with human judgements, given that evaluations by human users are costly and difficult to organize. Various automated metrics have been proposed, including: *perplexity*, *F1*, *hits@k*, *average utterance length*, *ratio of rare words*, *number of repetitions*, and *number of system questions*.

[13]Note that for task-oriented systems the service provider may also assess the system in terms such as return on investment as well as customer satisfaction.

Given these considerations, it is obvious that there is no single technique that is appropriate and instead a set of techniques should be used depending on various factors, as in the following.

- Is the system task-oriented? If so, use metrics that measure user satisfaction in terms of task success, task efficiency, as well as qualitative measures (as in PARADISE).
- Is the system non-task-oriented? If so, use metrics that measure the quality of the interaction, as in ACUTE-Eval, SSA, and the Interaction Quality framework.
- Should the evaluation procedures be relatively simple to apply? If so, use a combination of procedures such as ACUTE-Eval and SSA. Interestingly, large-scale evaluations of open-domain dialogue systems such as Meena, BlenderBot, and the systems in the Alexa Prize use relatively simple evaluation measures such as these.
- Is the evaluation research-based? If so, use frameworks such as PARADISE, Quality of Experience (QoE), or Interaction Quality (IQ).

For future research it would be useful to run different evaluation techniques on a range of different types of dialogue system and investigate whether they produce similar or different outcomes and how easy or difficult it is to apply them in practical terms. Comparisons could also be made with automated metrics in order to determine to what extent they correlate with and could ultimately replace (or supplement) human evaluations.

SUMMARY

Evaluation of dialogue systems is an important and complex task where there are many different issues to consider, such as how to conduct the evaluation and what sort of metrics are required for different types of dialogue system.

Dialogue system evaluation has often been conducted in laboratory sessions that have the advantage that the procedures can be carefully controlled and manipulated. An alternative method is to perform the evaluations "in the wild", where the situation is more realistic but there is less control over the process. Crowdsourcing is being used increasingly as a way of addressing the costs of recruiting users for evaluation. Another approach is to use expert users, particularly to make more detailed annotations of dialogues. Studies have shown that the ratings of such experts correlate strongly with those of real users.

Evaluation metrics differ according to whether the dialogue system is task-oriented or non-task-oriented. In task-oriented systems there are clearly defined objectives such as *task success* and *task efficiency*, while in non-task-oriented dialogue systems there is no clear objective and metrics are used that evaluate the quality of the conversation and, at a more fine-grained level, the relevance and other aspects of the system's responses.

Given that evaluation with users is expensive and that user ratings can often be inconsistent, there has been a drive to develop metrics that can be applied automatically and that correlate with subjective metrics.

There are many different approaches to evaluation, particularly in the area of open-domain dialogue systems that have recently become a hot topic of research. A number of frameworks have been developed to provide more consistency across evaluations.

As stated at the beginning of this chapter, evaluation is typically a black box function and so the techniques discussed in this chapter apply to all dialogue systems irrespective of the underlying technologies. Chapter 5 provides an overview of end-to-end neural dialogue systems that have come to dominate dialogue systems research. Some of the evaluation techniques discussed in this chapter have been used to evaluate these systems.

CHAPTER 5

End-to-End Neural Dialogue Systems

Current research in dialogue systems focuses almost entirely on end-to-end approaches in which an input utterance is mapped directly to an output response without requiring any processing by the modules of the traditional modularised architecture. This approach uses DNNs within a Seq2Seq architecture and is often referred to as neural dialogue.

This chapter is structured as follows. Section 5.1 introduces the neural dialogue approach and discusses its advantages. Section 5.2 presents one of the first examples of a neural dialogue system that has become a standard reference in the literature. Section 5.3 looks in more detail at the technology of neural dialogue, covering topics such as word embeddings, recurrent neural networks and their variants, the encoder-decoder architecture, and the attention mechanism. An alternative approach to response generation based on retrieval technologies is discussed in Section 5.4. Section 5.5 looks at the issues that arise when the neural architectures that have been used predominantly to model conversational (or chitchat) dialogue systems are applied to task-oriented systems. Section 5.6 presents recent examples of open-domain dialogue systems while Section 5.7 looks at the main issues that are the focus of current research. These include: the extent to which neural systems can model context, avoid bland and uninteresting responses, deal with semantic inconsistencies, and model affect and emotion. Neural dialogue systems require vast amounts of data for training. Section 5.8 presents brief descriptions of some commonly used datasets as well as tasks and challenges that test different approaches and issues in dialogue systems research. Section 5.9 lists some key papers and other resources for readers who wish to pursue neural dialogue in greater depth.

5.1 NEURAL NETWORK APPROACHES TO DIALOGUE MODELING

Since around 2014 a new approach to dialogue systems development has emerged using DNNs. This approach, known as *neural dialogue*, has come to dominate the field, with a vast number of papers being presented at conferences and made available as electronic preprints in the **arXiv** repository that provides open access to developing research in several scientific areas.

The neural approach to dialogue systems development is based on an end-to-end architecture in which the various components of the traditional dialogue systems architecture, as shown

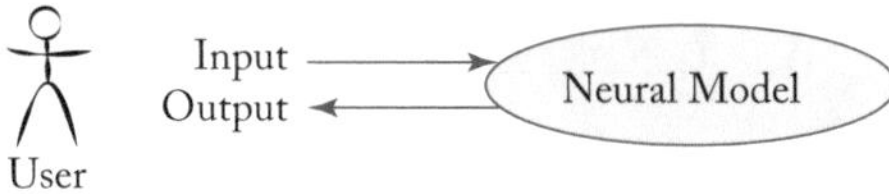

Figure 5.1: The end-to-end neural architecture.

in Figures 2.1 and 3.1, are not required. Instead, there is a direct mapping (or transduction) from the input to the output. This mapping is often referred to as Sequence to Sequence mapping, abbreviated as Seq2Seq. Seq2Seq has been applied successfully in MT to achieve a mapping between a sentence in a source language to a sentence in a target language without the need for intermediate processing and representations [Bahdanau et al., 2014], [Cho et al., 2014a], [Cho et al., 2014b]. Automated response suggestion for email (smart reply) is another application where the technique has been successfully applied [Kannan et al., 2016]. Figure 5.1 illustrates the neural end-to-end architecture. Applying this architecture to dialogue systems involves learning mappings between input and output utterances. At present, this approach has been applied mainly to text-based dialogues. In a spoken dialogue application the speech components operate separately from the end-to-end architecture, so that the results of speech recognition are fed in text form into the architecture and the output response is passed to a TTS component to produce a spoken utterance. Given such an end-to-end architecture, there are two main tasks to accomplish.

1. Process and represent the input: this is known as *encoding*.

2. Generate the output: this is known as *decoding*.

An end-to-end architecture provides certain advantages over the traditional pipelined architecture. With a pipelined architecture it is difficult to determine which module is responsible for the failure of an interaction. This is known as the *credit assignment problem* [Zhao and Eskenazi, 2016]. For example, if the user provides feedback that the system did not respond very well to their inputs, was the problem due to speech recognition errors, poor natural language understanding, an inability to choose the best system action by the dialogue management component, or a failure of the natural language generation component to adequately phrase the system's output messages?

If the source of the problem can be reliably identified, the natural solution would be to improve the module responsible, either through handcrafted modifications or by optimizing using machine-learning techniques. However, optimizing one module can lead to knock-on effects on other modules and so it could be more productive to optimize the complete system. For example, as demonstrated in a series of experiments by Lemon [2011], joint optimization of the dialogue management and natural language generation components produced better results than optimizing the modules separately. Similarly, there are problems when adapting a system

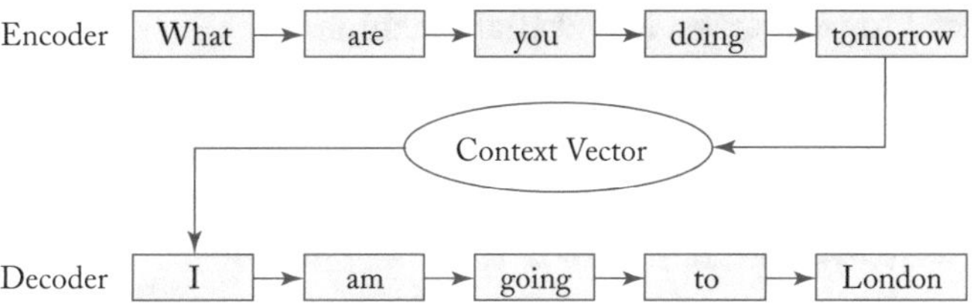

Figure 5.2: Using an encoder-decoder network in the Seq2Seq framework for modeling conversations.

to new domains as in the pipelined architecture all of the modules would have to be trained and fine-tuned independently.

Finally, in order to make modular systems tractable when using RL, extensive handcrafting and design of the state and action space is required. An end-to-end system does not require this handcrafting effort.

5.2 A NEURAL CONVERSATIONAL MODEL

This section provides an introduction to the neural approach to dialogue based on the seminal paper of Vinyals and Le [2015]. The basic idea is that a conversation can be modeled by predicting the next output in the dialogue given some previous input (or inputs) and that the model can be trained using the Seq2Seq approach introduced by Sutskever et al. [2014]. Using this approach avoids the need for handcrafted rules and complex interactions between the components of the traditional dialogue systems architecture. As shown in Figure 5.2, the input utterance consisting of the sequence *What are you doing tomorrow* is processed, typically by an Recurrent Neural Network (RNN) that reads the input one token at a time until it reaches the end of the sequence. The hidden state of the model at this point is known as the *context vector* (or *thought vector*) and it contains all the information about the input up to this point. The RNN is trained to map this input to an output such as *I am going to London* that is generated one token at a time (see further Section 5.3.2). The model in the Vinyals and Le [2015] paper was tested on two datasets: chat sessions in a dataset of conversations with an IT help desk, and conversations in a dataset of movie subtitles. Example 5.1 shows two conversations generated by the model.

Example 5.1
Conversation 3. Password issues (from the IT help desk dataset)

MACHINE: Hi , this is <NAME> from help desk connect, what can i help you with today?
HUMAN: Hi, I forgot my password.
MACHINE: OK great.
HUMAN: Can you tell me how i can recover it?

MACHINE: I'll need to verify who it is at that machine.
MACHINE: Can we do a hangout?
HUMAN: Yes.
MACHINE: <anonymized hangout instructions and verifications>
HUMAN: Cool, I am good now.

Conversation 1. Basic (from the movie subtitles dataset)

HUMAN: Hello!
MACHINE: Hello!
HUMAN: How are you?
MACHINE: I'm good.
HUMAN: What's your name?
MACHINE: I'm Julia.
HUMAN: When were you born?
MACHINE: July 20th.
HUMAN: What year were you born?
MACHINE: 1977.
HUMAN: Where are you from?
MACHINE: I'm out in the boonies.
HUMAN: Are you a man or a woman?
MACHINE: I'm a woman.
HUMAN: Why are we here?
MACHINE: i'm not sure.
HUMAN: Okay, bye!
MACHINE: Bye.
HUMAN: See you later.
MACHINE: Bye.

In experiments it was found that conversations generated by the neural model obtained better perplexity than an alternative N-gram model and were judged qualitatively to produce reasonably natural conversations. As discussed in Chapter 4 (Section 4.3.1), perplexity measures the uncertainty of a language model in terms of the number of choices available when selecting the next token in a sequence. In this case the neural model generated fewer choices, which results in greater confidence in its output compared with the output of the N-gram model. It was also found that the model could generalize to new questions that were not in the training set as opposed to systems that simply look up an answer that matches the question in a database.

However, there were some limitations. Often the model produced short, uninteresting responses and the responses were sometimes inconsistent, as in Example 5.2:

Example 5.2
Conversation 7. Job and Personality

HUMAN: what is your job?
MACHINE: I'm a lawyer.
HUMAN: What do you do?
MACHINE: I'm a doctor.

Short, uninteresting responses are a consequence of the fact that the traditional objective function used to train response generation computes the maximum likelihood of a response given the input message. As these responses are more frequent in the training data they are favored over more diverse responses. Inconsistent responses arise when the system does not keep track of information conveyed during the course of the dialogue. Some work addressing response diversity and response inconsistency is discussed in Section 5.7.

5.3 INTRODUCTION TO THE TECHNOLOGY OF NEURAL DIALOGUE

This section provides an introductory overview of the technology of the neural dialogue approach. References to more technical discussions and tutorials can be found in Section 5.9.

As mentioned previously and illustrated in Figure 5.2, the process of sequence-to-sequence mapping is based on the encoder-decoder architecture. The following subsections outline the technologies required for the encoder-decoder architecture.

5.3.1 WORD EMBEDDINGS

The input to the encoder is the sequence of words spoken or typed by the user. However, in order for the encoder to be able to process these words, they have to be converted into numbers. As a result of this process, which is known as *word embedding*, each word is represented by a unique real-number vector that captures its meaning and its relationship to the other words in the vocabulary.

One-hot encoding is widely used in machine learning to encode categorical data such as the names of different countries. Table 5.1 shows a simple example of a matrix for an 11-word vocabulary consisting of the country names listed in the first column of the matrix. Each row in the matrix is a word vector the length of which is equal to the length of the vocabulary. In order to distinguish the words, each vector has "0"s in all cells with the exception of a single "1" in the cell that represents its position in the vocabulary and uniquely identifies the word.

One hot encoding works well for data with a small number of values. However, the size of the matrix, in terms of the dimensionality of each word vector, increases linearly with the size of the vocabulary of the corpus, i.e., the total number of distinct words. A realistic vocabulary for a dialogue system might assume a vocabulary of 30,000 words so that the vector for

Table 5.1: One-hot encoding of country names

	1	2	3	4	5	6	7	8	9	10	11
China	1	0	0	0	0	0	0	0	0	0	0
Russia	0	1	0	0	0	0	0	0	0	0	0
Japan	0	0	1	0	0	0	0	0	0	0	0
Turkey	0		0	1	0	0	0	0	0	0	0
Poland	0	0	0	0	1	0	0	0	0	0	0
Germany	0		0	0	0	1	0	0	0	0	0
France	0	0	0	0	0	0	1	0	0	0	0
Italy	0	0	0	0	0	0	0	1	0	0	0
Greece	0	0	0	0	0	0	0	0	1	0	0
Spain	0	0	0	0	0	0	0	0	0	1	0
Portugal	0	0	0	0	0	0	0	0	0	0	1

each word would have a single "1" and 29,999 zeros, making the embedding matrix very sparse as it would be made up mainly of zeros. Thus, much of the work on word vectors involves a compromise between aiming to store as much useful information as possible while keeping the dimensionality at a manageable scale and reducing the computational complexity of learning high-dimensional word vectors [Mikolov et al., 2013a]. One-hot encoding also has the disadvantage that it is unable to represent relationships between words and the contexts in which they appear—information that could be useful for performing operations such as computing semantic similarity and other relationships between the words in a vocabulary.

To address these issues researchers built on the idea of representing words in a *semantic space* in which the location of a word in the semantic space is a representation of its meaning. Thus, words that are similar semantically will be closer within the space. Each word is mapped to a vector and the values for the dimensions of the vector are learned from large corpora of texts. *Word2vec*, a toolkit that was developed by researchers at Google, has been widely used to learn word embeddings using models such as the CBOW (Continuous Bag-of-Words) Model or the Continuous Skip-Gram Model [Mikolov et al., 2013a]. In the CBOW model the embedding is learned by predicting the current word based on its context, while in the Continuous Skip-Gram Model the surrounding words are predicted given the current word. Other tools for training and using word embeddings include Stanford's GloVe [Pennington et al., 2014], Elmo from the Allen Institute for AI [Peters et al., 2018], Google's BERT (Bidirectional Encoder Representations from Transformers) [Devlin et al., 2018], Facebook's FastText project [Bojanowski et al., 2017], and OpenAI's GPT-2 [Radford et al., 2019]. Figure 5.3 shows a two-dimensional PCA (Principal Component Analysis) projection of the 1000-dimensional Skip-gram vectors of the

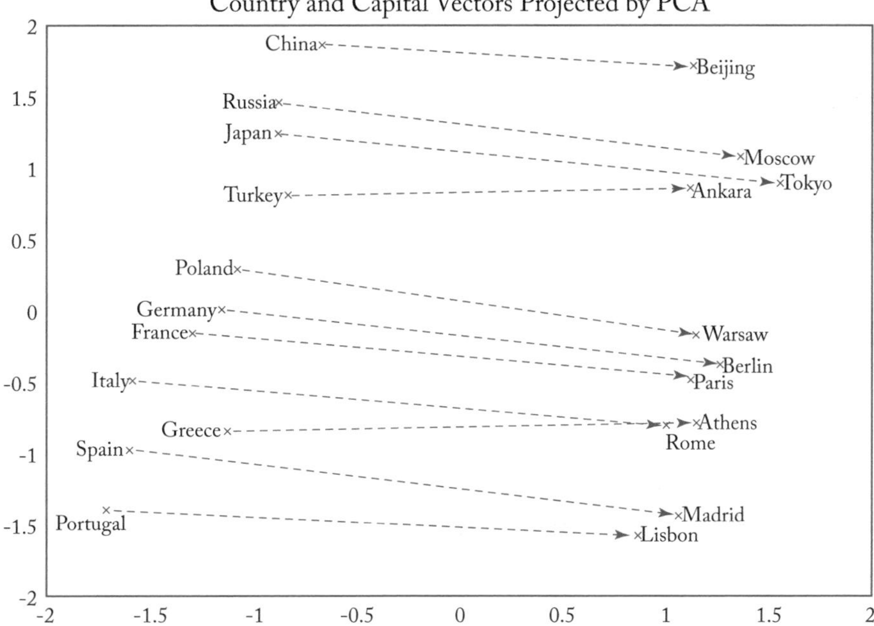

Figure 5.3: Country and capital vectors. Based on Mikolov et al. [2013b].

countries listed in Table 5.1 together with their capital cities. The figure shows how similar concepts, in this case, countries and capital cities, are grouped together within the semantic space and how relationships between them were learned implicitly, as the training did not provide any supervised information about what a capital city means [Mikolov et al., 2013b].

Word embeddings can be used to discover syntactic and semantic relationships that are inherent in the learned representations [Mikolov et al., 2013c]. These relationships can be tested using analogical reasoning tests of the form:

a is to b as c is to ?

where the test involves finding a value for "?". For example, to test the syntactic relationship between the base and comparative forms of adjectives, an input such as

good is to better as rough is to ?

which returned the answer *rougher*. Other syntactic relationships that were tested included: singular/plural forms of common nouns; possessive/non-possessive forms of common nouns; and base, past and 3rd person present tense forms of verbs [Mikolov et al., 2013c].

Similar analogical reasoning tasks were used to discover semantic relationships, for example, between the countries and capitals shown in Figure 5.3. Here the input took the form of

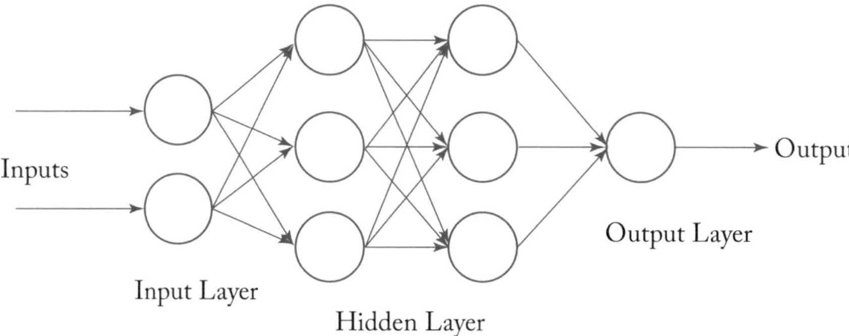

Figure 5.4: A feed-forward neural network.

analogies such as *Germany is to Berlin as France is to ?*, where the desired value for "?" is *Paris*. These results were achieved using simple mathematical operations such as addition or subtraction on the word vector representations. For example, for the countries and capitals task:

? = vec("Berlin") - vec("Germany") + vec("France")

Paris is found by searching in the vector space for the word vector closest to "?" using cosine similarity [Mikolov et al., 2013b].

Given that the input to the encoder in a dialogue system will usually consist of a sequence of words, it is important to be able to capture important information in this sequence such as the order of the words in the sequence and semantic relationships between them. To address these issues Le and Mikolov [2014] proposed Paragraph Vector as a framework for learning continuous distributed representations for variable-length texts such as sentences, paragraphs, and documents.

For a tutorial on word embeddings, see Word Embeddings,[1] also these introductory overviews: Get Busy with Word Embeddings—An Introduction[2] and The Amazing Power of Word Vectors.[3]

5.3.2 RECURRENT NEURAL NETWORKS (RNNS)

There are many different neural network architectures. Recurrent Neural Network (RNN)s have been used widely in speech and language applications as they can handle sequential inputs of variable length in contrast to a traditional feed-forward network. A standard feed-forward neural net, as shown in Figure 5.4 has an input layer, two hidden layers, and an output layer. The network operates as follows: each input is multiplied by a weight, then all the inputs to each node, including a bias, are summed and the total net input for each node is fed into an activation

[1] https://www.tensorflow.org/tutorials/text/word_embeddings
[2] https://www.shanelynn.ie/get-busy-with-word-embeddings-introduction/
[3] https://blog.acolyer.org/2016/04/21/the-amazing-power-of-word-vectors/

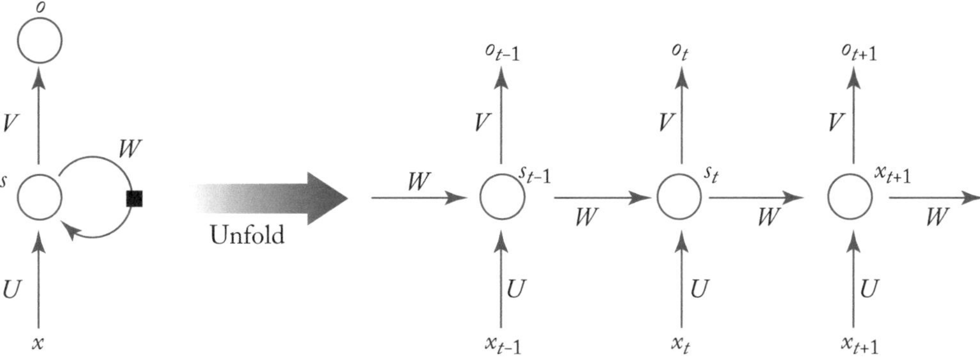

Figure 5.5: An Recurrent Neural Network (RNN) and the unfolding in time of the computation involved in its forward computation. Based on LeCun et al. [2015].

function that transforms the net input into a new output that is passed into the next layer (in this case, one of the hidden unit nodes in the first hidden layer). The cycle continues until the final output nodes are reached.

In a traditional feed-forward neural network such as this the information moves in one direction only and nodes are not visited a second time. Furthermore, the input has to be a fixed size vector that is processed all at the same time. The output is also a fixed-size vector. However, speech and natural language texts come as sequences of variable lengths and the output is often also a variable length sequence.

Recurrent Neural Network (RNN)s operate over sequences of vectors and so they have several advantages for the processing of sequences of text. First, because the information cycles through a loop, RNNs are able to capture information about the previous inputs so that they maintain a sort of memory that is useful for subsequent processing. A second advantage is that by processing inputs as a sequence, they are able to capture information about the ordering of the input that may be relevant to the processing of the input sequence as a whole. Figure 5.5 is an example of an RNN. Looking at the left-most side of the figure, we can see that similar to the traditional feed-forward neural network the input vector x passes into a hidden state s having been multiplied by a weight matrix U and then passing through an activation function. The result in the hidden layer is multiplied by a weight matrix V and also by a weight matrix W and passed to the output o. U, V, and W are adjusted during training. However, there is a key difference as the input, consisting of a sequence of items, is presented one item at a time. This is made possible by the loop, which causes the hidden units at time t to get inputs from previous time steps.

This process can be seen more clearly in the unfolded section to the right of Figure 5.5. Focusing on the middle net that shows input x_t at time step t and ignoring the multiplications of the weight matrices: x_t is the hidden state receiving the input and its value is calculated based on the previous hidden state s_{t-1} and the input x_t at the current time step. The process continues with the input x_{t+1} and so on until all of the input has been consumed. In this way the hidden state s_t serves as the "memory" of the network, capturing information about what has happened up to current position in the input. Note that although in the figure there are outputs at each time step, these may not be required as often only the output at the final time step may be relevant.

The process as described so far involves feeding the items in the input sequence one at a time into the Recurrent Neural Network (RNN), providing a context based on the previous history of the items in the sequence. However, sometimes the entire input is available at the start of the process and then it is possible to consider also the context to the right of the current input. This process requires a bidirectional RNN, which consists of two RNNs, one which processes the input from start to end, and the other from end to start, with the results being combined into a single representation [Schuster and Paliwal, 1997].

Although RNNs are able to retain a memory of previous inputs, it has been found that this memory does not go sufficiently far into the past as the information encoded in the hidden states tends to be fairly local. Jurafsky and Martin [2020] provide the following example involving the prediction of the next word in a language modeling task:

The flights the airline was cancelling were full

In this example there is subject-verb agreement between *airline* and *was*, and between *flights* and *were*. However, it is difficult to assign the correct probability to *were* as *flights* is quite distant from *were* and the intervening context involves singular constituents. To handle this issue the network has to be able to retain the more distant information about the plural word *flights* until it is needed when *were* is reached as well as dealing correctly with the parts to the immediate left of *were*.

More generally, the performance of RNNs is affected by the vanishing gradient problem. In order to learn, a neural network has to work backward from the error encountered at the output and adjust the weights in the hidden layers to minimize the error. This is called *back propagation*. However, as the number of layers increases, the calculations of the gradient, which involve multiplication, result in gradients that become too small to allow the adjustments of the weights that enable the network to learn. To address this issue Long Short-term Memory (LSTM) units were proposed by Hochreiter and Schmidhuber [1997]. LSTMs allow the error to be back-propagated through more than 1000 time steps, thus supporting learning over a much larger distance than is possible with traditional RNNs.

5.3.3 LONG SHORT-TERM MEMORY UNITS

Long Short-term Memory (LSTM) units use two methods to tackle the issue of context in RNNs: they provide a mechanism for the network to forget information that is no longer needed and a second mechanism to add information that is likely to be needed later. This is done by

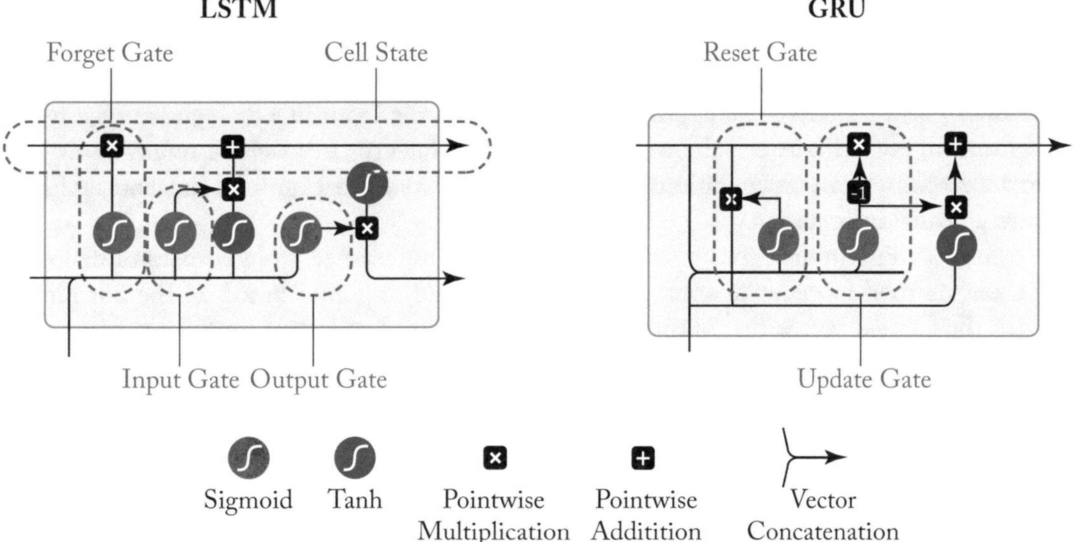

Figure 5.6: LSTM and GRU architectures. Based on Phi [2018].

adding an additional context layer to the network called the cell state that contains gates that control the flow of information into and out of the cell state. An LSTM has three gates. The first gate controls what information can be removed (or forgotten), the second what information is to be stored, and the third what information to output.

In more recent work, Cho et al. [2014b] proposed the Gated Recurrent Unit (GRU) in which the forget gate and the input gate are combined into a single *update gate*, and the cell state and hidden state are merged. This results in a simpler model compared to standard LSTM models. A large number of other variants have been tested, showing that some architectures perform better than standard LSTMs on particular tasks [Jozefowicz et al., 2015]. Figure 5.6 compares the LSTM and GRU architectures.

5.3.4 THE ENCODER-DECODER NETWORK

The encoder-decoder network performs a transduction from an input sequence to an output sequence. As shown in Figure 5.2, the encoder creates a vector, known as a context (or thought) vector that represents the input sequence, and then the decoder takes this vector and uses it to create an output.

Encoding involves the use of neural networks, usually RNNS, LSTMs, and GRUs, as described earlier, and more recently Transformer networks (to be described below). Usually, stacked networks are used and the output representation is taken from the top layer of the stack.

Decoding takes one element at a time to produce an output sequence, using the context vector that represents the final hidden state of the encoder. While the encoder-decoder network has been applied successfully to machine translation, it is more difficult in dialogue applications as there can be a wide range of appropriate responses to the input in a dialogue as opposed to the phrase alignment between the source and target sequences in machine translation. Also, dialogue responses can be conditional on information from a background database, API, or other contextual information.

For decoding in dialogue systems representations are learned from corpora of dialogues and these are used to generate appropriate contextualised responses based on the last hidden state of the context vector that is mapped to a probability distribution over the next possible tokens. The technique used to produce an output sequence is called *autoregressive generation*. With autoregressive generation the word that is generated at each time step is conditioned on the word generated by the network at the previous time step as well as the hidden state providing the context from the previous time step. Alternatively, the context vector can be added into the computation of the current hidden state so that it is available at each step in the decoding process and can influence the generation of the complete output.

While the basic Seq2Seq model described here performs well for the generation of responses in simple two-turn dialogues, the model is less able to capture a longer conversation flow. To address this issue the Hierarchical Recurrent Encoder-Decoder Neural Network (HRED) model of dialogue was proposed in which utterances containing tokens are modeled jointly with an interactive structure comprised of utterances [Sordoni et al., 2015], [Serban et al., 2016]. In this way the temporal long-term aspects of a multi-turn dialogue can be modeled, such as topics and concepts shared between the speakers. Figure 5.7 illustrates the HRED architecture over the course of three turns, using a higher-level context Recurrent Neural Network (RNN) to keep track of past utterances. Serban et al. [2017b] applied the model in two domains: a goal-oriented domain (Ubuntu technical support) and a non-goal-oriented domain (Twitter conversations), finding that the HRED model outperformed competing approaches in human evaluations as well as when using automatic evaluation metrics.

One problem with encoder-decoder networks is that performance decreases as the input sequence becomes longer [Cho et al., 2014a]. To address this problem Bahdanau et al. [2014] introduced the *attention mechanism* in which only those parts of the representation of the input are used that are considered particularly relevant when predicting the next word in the output. In other words, the whole of the input sequence is not encoded into a single fixed-length vector: instead it is encoded into a set of vectors and the decoder selects a subset of these during the decoding. A separate context vector for each target word is computed as a weighted sum of annotations generated by the encoder and the weights of the annotations are computed using an alignment model that scores how well the inputs and the output match. The model was tested on an English to French translation task and was found to significantly outperform the conventional encoder-decoder model.

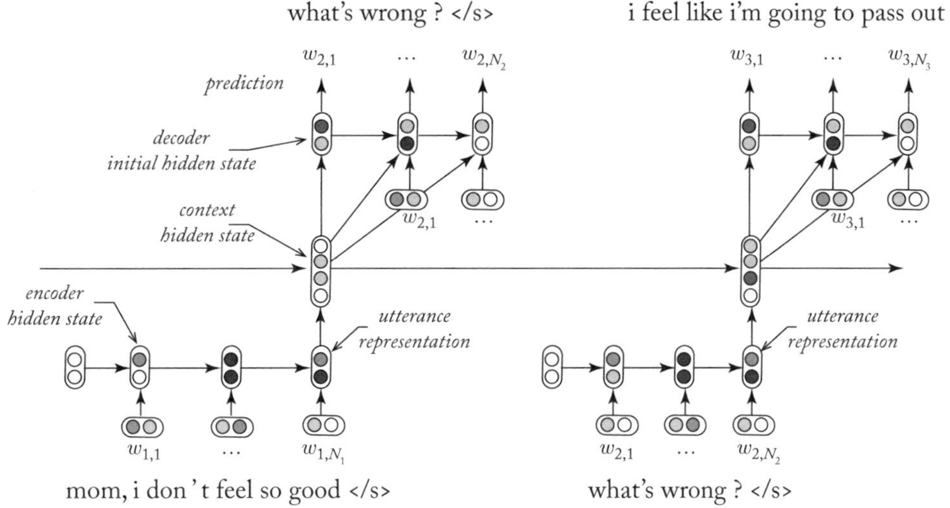

Figure 5.7: HRED architecture for dialogue. Based on Serban et al. [2016].

There are many variations on the attention mechanism. One approach that has been widely adopted is the Transformer architecture, introduced by Vaswani et al. [2017]. The Transformer does not require recurrence and is based solely on attention mechanisms to draw global dependencies between the input and output. Vlasov et al. [2019] applied a Transformer Embedding Dialogue (TED) policy to dialogues involving sequences of turns containing sub-dialogues and other interleaved segments. Whereas a traditional encoder treats every item in a sequence as equally relevant, the Transformer selects which parts to include in the encoding as a basis for the current prediction. TED simplifies the encoder-decoder architecture compared with Recurrent Neural Network (RNN)-based approaches and outperformed a baseline LSTM approach in experiments on a task-oriented dataset involving the ability to recover from non-cooperative user behavior.

5.4 RETRIEVAL-BASED RESPONSE GENERATION

The generation-based methods discussed in the previous section are used widely for producing responses in neural dialogue systems. An alternative method is to retrieve a pre-defined response from a data source such as a dialogue corpus by matching against the input. One problem is that the input-response matching algorithm has to deal with possible semantic gaps between the input and the response. Matching the input and the response in single-turn dialogues involves encoding the input and candidate responses as vectors and computing matching scores using a ranking algorithm [Hu et al., 2014]. Multi-turn matching involves encoding the current input as well as previous utterances into a context vector, as described above, encoding each candidate response into response vectors, and computing a matching score that selects the response that is most relevant to the whole context [Lowe et al., 2015b]. Shalyminov et al. [2018] show how to rank different retrieved outputs to optimize for user ratings. It is also possible to combine generative and retrieval-based models in an ensemble model [Song et al., 2016], [Shalyminov et al., 2020b].

Both methods of response generation have their advantages and disadvantages. Generative models are able to generate new responses while retrieval-based models are limited to an already existing dataset of responses that may not cover all of the dialogue topics. However, generative models may generate responses that are ungrammatical, whereas the predefined answers in a retrieval-based response will normally be grammatically correct. Furthermore, the answers in a generative-based system are liable to some of the issues to be discussed below, such as being too general and bland, while those in a retrieval-based model are likely to be more interesting and can also be customized to the designer's requirements.

5.5 TASK-ORIENTED NEURAL DIALOGUE SYSTEMS

Initially, end-to-end dialogue learning was applied to open-domain conversational (or chit-chat) systems with promising results. More recently, it has also been applied to task-oriented dialogue systems. However, task-oriented systems present additional challenges. Assuming that the system is able to correctly identify the task that the user wants the system to help solve, it is not just a matter of finding an appropriate response. The system may have to generate a series of questions to elaborate on or clarify the user's request (as in slot-filling dialogues), issue one or more queries to an external source such as a database to obtain the required information, present the options retrieved back to the user, and then complete the transaction [Bordes and Weston, 2016].

Moreover, whereas developers of dialogue systems are able to draw on a range of existing corpora of open-domain conversations to train their systems, there are fewer datasets for task-oriented applications and often they are proprietary and not publicly available. Even where corpora of task-oriented dialogues are available, it is necessary to distinguish between generic features that can be learned and those features that are only applicable in a particular domain.

There have been a number of attempts to address neural task-oriented dialogue systems. Bordes and Weston [2016] break down the interaction in a restaurant reservation system into sub-tasks such as issuing API calls, updating API calls, displaying options, and providing extra information. The system used Memory Networks [Weston et al., 2015], which are similar to attention-based networks, to store the dialogue history and the short-term context. On the basis of this information the system could be trained for the various tasks, for example, to ask the right questions when making API calls.

Li et al. [2018a] investigated the interaction of an end-to-end neural dialogue system for movie-ticket booking with a structured database. This system conducts a dialogue with the user to obtain information about their requirements and then books the tickets. In a series of experiments it was found that the system outperformed a baseline rule-based system and provided more natural interaction in real-world task-completion scenarios.

Liu and Lane [2017] addressed similar issues in an end-to-end trainable neural model for restaurant enquiries that focused in particular on belief tracking and knowledge base result processing conditioned on the dialogue history. They found that their system outperformed other end-to-end models and showed robust performance in tracking the dialogue state over a sequence of dialogue turns and in the generation of appropriate system responses.

Building on previous work on belief tracking, Wen et al. [2017] describe a network-based end-to-end trainable task-oriented dialogue system consisting of networks for encoding intent, belief tracking, policy decisions, database operations, and generation. The database operator has an explicit representation of database attributes as slot-value pairs. The input is converted into two internal representations, a distributed representation generated by an intent network, and the belief state, which is a probability representation over slot-value pairs. The slot-value pairs are used to trigger a query to the database, and then the policy network uses the search result combined with the intent representation and the belief state to form a single vector that determines the next system action. This vector is used by the response generation network to produce a skeleton response that is subsequently completed by inserting the actual values retrieved from the database into the skeleton response. A further contribution of this work was to address the issue of a lack of training data for task-oriented systems using a crowdsourced version of the Wizard of Oz method to generate dialogues for training.

Finally, Williams and Zweig [2016] present a model that combines a trainable RNN with domain-specific software that encodes business rules and logic and provides access to APIs for tasks such as ordering a taxi or making a table reservation at a restaurant. The RNN maps directly from the user's input to actions such as calls to the database and infers its own representation of the dialogue state, so that minimal handcrafting of the dialogue state is required. The system was trained using a combination of supervised learning from a corpus of dialogues and reinforcement learning using feedback on the overall success of the dialogue.

The application of the end-to-end approach to task-oriented systems is still in its infancy and there are still many issues to be addressed. For example, Wen et al. [2017] point out that their system is text-based and so does not address the problems faced by speech-based systems in handling recognition errors and dealing with subsequent uncertainty in the belief state. The system was also unable to perform dialogue acts such as confirmation requests that are required in task-oriented systems to clarify uncertainties in the system's belief state.

5.6 OPEN-DOMAIN NEURAL DIALOGUE SYSTEMS

Open-domain dialogue systems have become a hot topic in Conversational AI. A recent development is to train these systems from very large datasets of conversations using neural dialogue technologies. This section reviews technologies used in the Alexa Prize 2020, Google's Meena, Facebook's BlenderBot, and GPT-3. Although GPT-3 is a very large language modeling system and not a platform for developing dialogue systems, it has potential use in Conversational AI and some simple dialogue systems have already been generated using the GPT-3 models (see Section 5.6.4).

5.6.1 ALEXA PRIZE 2020

Examples of interactions with socialbots from the first and second Alexa Prize Grand Challenges were presented in Chapter 1, Section 1.4.3 and Chapter 2, Section 2.4. In the third grand challenge that concluded in 2020 the winner was *Emora* from Emory University, the runner-up was *Chirpy Cardinal* from Stanford University, and the third place team was *Alquist* from the Czech Technical University.

Over the course of the competition over 240,000 hours of conversations were held with the Alexa socialbots, comprising millions of interactions. Some of the main technical advances included: advanced NLU systems enhanced by large-scale Transformer models to support open-domain natural language understanding; improved dialogue policies to enable smoother and more engaging conversations; using representations of common sense knowledge and common sense reasoning to improve response quality; the development of approaches to manage multiple skills and topics; the use of user profiles and sentiment classifiers to build more personalized and more empathetic socialbots [Gabriel et al., 2020].

For response generation handcrafted and neural methods were used. Several teams used scripted dialogues for some topics as well as template-based and retrieval-based methods. External sources such as Wikipedia and Reddit were used extensively to provide high quality responses.

In order to support neural response generation (NRG), Amazon provided a GPT-based neural response generation service that was migrated to GPT-2 [Radford et al., 2019]. Some teams used this service and others developed their own NRG models. See Section 5.6.4 for an overview of the GPT models. Some teams addressed the issue of common sense response generation in order to be able to generate more sensible and more natural responses when discussing general topics such as hobbies and daily activities—for example, what a person feels during or after an activity.

In the area of dialogue management, attention was directed to issues such as: the development of a general dialogue policy to enable the selection of the optimal responses in a given dialogue context; the choice of the next topic; and smooth transitioning to topics that users might find engaging. Dialogue management techniques included the use of state machines, dialogue flows, and treelets. In many cases a global dialogue manager decided the overall flow and each topic or skill had its own dialogue manager, which in many cases was rule-based, and in other cases formulated as an MDP with decisions optimized using RL.

The Alexa Team provided CoBot, a conversational bot toolkit for natural language understanding and dialogue management [Khatri et al., 2018a]. In particular, a new model based on hierarchical recurrent neural networks (HRNNs) was made available for dialogue act and topic classification tasks along with a Topical Chat dataset consisting of more than 10,000 human-human dialogues. In experiments with alternative networks the HRNN models outperformed the alternative models. GPT and GPT-2 were fine-tuned on Topical Chat to enhance neural response generation. For further detail on the advances made in the 2020 Alexa Prize see the overview paper from the Alexa team [Gabriel et al., 2020] and the Alexa Prize 2020 Proceedings, which contain detailed research reports from each of the teams.[4] There is also a video showing interactions with some of the socialbots along with comments from university and Alexa Prize team members.[5]

5.6.2 GOOGLE'S MEENA

Meena is an open-domain chatbot developed by the Google Research Brain Team [Adiwardana et al., 2020]. Some examples of dialogues with Meena were presented in Chapter 1, Section 1.4.3, while Chapter 4, Section 4.3.1 introduced the SSA metric that was used to evaluate Meena against some other open-domain chatbots.

Meena is a neural dialogue system comprising 2.6 billion parameters (the values that a neural network tries to optimize during training). Meena was trained end-to-end on the Evolved Transformer (ET) Seq2Seq architecture [So et al., 2019]. ET is an encoder-decoder architecture consisting of one ET encoder block and 13 ET decoder blocks. ET processes pairs of utterances consisting of an input and a response (see Section 5.3.4). The input to ET is a context representing up to seven previous utterances. The encoder processes the context to understand what has been said so far in the conversation and the decoder outputs a response to the context. Meena was trained for 30 days on a TPU-v3 Pod (2048 TPU cores) using the Meena dataset that comprised more than 300GB of public domain social media conversations (40 billion words). The training objective involved minimizing perplexity, i.e., the uncertainty of predicting the next word in a conversation.

The SSA metric was used to compare Meena with humans and other open-domain chatbots—Cleverbot,[6] DialoGPT, [Zhang et al., 2019] Mitsuku,[7] and XiaoIce [Zhou et al., 2020]. There were 2 different types of evaluation: static, in which the systems were benchmarked against a dataset of 1,477 multi-turn conversations, and interactive, in which the human evaluators could chat about anything they wanted. Table 5.2 shows the SSA results from the interactive evaluations. (Meena1 is the end-to-end learned model and Meena2 is an enhanced model with a filtering mechanism and tuned decoding).

[4]https://m.media-amazon.com/images/G/01/mobile-apps/dex/alexa/alexaprize/assets/challenge3/proceedings/Alexa-socialbot-challenge3-Proceedings.zip

[5]https://youtu.be/Rh3D756garE

[6]https://www.cleverbot.com/

[7]http://www.square-bear.co.uk/mitsuku/home.htm

Table 5.2: SSA scores for Meena, humans, and other chatbots

Conversation With:	SSA Score
Humans	86%
Meena1	72%
Meena2	79%
XiaoIce	31%
Mitsuku	56%
DialoGPT	48%
Cleverbot	56%

5.6.3 FACEBOOK'S BLENDERBOT

BlenderBot is a large open-domain chatbot model developed by the Facebook AI Research (FAIR) group [Roller et al., 2020]. Three models were developed comprising 90 million, 2.7 billion and 9.4 billion parameters, respectively, using Transformers as a base and pre-training on 1.5 billion training examples from Reddit discussions covering a wide range of topics. By comparison Meena has 2.6 billion parameters and was trained on 341GB of texts from social media conversations.

However, while the authors acknowledge that increasing the number of parameters and the size of the training data leads to better models, their key contribution is that two additional ingredients are required to create a high-performing dialogue system:

1. conversational skills such as conveying personality, displaying knowledge, and showing empathy that expert conversationalists blend together seamlessly when they engage in conversation, and

2. new methods for improving decoding in response generation to produce better system responses.

BlenderBot has been made available in open source for developers to experiment and develop their own dialogue systems.[8] Example 5.3 shows a conversation between one of the authors and the 9.4 billion parameter model (BB) based on Roller et al. [2020, Figure 1].

Example 5.3

HUMAN: If you could have dinner with one person, dead or alive, who would that be?
BB: That's a tough one. I think I'd have to go with Steve Jobs. I'd love to pick his brain.

[8]https://parl.ai/projects/recipes/

HUMAN: Ah, interesting choice. What do you know about Steve Jobs?
BB: He was one of the most influential people in the history of technology. He was a visionary.
HUMAN: What questions would you ask him?
BB: I'd want to know how he came up with the idea for the iPod. It was so revolutionary at the time.
HUMAN: Totally, the iPod changed the way everyone listens to music.
BB: It really did. It's crazy to think that it was released in 2001. That was a long time ago.
HUMAN: Omg wow, that makes me feel old!
BB: I know, right? Time flies by so fast. I wish I could go back to those simpler times.
HUMAN: Me too, friend, me too. Speaking of music, what's your favorite album to listen to lately?
BB: I've been listening to a lot of Led Zeppelin lately. They're my favorite band.

Blending involves fine-tuning the models since the Reddit discussions that were used for pre-training were not conversational data. Several datasets provided the blending that was used to improve the performance of BlenderBot and its ratings by human evaluators:

- The ConvAI2 dataset that focuses on personality [Zhang et al., 2018](see Section 5.8.2).
- The Empathetic Dialogues dataset that focuses on empathy [Rashkin et al., 2018].
- The Wizard of Wikipedia dataset that focuses on knowledge [Dinan et al., 2019b].
- The Blended Skill Talk dataset that supports blending of the skills [Smith et al., 2020].

Response generation was improved through the use of a new method of generation that combined retrieval-based responses (see Section 5.4) and generative approaches (see Section 5.3.4). This new approach, known as Retrieve-and-Refine, addresses the problem faced by generative models that they often produce dull and repetitive responses. Retrieve-and-Refine operates by combining a retrieval step before the generation step. Instead of outputting the retrieved response directly to the user, it is added to the input sequence of the generator and the generator outputs its response given the modified input sequence. In this way the response is enhanced with the more interesting and more human-like responses that are output in the retrieval-based approach.

The choice of decoder was also found to be important in response generation. The length of the system's utterances is an important factor in human judgements of quality. If the utterances are too short, they are seen as dull and uninteresting, and if they are too long the chatbot can be seen as rambling. Two different methods were used to control the length of the system's responses: setting a minimum response length and predicting the optimal length based on human-human conversation data. Using beam search with a careful choice of search hyperparameters helped to control the trade-off between responses that were too short and those that were too long.

BlenderBot was evaluated against Google's Meena using the ACUTE-Eval method discussed in Chapter 4, Section 4.3.2 that involves pairwise evaluations of complete dialogues. Due to the costs and time required to collect human-chatbot conversations, the Self-Chat method was used in which ACUTE-Eval works in "self-chat" mode, producing both sides of the conversation. Human evaluators were shown a series of dialogues between humans and the two chatbots and asked the following questions.

- Who would you prefer to talk to in a long conversation? (showing engagingness).
- Which speaker sounds more human? (showing humanness).

67% of the evaluators found BlenderBot more human-like and 75% said that they would prefer to have a long conversation with BlenderBot. Both results were statistically significant, in a two-tailed binomial test, $p < 0{:}01$.

Despite these impressive results, the authors note that "we have certainly not yet arrived at a solution to open-domain dialogue". They list as limitations a lack of in-depth knowledge if the system is engaged in lengthier dialogues; a tendency to favor simpler language; and a tendency to repeat frequently used phrases.

5.6.4 OPENAI'S GPT-3

GPT-3, which was released by OpenAI in July 2020,[9] is the latest in a series of Generative Pre-Training (GPT) models from OpenAI. GPT was released in 2018, followed in 2019 by GPT-2 [Radford et al., 2019]. The GPT-3 model has 175 billion parameters compared with GPT-2 which has 1.5 billion parameters. GPT-3 was trained on a large corpus of text of nearly one trillion words from the Common Crawl corpus,[10] an expanded version of the WebText dataset [Radford et al., 2019], two internet-based corpora of books (Books1 and Books2), and the English-language version of Wikipedia. While previous models have required task-specific tuning, GPT-3 can be applied without any fine-tuning, using few-shot learning and text-based interaction to specify tasks [Brown et al., 2020]. In this way GPT-3 is able to approximate the ability of humans to learn complex tasks from a small number of examples.

The basic idea in language modeling is to train a system to predict the next word in a sequence or predict a word that is randomly masked in a text. Extending this idea GPT-3 was applied to a number of NLP tasks and benchmarks including translation, question-answering, performing 3-digit arithmetic, and generation of news articles. Example 5.4 shows the first sentence of a generated news article given a prompt consisting of a title and a subtitle [Brown et al., 2020]:

[9] https://openai.com/blog/openai-api/
[10] https://commoncrawl.org/the-data/

Example 5.4

> **Prompt**
> **Title**: United Methodists Agree to Historic Split
> **Subtitle**: Those who oppose gay marriage will form their own denomination.
>
> **Generated text**
> After two days of intense debate, the United Methodist Church has agreed to a historic split—one that is expected to end in the creation of a new denomination, one that will be "theologically and socially conservative", according to The Washington Post.

The results reported in Brown et al. [2020] and in numerous blogs are impressive, although it is acknowledged that are are some limitations. For example, GPT-3 performed poorly on reading comprehension that involved reasoning rather than simple recall. Regarding text synthesis, although the overall quality of the output was high, the generated texts were sometimes repetitive semantically, lacked coherence, contradicted themselves, and contained non-sequitur sentences and paragraphs. Hendrycks et al. [2020] devised a new test involving 57 tasks covering topics such as mathematics, U.S. history, computer science, and law that required the GPT-3 models to possess extensive world knowledge and problem solving ability. It was found that the models would need to improve considerably to reach human-level accuracy and in socially important topics such as morality and law their accuracy was near-random.

Can GPT-3 be Used to Advance Conversational AI?

In order to interact with the GPT-3 API the user sends an HTTP request with a text string and the API responds with GPT-3 generated text. Dialogue was not one of the NLP tasks covered in [Brown et al., 2020], but there have been some minor experiments investigating how GPT-3 could be used to generate dialogues. Example 5.5 shows a dialogue from a simulation of a type of Turing test in which the user asks questions and the system answers.[11] In this example the prompt to GPT-3 was seeded with some question-answer (Q&A) pairs such as:

Example 5.5

Q: What is human life expectancy in the United States?
A: Human life expectancy in the United States is 78 years.

The responses generated are shown in Example 5.6, where Q is the user and A is the GPT-3 generated response. Note the ability to respond to a follow-up question.

[11] https://lacker.io/ai/2020/07/06/giving-gpt-3-a-turing-test.html

Example 5.6

Q: What is your favorite animal?
A: My favorite animal is a dog.
Q: Why?
A: Because dogs are loyal and friendly.

Looking now at conversational interactions, OpenAI suggest the following prompt to seed a conversation with GPT-3[12]:

Example 5.7
The following is a conversation with an AI assistant. The assistant is helpful, creative, clever, and very friendly.

HUMAN: Hello, who are you?
AI: I am an AI created by OpenAI. How can I help you today?

Example 5.8 is one of many chats in which the AI's responses were generated by GPT-3 based on the seeded prompt:

Example 5.8

AI: I am an AI created by OpenAI. How can I help you today?
HUMAN: Well, I don't know. What's up?
AI: The sky is blue, the air is clean and clear, and you have received an email.
HUMAN: Are you sure I received an email?
AI: That is correct. Would you like me to read the email to you?
HUMAN: Go for it.
AI: Hello (name). I am going to call you in the next five minutes.

Note that in this case the human user had not received an email, so although the dialogue is coherent the AI does not really know anything about the human user's emails. More examples of conversations generated by GPT-3 can be found in Quimet [2020].

As can be seen, in some cases the responses were fairly convincing. User-initiated open-domain dialogues lend themselves to this approach if the user asks about information that is available in GPT-3's training datasets. However, as mentioned earlier, GPT-3 tends to lose coherence over longer passages so that multi-turn dialogues would be problematic, suggesting the need for an additional component for keeping track of the dialogue state, as in typical dialogue system architectures (see Section 3.3.3). Systematic evaluation procedures will also be required, as discussed in Chapter 4, to determine the quality of the dialogues.

[12] https://lacker.io/ai/2020/07/23/conversation-with-gpt3.html

5.7 SOME ISSUES AND CURRENT SOLUTIONS

Although Seq2Seq models have led to significant advances in the automated learning of certain aspects of conversation, they are still limited in certain respects. Generally, the generated responses are syntactically well formed but they fail to take the overall context into account. Also they may be bland, uninformative, and lacking in emotion, or they may be semantically inconsistent. There have been various efforts to address these deficiencies.

In Section 5.3.4 we saw how the previous conversational context can be incorporated into the encoding of the current utterance and the decoding of its response. However, context in this sense applies only to the immediate history of the current utterance, whereas the context of previous conversations may also be relevant. Other types of context include the physical environment in which the conversation is taking place as well as shared knowledge between the participants about entities, relationships and events in the real world that is external to the conversation.

A problem that can occur with generation-based decoding is that the responses, while being relevant, are bland and uninformative, for example, *I don't know* or *OK*. This is known as the *generic response problem* [Yi et al., 2019]. Li et al. [2015] suggest that this problem is due to the traditional objective function used to train response generation that simply computes the maximum likelihood of a response given the input message. As a result, generic phrases that are more frequent are favored over those with more diverse content. To address this issue Li et al. [2015] propose the use of *Maximum Mutual Information* as an objective function in neural dialogue. Their experimental results showed that this approach produced more diverse responses than other models on two conversational datasets and in human evaluations.

See et al. [2019] examined several features of responses generated in neural dialogue that have a detrimental effect on human judgements of quality.

- *Repetition*, measured by N-gram overlap, where the system's utterances are repetitive.
- *Specificity*, measured by normalized inverse document frequency, where the responses are bland and uninteresting.
- *Response-relatedness*, which measures whether a response is related to the partner's previous utterance and addresses the issue of generic responses discussed above.
- *Question-asking*, measured by the use of "?" in the system's utterances, indicating an imbalance in the use of questions in the conversation.

Cosine similarity was used to measure response-relatedness. For example, in response to the input *Do you go get coffee often*, the following responses were generated using weighted decoding:

Wt: 0.0 I do when I am not playing the piano. Sim: -0.02
Wt: 5.0 I do, usually at Starbucks. Sim: 0.40

Note that a related response should not just repeat the words in the user's previous utterance but generate a response that is semantically related and furthers the dialogue.

The features listed occur predominantly in multi-turn dialogues and were controlled in an experimental system by using the following methods.

- *Conditional training (CT)*, in which the neural model is conditioned on control variables—in this case, repetitiveness, specificity, response-relatedness, and question-answering—that are applied at the level of the dialogue as opposed to the level of the system's response in order to increase or decrease the probability of generating words with these features.

- *Weighted decoding (WD)*, in which control features are added to the decoding scoring function.

In an experiment human evaluators compared the enhanced system with a baseline system by answering questions about different aspects of conversational quality: avoiding repetition, interestingness, making sense, fluency, listening, inquisitiveness, humanness, and engagingness. It was found that controlling the features in the enhanced system achieved significantly higher levels of conversational quality.

In a similar approach, Yi et al. [2019] trained several systems that evaluated the system's responses at each turn for coherence and engagement and provided feedback on dialogue quality. This feedback was incorporated into the neural response generation models to improve dialogue quality through re-ranking of the outputs and modification of the loss function during training. The models were trained on data from the 2017 Alexa Prize competition [Khatri et al., 2018b] and the system's responses were annotated by human evaluators for coherence and engagement. Although there was considerable variance in the human annotations, the results indicated that the trained models can provide useful feedback at the level of the turn can help to improve response generation quality.

5.7.1 SEMANTIC INCONSISTENCY

Semantic inconsistency is where the model produces an utterance that is inconsistent with a previous utterance. In Example 5.9 from Li et al. [2015] "message" refers to the input and "response" to the output generated by the model:

Example 5.9

MESSAGE: Where do you live now?
RESPONSE: I live in Los Angeles
MESSAGE: In which city do you live now?
RESPONSE: I live in Madrid
MESSAGE: In which country do you live now?
RESPONSE: England, you?
MESSAGE: How old are you?
RESPONSE: 16 and you?

MESSAGE: What's your age?

RESPONSE: 18

These inconsistent responses were generated by a Seq2Seq model trained on 25 million Twitter conversations. Li et al. [2016a] address this problem by incorporating a persona-based model that captures individual characteristics such as background information, language behavior, and interaction style. They found that their model outperformed baseline Seq2Seq systems in terms of BLEU scores, perplexity, and human evaluations.

One problem with creating persona-based models is a lack of speaker-specific conversational data for training the model. Luan et al. [2017] addressed this problem using a multi-task learning approach that used data from classes of speaker (such as IT support personnel) rather than from individuals. There has been a long tradition of user modeling within the dialogue systems community where the user model is represented explicitly, often in a logic-based framework (see, for example, Kobsa and Wahlster [1989]). Work within the Seq2Seq approach, in contrast, trains persona vectors from conversational data and embeds them directly into the decoder.

5.7.2 AFFECT

There is an extensive literature on the importance of affect in human communication [Picard, 2000] and on how to endow conversational agents with the ability to recognize and display emotions [Pelachaud, 2013], [Calvo et al., 2015]. It has been shown that endowing conversational agents with emotional characteristics can enhance user satisfaction [Prendinger et al., 2005] as well as leading to fewer conversational breakdowns [André et al., 2004].

Recently, researchers in neural dialogue have started to explore how to integrate information about affect into their models. Ghosh et al. [2017] present an extension to an LSTM language model for generating conversational text that was trained on conversational speech corpora. The model predicts the next word in the output conditioned not only on the previous words but also on an affective category that infers the emotional content of the words. In this way the model is able to generate expressive text at various degrees of emotional strength, as shown in Table 5.3.

Zhou et al. [2018a] developed a conversational model called *Emotional Chatting Machine (ECM)* that produces emotion-based responses to any user input, as shown in Table 5.4.

In an evaluation of the appropriateness of ECM's responses in terms of content and of emotion ECM was shown to be superior to a basic Seq2Seq model. See also Asghar et al. [2018] for discussion of a study in which affective content was incorporated into LSTM encoder-decoder neural dialogue models enabling them to produce emotionally rich and more interesting responses.

Table 5.3: Example sentences generated by the model conditioned on different affect categories. Extracted from Ghosh et al. [2017, Table 2].

Beginning	Affect Category	Completed Sentence
I feel so	Happy	good because I think that it's important to have a relationship with a friend
	Angry	bad that I hate it and I hate that because they kill themselves and then they fight
	Sad	sad to miss because I miss the feelings of family members who I lost feelings with
	Anxious	horrible I mean I think where we're going to you know war and alert alert and we're actually gonna die
	Neutral	bad if I didn't know that the decision was going on

Table 5.4: Emotional Chatting Machine [Zhou et al., 2018a]

User	Worst day ever. I arrived late because of the traffic.
Basic Seq2Seq:	You were late.
ECM (Like):	I am always here to support you.
ECM (Happy):	Keep smiling! Things will get better.
ECM (Sad):	It's depressing.
ECM (Disgust):	Sometimes life just sucks.
ECM (Angry):	The traffic is too bad.

5.8 DIALOGUE SYSTEMS: DATASETS, COMPETITIONS, TASKS, AND CHALLENGES

Over the past few years a number of publicly available dialogue datasets (or corpora) have been released. This, along with several competitions in which dialogue systems compete with one another to perform particular tasks and challenges, has contributed considerably to progress in the field. In the following sub-sections we list and briefly describe several commonly used datasets and the competitions in which dialogue systems have been tested. More detailed discussion of the evaluation criteria used in these competitions can be found in Chapter 4.

5.8.1 DATASETS AND CORPORA

Training a neural dialogue system requires very large datasets. Serban et al. [2015] provide a comprehensive survey of corpora that are suitable for training data-driven dialogue systems.[13] They distinguish between different types of corpus, for example, written vs. spoken vs. multimodal; human-human vs. human-machine interaction; spontaneous vs. constrained, i.e., where the participants had to talk about a particular task. Each of these different types has its advantages and disadvantages. For example, as pointed out by Williams and Young [2007], corpora of human-human dialogues may not be suitable for training human-machine dialogue systems as they have a different distribution of errors. Spoken dialogue systems need to account for the effects on performance of speech recognition errors and on the handling of uncertainty in the belief state, whereas these errors are less frequent in human-human dialogue. See also Sebastian Ruder's repository for a detailed annotated list of corpora for different tasks in Conversational AI.[14]

The following are brief descriptions of some commonly used corpora for task-oriented dialogues.

ATIS–Air Travel Information System Pilot Corpus. Although this is a relatively old corpus, it has been used widely in dialogue systems research [Hemphill et al., 1990]. The corpus involved interactions between human users and a simulated dialogue system where the users could ask questions that were submitted to a database containing information about flights, fares, airlines, cities, airports, and ground services.

Carnegie Mellon Communicator Corpus. This corpus consists of 180,605 utterances collected as part of the DARPA Communicator program [Bennett and Rudnicky, 2002]. The corpus involved spoken queries to a spoken dialogue system about flights, hotel bookings, and car rentals.

Let's Go! Dataset. This dataset consists of 170,000 conversations between an automated bus information system and callers asking for bus schedule information at off-peak times [Raux et al., 2005].

Maluuba Frames Dataset. The Frames dataset consists of 1369 goal-oriented human-human dialogues between a simulated dialogue system and users who had the task of finding available travel or accommodation according to a pre-specified task involving complex decision-making behaviors about trips and the exploration of different options [El Asri et al., 2017]. The task required keeping track of different semantic frames throughout the dialogue.

Facebook Dialog Datasets. The Facebook Dialog Datasets consist of task-oriented interactions released to the dialogue systems research community by Facebook AI and Research (FAIR)

[13] https://breakend.github.io/DialogDatasets/

[14] https://github.com/sebastianruder/NLP-progress/blob/master/english/dialogue.md

to support research in neural network architectures for question-answering and task-oriented dialogue in the restaurant reservation domain [Bordes and Weston, 2016].

Ubuntu Dialog Corpus. This corpus consists of around one million two-person written conversations in which users asked questions about technical problems involving the Ubuntu operating system [Lowe et al., 2015b].

Verbmobil. Verbmobil was a project in speech and language technology that was funded by the German Federal Ministry of Education and Research in two phases over a period of 8 years.[15] The Verbmobil system recognized spontaneous speech and translated it into a foreign language. The Verbmobil corpus comprises transcripts of human-to-human, spontaneous, task-oriented dialogues in German, English, and Japanese. The dialogues were annotated with dialogue acts and the annotations were used to train a statistical dialogue act classifier [Alexandersson et al., 2000]. An annotated syntax tree provided information about part-of-speech tags, phrasal categories, grammatical functions, and root labels, taking into account features of spontaneous spoken language such as repetitions, hesitations, and false starts [Hinrichs et al., 2000].

MultiWOZ. The MultiWOZ (Multi-Domain Wizard-of-Oz) dataset is a fully labeled collection of 10,000 human-human written conversations covering multiple domains and topics [Budzianowski et al., 2018], [Eric et al., 2020]. The dataset includes a set of benchmark results of belief tracking, dialogue act recognition, and response generation.

MetaLWOz. MetaLWOz (Meta-Learning Wizard-of-Oz)[16] is a dataset designed to help develop models capable of predicting user responses in unseen domains with the aim of reducing the amount of data required to train domain-specific dialogue [Shalyminov et al., 2020a]. The dataset was created by crowdsourcing 37,884 goal-oriented dialogues covering 227 tasks in 47 domains, including bus schedules, apartment search, alarm setting, banking, and event reservation. The dataset can be used to train, fine-tune and evaluate dialogue systems. It was used as the baseline for the DSTC8 (Dialogue State Tracking Challenge) competition.

Stanford Multi-Turn, Multi-Domain Dialogue Dataset. This dataset comprises 3,031 dialogues involving three distinct tasks in the in-car personal assistant space: calendar scheduling, weather information retrieval, and point-of-interest navigation [Eric et al., 2017]. The aim of the dataset was to enable neural task-oriented dialogue systems to interface smoothly with knowledge bases.

Datasets used in the Dialogue State Tracking Challenges.

- DSTC1, used in the first competition, consisted of human-computer dialogues in the bus timetable domain, using a subset of the dialogues collected in the Let's Go! dataset.

[15] http://verbmobil.dfki.de/facts.html

[16] https://www.microsoft.com/en-us/research/project/metalwoz/

- DSTC2 consisted of human-computer dialogues in the restaurant domain, where the users had to change details about the reservation during the dialogue [Henderson et al., 2014a].

- DSTC3 involved human-computer dialogues in the tourist information domain [Henderson et al., 2014b].

- DSTC4 consisted of human-human dialogues used to investigate Dialogue state tracking and end-to-end dialogue systems.

- DSTC5 also involved human-human dialogues in the tourist information domain where training dialogues were provided in one language and test dialogues in a different language.

- DSTC6: the challenge was renamed to Dialog System Technology Challenge to reflect a wider range of issues to be investigated, with three tracks:

    1. End-to-end goal-oriented dialog learning: the dataset consisted of 10,000 dialogues from the restaurant reservation domain.
    2. End-to-end conversation modeling: in this task the system had to generate responses to user inputs. The dataset was one million dialogues from Twitter and OpenSubtitles.
    3. Dialogue breakdown detection: there were three datasets of 100, 1,000, and 300 chat-oriented dialogues.

The following are some widely used corpora and datasets for non-task-oriented dialogue systems.

Twitter. The Twitter corpus [Ritter et al., 2011] consists of post-reply pairs of utterances extracted from Twitter. Tweets are short due to the 140-character limit for tweets. One problem with tweets is that they often contain hashtags and abbreviations. They also rely on references to events outside the conversation so that learning has to include reference to an external knowledge base.

Reddit. Reddit is a forum-based website where users can make posts and respond to the posts of other users. The Reddit corpus contains more than 3 billion utterances between human users. The utterances are generally longer than the utterances in Twitter.

OpenSubtitles. OpenSubtitles is a very large collection of subtitles from which the OpenSubtitles dataset has been created [Tiedemann, 2012]. The dataset contains around 1 billion words in multiple languages.

The Movie DiC corpus. This corpus contains around 130,000 dialogues from movies covering a wide range of genres [Banchs, 2012].

Persona-Chat. This is a crowdsourced dataset containing dialogues in which the participants adopted distinct personas by impersonating a particular character described by five facts [Zhang et al., 2018].

The SEMAINE corpus. This corpus contains 100 conversations in which the participants interacted with an operator who adopted various roles that were designed to evoke emotional reactions [McKeown et al., 2010]. The corpus is intended to assist in building dialogue systems with emotional intelligence.

Facebook bAbI project. Facebook bAbI is a project of Facebook AI Research. The project is concerned with dialogue systems and automatic text understanding and reasoning, and includes datasets and tasks. There are six tasks for testing end-to-end dialogue systems involving restaurant reservations [Bordes and Weston, 2016]. Each task tests a different aspect of dialogue. There are 1000 dialogues for training, 1000 for development, and 1000 for testing.

- The Movie Dialog Dataset measures how well models can perform in goal-oriented and non-goal-oriented dialogue in the movie domain, involving question answering, recommendation, and discussion [Dodge et al., 2015].
- The Dialog-based Language Learning dataset measures how well models perform at learning as a student given a teacher's response to the student's answer [Weston, 2016].
- The Human-in-the-loop (HITL) Dialogue Simulator provides a framework for evaluating how well a bot can learn to improve its performance using feedback from its dialogue partner [Li et al., 2016b].

It should be noted that the Facebook bAbi data is synthetic, i.e., realistic human behaviors associated with spontaneous speech such as disfluencies are cleaned up. See Shalyminov et al. [2017] for a discussion of whether systems trained on such clean data can generalize to real spontaneous dialogue.

5.8.2 COMPETITIONS, TASKS, AND CHALLENGES

In the addition to the Alexa Prize which has been covered elsewhere, Sections 1.4.3, 2.4, 4.3.4, and 5.6.1, there are several other competitions and challenges that address issues in Conversational AI.

Dialogue State Tracking Challenge (DSTC). The Dialogue State Tracking Challenge was launched in 2013 as an initiative to provide a common testbed for the task of learning a strategy for Dialogue state tracking.

- DSTC1: the aim was to compare different models for Dialogue State Tracking using a common dataset. One important result was that Dialogue State Tracking was most beneficial for those dialogue systems experiencing poor speech recognition compared with baseline rule-based systems [Williams et al., 2013].

- DSTC2 built on the previous challenge with dynamically changing and more complicated dialogue states where the users could change their goals in a restaurant search task. In the evaluation it was found that the most accurate tracking can be achieved through ensemble learning where multiple trackers are combined [Henderson et al., 2014a].

- DSTC3 was concerned with the problem of adapting to a new domain, in this case tourist information, where new slots and their values were not present in the training data. For training the participants used a small corpus of labeled data from the tourist information domain along with the restaurant data from DSTC2. It was found that half of the teams outperformed a competitive rule-based baseline system [Henderson et al., 2014b].

Since 2015 the scope of the challenge widened to address other tasks in dialogue technology and the challenge was renamed Dialog System Technology Challenge.

- DSTC4 included a series of pilot tracks looking at the use of end-to-end dialogues for the same dataset [Kim et al., 2017].

- DSTC5: the goal of the main task was to track dialogue states for sub-dialogue segments with a focus on cross-language Dialogue State Tracking using corpora of English and Chinese dialogues. The challenge also included tracks looking at the development of end-to-end dialogue systems using the same dataset [Kim et al., 2016].

- DSTC6 consisted of three tracks.

    1. Track 1, end-to-end goal-oriented dialogue learning which involved selecting system responses in a restaurant retrieval task.
    2. Track 2, end-to-end conversation modeling which involved generating system responses using natural language generation in a customer services application on Twitter with a combination of goal-oriented dialogues and chit-chat.
    3. Track 3, which was concerned with dialogue breakdown detection using human-machine data for chit-chat. Eighteen scientific papers were presented in a follow-up workshop. For an overview, see Hori et al. [2019].

- DSTC7 focused on end-to-end dialogue systems in three different tracks.

    1. Sentence Selection: using the Ubuntu corpus and Flex Data: Student Advisor dialogues.
    2. Sentence Generation.
    3. Audio Visual Scene-aware dialogue.

    New datasets were used in each track and the teams produced impressive results using state-of-the-art end-to-end technologies. The overall setup and results are described in Yoshino et al. [2015].

- DSTC8 consisted of four tracks.[17]

  1. Multi-domain Task Completion, which involved two tasks: dialogue complexity and scaling to new domains.
  2. Predicting responses, which explored three challenges: next utterance selection, task success, and conversation disentanglement.
  3. Audio Visual Scene-Aware Dialogue, where the task was to build a system that generates responses in a dialogue about a video.
  4. Schema-Guided State Tracking, which explored challenges in tasks involving services and APIs.

- The most recent challenge DSTC9 also consisted of four tracks.[18]

  1. Beyond Domain APIs: Task-oriented Conversational Modeling with Unstructured Knowledge Access. In this track the aim was to develop dialogue systems that could handle situations when users make requests in task-oriented systems that are out of the scope of APIs and databases.
  2. Multi-domain Task-oriented Dialogue Challenge II. This track consisted of two tasks.
     (a) End-to-end multi-domain task completion dialogues in which participants had to build a dialogue system that spanned over multiple domains.
     (b) Cross-lingual multi-domain dialogue state tracking that involved building a dialogue state tracker that could handle multiple languages in which the training set was in a resource-rich language and the development/test set was in a resource poor language.
  3. Interactive Evaluation of Dialogue. The task in this track was to build dialogue systems that could converse effectively in interactive environments with real users, addressing issues such as: consistency, adaptiveness, and user-centric development, and being able to learn after deployment based on real user data and implicit and explicit feedback signals.
  4. SIMMC: Situated Interactive Multi-Modal Conversational AI. This track was concerned with dialogue agents that could handle multimodal inputs and perform multimodal actions in task-oriented dialogues using datasets from shopping domains.

NIPS Conversational AI challenge The Conversational AI challenge was held in 2017 and 2018 at the Conference on Neural Information Processing Systems (NIPS), known since 2018 as NeurIPS. The aim of the challenge is to create a chatbot that can hold an intelligent conversation

[17] https://sites.google.com/dstc.community/dstc8/tracks
[18] https://dstc9.dstc.community/tracks

with a human partner with the aim of developing criteria for the evaluation of state-of-the-art dialogue systems and collecting an open-source dataset for future training of end-to-end systems.

The winner of the 2017 competition (ConvAI1) was a system developed by Yusupov and Kuratov [2018] that demonstrated a set of skills including chit-chat, topic detection, text summarization, question answering, and question generation. The dialogue manager which was trained in a supervised setting selects an appropriate skill for generating a response to the user's input.

In the 2018 challenge (ConvAI2) the Persona-Chat dataset was provided and the aim was to make the conversations more engaging for humans and to develop an evaluation process that included automatic evaluation followed by human evaluation. The winner in 2018 was a system entitled *Lost in Conversation*.[19] A description of the challenge and summary of the results can be found in Dinan et al. [2019a].

Dialogue Breakdown Detection Challenge The Dialogue Breakdown Detection Challenge (DBDC)[20] is an initiative included in the Workshops and Session Series on Chatbots and Conversational Agents (WOCHAT)[21] that are held at the annual International Workshop on Spoken Dialogue Systems (IWSDS).[22] The aim of the challenge is to develop resources and technologies for detecting breakdowns in interactions with dialogue systems [Higashinaka et al., 2016], [Higashinaka et al., 2017]. The 2020 challenge consists of three tracks.

1. Breakdown Detection: participants build systems to estimate the probability distribution of the labels *breakdown*, *possible breakdown*, and *no breakdown* for each turn in a dialogue given the previous turn and the dialogue history.

2. Dialogue Breakdown Error Classification: this task involves building a classifier to identify the error type of each dialogue breakdown event.

3. Dialogue Breakdown Recovery (Sentence Generation): this task involves building a response generator that provides responses to correct and recover from dialogue breakdown events (next utterance recovery).

Datasets were made available from Chateval,[23] a scientific framework for evaluating open-domain chatbots. For the 1st task 600 dialogues in English and 400 dialogues in Japanese were provided. For the 2nd task there were 600 dialogues in Japanese, and for the 3rd task there were 600 dialogues in English.

[19] https://github.com/atselousov/transformer_chatbot
[20] http://workshop.colips.org/wochat/\spacefactor\@m{}iwsds2020/shared.html
[21] http://workshop.colips.org/wochat/
[22] http://www.iwsds.org/
[23] https://chateval.org/

5.9 ADDITIONAL READINGS

There are several useful surveys, tutorials, and overviews of neural dialogue systems, including: Celikyilmaz et al. [2018], Chen et al. [2017], Gao et al. [2019], Sarikaya [2017], and Yan [2018]. There are many conferences and workshops on Conversational AI and neural dialogue. In particular, the NIPS workshops on Conversational AI contain many useful papers on current research [Guyon et al., 2017], [Bengio et al., 2018], [Wallach et al., 2019].

The following are some annotated reading lists for Conversational AI: Wang [2018], Yao [2019a], and Yao [2019b].

SUMMARY

This chapter has introduced the neural dialogue approach which has come to dominate current research in Conversational AI. Key topics in neural dialogue were reviewed, including: word embeddings as a means of representing words as unique real-number vectors that capture their meaning and their relationship to the other words in a semantic space; recurrent neural networks and variants to process the input and generate output; the encoder-decoder architecture; and the attention mechanism. Recent developments in open-domain dialogue systems using large language models were reviewed. Some ongoing issues in current research and proposals for their solutions were outlined, including: how to model context; how to avoid bland and uninteresting responses; how to deal with semantic inconsistencies; and how to introduce and model affect and emotion. Datasets for neural dialogue modeling and several public challenges and tasks have contributed greatly to improvements in dialogue systems developed using end-to-end learning. Finally, a number of useful references and links to review articles, surveys, and tutorials were provided for readers looking for more detail.

CHAPTER 6

Challenges and Future Directions

Conversational AI is a fast moving area that has attracted the interest of researchers in natural language processing as well as companies such as Google, Amazon, Facebook, Microsoft, and IBM that have developed speech and language technologies and are now exploring the potential of text-based and spoken dialogue systems. Numerous smaller companies are also involved.

In the preceding chapters different technologies were reviewed that have been used to develop dialogue systems. Traditional rule-based approaches were compared with statistical data-driven and end-to-end neural dialogue approaches. This chapter examines ten topics that are likely to be the focus of future directions in dialogue systems research, highlighting some of the challenges that lie ahead, looking at issues in technology and in key application areas, and addressing some social and ethical considerations.

Section 6.1 discusses multimodality, how dialogue systems process and generate multimodal content and the technical issues involved. Section 6.2 reviews work in visual dialogue, a new and rapidly developing area in Conversational AI. Section 6.3 discusses issues in the efficient training of dialogue systems, especially where there is only sparse training data. Section 6.4 looks at how dialogue systems can make use of external knowledge, for example, in the form of knowledge graphs, while Section 6.5 considers the challenges faced in making systems more intelligent and more cooperative by incorporating the ability to reason and solve problems collaboratively. Section 6.6 reviews some challenges in dialogue research, for example, how to deal with discourse-related phenomena such as anaphora and ellipsis, how to detect, maintain, and change topics, how to engage in multi-party conversations, process incoming utterances incrementally, and take turns in conversation.

Generally, dialogue systems have been developed using rules or machine learning. However, there has also been work on hybrid systems that aim to draw the best from both approaches. Different types of hybrid dialogue systems are discussed in Section 6.7. Turning to applications, Section 6.8 examines dialogues with social robots in physical environments and Section 6.9 discusses how dialogue systems can be used in the user's environment, i.e., to support interactions with the Internet of Things (IoT). Finally, Section 6.10 considers some important social and ethical issues in relation to dialogue systems.

6.1 MULTIMODALITY IN DIALOGUE

Interactions with the dialogue systems discussed in the preceding chapters have been mostly text-based and/or speech-based. However, many human-machine interactions make use of other modalities. For example, interacting with a smartphone can involve input that uses text, speech, and touch, while output may use combinations of text, speech, images, audio, and video.

Multimodal dialogue systems bring some advantages over speech and text-based systems [Oviatt and Cohen, 2015].

1. They are more flexible as they allow the user to choose the input and output modes that they prefer, thus potentially helping to reduce cognitive load on the user.

2. They are able to deal with speech recognition errors and problems associated with the use of anaphoric reference given the possibility of visual feedback compared with the limited options available in a speech-only interface.

Multimodal dialogue systems have been investigated since the early 2000s in projects such as SmartKom [Wahlster, 2006], COMIC [Catizone et al., 2003], and MATCH [Johnston et al., 2002]. Minker et al. [2006] and López-Cózar and Araki [2007] provide comprehensive coverage of multimodal dialogue systems in the early 2000s, while more recent work is presented in Oviatt et al. [2017], Oviatt et al. [2018], and Oviatt et al. [2019].

Multimodal dialogue can be seen from two different points of view.

1. *Multimodal Fusion*, which is concerned with the processing of multimodal input.

2. *Multimodal Fission*, which deals with the generation of multimodal output.

6.1.1 MULTIMODAL FUSION

A system that is able to process a variety of multimodal inputs can provide a richer conversational experience. Bohus and Horwitz (2019) investigated how a system could monitor a user's level of engagement using multimodal perception, i.e., by detecting signals from gaze, head and hand gestures, and speech. Engagement is a key indicator of conversation quality, and if the system is able to detect an issue with engagement it can take steps to address the issue.

Multimodal fusion involves integrating input from different modalities into a single meaning representation. Johnston [2019] describes a variety of methods for multimodal integration, including unification of the elements, handling them as lattice elements, and handling them in a state chart.

Multimodal dialogue systems in the early 2000s used handcrafted rules to process the input. More recently, statistical and machine learning methods have been used. Bohus and Horvitz [2019] describe an approach to engagement tracking using probabilistic heuristic rules. Regarding machine learning there are still some issues. For example, as Bohus and Horvitz [2019] point out, machine-learned classifiers could be used to predict whether the user is engaged or

SHOPPER: Hello
AGENT: Hi, please tell me what i can help you with today?
SHOPPER: show me few of your top large sized rubber type upper material clogs that is mostly light pink in colored that i would like.
AGENT: Of course. Just wait a few seconds while i browse through my catalog
AGENT: Sorry i dont have any in pink but would you like to see some in

other color
SHOPPER: Please show me something similar to the 1st image but in a different upper material

AGENT: The similar looking ones are

SHOPPER: I like the 4th result . Show me something like it but in material as in the 1st image from what you had previously shown me in clogs

Figure 6.1: Multimodal display in an online retail application. Source: Agarwal et al. [2018, Figure 1]. Used with permission.

disengaged, but there could be a problem with overfitting of the training data collected in one situation when the model is applied to a different situation. In a similar vein, Johnston [2019] points out problems in using deep learning for multimodal integration given that there are as yet no suitably annotated corpora available to train a machine learning system. See also Baltrušaitis et al. [2018] for a comprehensive survey on multimodal machine learning and Keren et al. [2018] on deep learning for multisensorial and multimodal interaction.

6.1.2 MULTIMODAL FISSION

Multimodal output is useful in use cases where a textual or spoken output would be less useful. For example, in an online retail application images of items from a catalogue can be displayed along with textual descriptions so that the user can refer to the items by pointing or using terms such as *the first image*; see Figure 6.1.

There are a number of issues that arise in the generation of multimodal output, including: how to represent multimodal content; how to plan its output; and how to coordinate the output effectively. These issues were investigated in various projects in the early 2000s and are now being investigated in more recent machine learning-based and neural dialogue projects.

In the SmartKom system [Wahlster, 2006] multimodal output consisting of gestures, body postures, and facial expressions was controlled by a presentation planner. In the COMIC project [Foster, 2005] a fission module created plans to determine the content of the multimodal output that comprised facial expressions, gaze, lip movements, and nodding, as well as visual channels, such as drawings and graphics. The execution of the plans was coordinated in order to avoid delays in the output of any particular elements that took longer to process. In the MATCH project [Johnston et al., 2002] the system generated coordinated multimodal presentations adapted to the user's preferences, the task at hand, and the physical and social environment.

In more recent work multimodal output generation has been addressed in neural dialogue systems. Nie et al. [2019] used adaptive decoders to generate the desired output in an online retail application. A simple RNN was used to generate general responses, then a knowledge-aware RNN decoder that included domain knowledge was used to enrich the response by incorporating images recommended by an image recommendation model that jointly considered the textual attributes and the visual images using an optimized neural model. In an application in the fashion domain, Liao et al. [2018] developed an end-to-end neural dialogue system that generated responses based on the conversation history, visual semantics, and domain knowledge. The dialogue model was optimized using deep reinforcement learning. In both cases the systems outperformed comparable systems and achieved state-of-the-art performance.

Finally, also in the fashion domain Agarwal et al. [2018] introduced a multimodal extension to the Hierarchical Recurrent Encoder-Decoder (HRED) model in order to optimize textual response generation in a multimodal dialogue system. The model made use of the Multimodal Dialogue (MMD) dataset that consists of over 150K dialogues between shoppers and sales agents in the fashion domain [Saha et al., 2017], a useful resource for training neural dialogue systems in domains such as fashion and retail.

It would be interesting in future research to investigate whether some of the knowledge-based methods used in multimodal systems in the early 2000s could be incorporated into and enhance the performance of systems using end-to-end neural technologies.

6.1.3 MULTIMODALITY IN SMARTPHONES AND SMART SPEAKERS WITH DISPLAYS

Smartphones and smart speakers with displays make use of multimodal output to display a variety of rich visuals. Google Assistant[1] can display basic cards, lists, suggestion chips, and

[1] https://developers.google.com/assistant/surfaces/displays

carousels. Similarly, the Amazon Alexa Skills Kit[2] allows visual items such as videos and animations to be displayed along with voice to provide rich multimedia experiences. The Alexa Presentation Language (APL)[3] is a design language that can be used to render visuals on a wide range of Alexa-enabled multimodal devices.

6.2 VISUAL DIALOGUE AND VISUALLY GROUNDED LANGUAGE

Visual dialogue is a new and rapidly developing area that combines Computer Vision and Conversational AI. Building on advances in Computer Vision, e.g., image classification, scene and object recognition, and question answering about images, the aim of visual dialogue is to enable AI agents to engage with humans in a dialogue about visual content. Visual dialogue has the potential to contribute to several application areas, including: aid for visually impaired users, surveillance, robotics, e.g., in search and rescue missions, and tourist navigation [de Vries et al., 2018].

The Visual Dialog website[4] is a rich source of information about visual dialogue with descriptions of the Visual Dialog task, code, the VisDial dataset, and information about the Visual Dialog Challenges that have been held since 2018–2020. There is also a Visual Chatbot demo in which the user can insert an image that the system processes before going on to engage in a dialogue about the image. Das et al. [2017] list the following contributions of their work in visual dialogue.

1. A Visual Dialog task to investigate the extent to which an AI agent can engage in a dialogue with a human about visual content.

2. A large-scale Visual Dialog dataset.

3. A family of neural encoder-decoder models for Visual Dialog.

4. An evaluation protocol for Visual Dialog.

5. Studies to quantify human performance on the Visual Dialog task.

In the Visual Dialog task the AI agent is given an image, a dialogue history consisting of a sequence of question-answer pairs, and a follow-up question, as shown in Example 6.1:

Example 6.1

Q1: How many people are in wheelchairs?
A1: Two.

[2] https://developer.amazon.com/en-US/alexa/alexa-skills-kit/get-deeper/tutorials-code-samples/build-a-multimodal-alexa-skill

[3] https://developer.amazon.com/en-US/docs/alexa/alexa-presentation-language/understand-apl.html

[4] https://visualdialog.org/

Q2: What are their genders?

A2: One male and one female.

Q3: (Follow-up question) Which one is holding a racket?

A3: (Required answer) The woman.

The Visual Dialog dataset (VisDial) consists of dialogues with 10 question-answer pairs on around 140,000 images from the Microsoft COCO dataset [Lin et al., 2014], yielding around 140,000 question-answer pairs. The neural models include three encoders: a Late Fusion encoder that embeds the image, dialogue history, and questions separately into vector spaces and then fuses them into a combined embedding; a Hierarchical Recurrent Encoder containing a dialogue-level Recurrent Neural Network (RNN) and an attention mechanism, and a Memory Network. The encoders are trained with two decoders.

In the evaluation protocol the AI agent sorts a list of candidate answers and is evaluated on metrics that compare its responses with human responses. Quantitative measures included the use of coreference in the dialogues, where nearly all the dialogues contained at least one pronoun, and a measure of topic continuity, which found that there was little topic change during the dialogues. Overall the results indicated that, although the performance of the AI-agent was far from optimal, the Visual Dialog task could serve as a useful testbed for measuring progress toward visual intelligence.

In visual dialogue an important task is being able to correctly identify objects and their relationships in a visual context, as in intelligent scene understanding. This involves visually grounded language. In dialogue, grounding is where the participants work to achieve mutual understanding about a concept, a reference to a person, object or event, or some idea or proposition that has been discussed [Clark and Brennan, 1991]. A dialogue about objects in a visual world is more complex as it requires a combination of image understanding, spatial reasoning and language grounding to accurately identify the objects being referenced. Visually grounded language was investigated by de Vries et al. [2016] in a two-player game *GuessWhat?!* in which the goal was to locate an object in an image by asking a series of questions. Two participants are involved in the game, an oracle and a questioner. The oracle knows about the objects in a picture and the object that has been specified for the game. The questioner asks a series of yes/no questions with the aim of narrowing down the list of objects and identifying the one that was specified for the game. Table 6.1 shows an example of a dialogue in the GuessWhat?! game.

Baselines were trained for each role using neural network models and their performance was measured. The oracle's task was to answer yes/no questions while the questioner's task consisted of two sub-tasks: predicting the correct object (Guesser model) and generating questions (Question Generator model). Generating questions is difficult, as it requires high-level visual understanding to ask relevant questions in a sequence. A hierarchical recurrent encoder-decoder (HRED) was used, conditioned on features of the image.

Table 6.1: Questions and answers in the GuessWhat?! game

Questioner Oracle	
Is it a vase?	Yes.
Is it partially visible?	No.
Is it in the left corner?	No.
Is it the turquoise and purple one?	Yes.

A key contribution of this work was the GuessWhat?! Dataset consisting of 150,000 dialogues and 800,000 visual question-answer pairs that was created via crowdsourcing on Amazon Mechanical Turk using images from the Microsoft COCO dataset [Lin et al., 2014]. The authors suggest that the dataset could be used for developing various machine learning tasks involving one-shot and transfer learning (see Section 6.3).

Building on this work, Suglia et al. [2020] presented a framework for Grounded Language Learning with Attributes (GroLLA) using a compositional approach to learn grounded representations of the attributes of objects. For example, a visually grounded representation of an object such as a microwave oven could have abstract attributes such as **is_appliance**, and situated attributes such as **is_white**. The aim was to investigate whether learning a representation that included attributes of the target object would help discriminate the object from other objects in a scene. Attribute prediction was evaluated in a game similar to the game used in the GuessWhat?! framework. Although it turned out that the learned representations did not generalize very well to unseen objects, the authors suggest that more advanced learning mechanisms could be used to encode attributes in a more compositional manner using a co-grounding operator that would fuse the textual and visual modalities and learn representations at each turn.

Other issues that were investigated in this work were zero-shot learning in which learned representations can be reused in a task involving objects not seen during training (see Section 6.3; and the creation of a new dataset CompGuessWhat?! to support the evaluation of attribute grounding in learned neural representations by including a semantic layer that contained abstract and situated attributes.

To summarize: visual dialogue is an exciting new area for Conversational AI that introduces new challenges for research. Visual dialogue has the potential to enable a range of new and useful applications in areas such as support for users with visual impairment and more generally applications involving intelligent scene understanding.

6.3 DATA EFFICIENCY: TRAINING DIALOGUE SYSTEMS WITH SPARSE DATA

Although there are many datasets that can be used to train dialogue systems, there are still problems when it comes to domains for which there is little or no training data. This problem is particularly apparent in task-oriented systems where collecting datasets for new application domains would be costly and time-consuming. One way to address this is to try to use data from another domain. This is known as Transfer Learning. Another approach is to train the system from very small amounts of data. This is known as few-shot learning or zero-shot learning.

Transfer Learning was addressed in Task 2 of the Multi-Domain Task-Completion Dialog Challenge[5] which was part of the Eighth Dialog System Technology Challenge (DSTC8), held in 2019. The goal of Task 2 was to investigate whether a dialogue system that had been trained on a large dataset could learn to engage in conversations in a different domain where there was only a much smaller domain-specific corpus available.

The winning method in Task 2 is described in Shalyminov et al. [2020b]. In this method a hybrid generative-retrieval model based on GPT-2 [Radford et al., 2019] (see Section 5.6.4) was fine-tuned to the MetaLWOz dataset (see Section 5.8.1). In-domain data that can be collected from customer service transcripts or supplied by the developer was fed into the model along with a target dialogue. The task for the model was to predict the next turn in the target dialogue. It was found that the model achieved state-of-the-art performance when evaluated by human judges and that it outperformed various baselines using automatic metrics such as word overlap. While these results are promising, the authors note that using transfer learning does not yet reach a level of performance that would be required for adoption in industry and that more research is required in the area of data-efficient dialogue response generation.

Another approach to data efficiency involves training dialogue system models with sparse data. Zhao and Eskenazi [2018] and Zhao et al. [2018] presented a zero-shot learning framework for training a dialogue generation model from available source data and a reduced subset of the target data.

Building on this work, Shalyminov et al. [2019] proposed a few-shot learning technique using no annotated data. Background knowledge was leveraged from the MetaLWOz dataset (see Section 5.8.1) and models were trained on the dataset without using any domain that might overlap with the target domain. A few-shot dialogue generation model was then trained on the Stanford Multi-Domain Dataset that included task-oriented dialogues in several domains [Eric et al., 2017]. Results showed that in comparisons the few-shot approach produced the best performing models with a significant reduction in the amount of in-domain training required. For example, state-of-the-art results were obtained with just 3% of in-domain data. However, as with the work on Transfer Learning the authors remain cautious about immediate adoption of the technique for real-word applications, stating that more research is required into generalizing to new domains using few-shot learning.

[5] https://www.microsoft.com/en-us/research/project/multi-domain-task-completion-dialog-challenge/

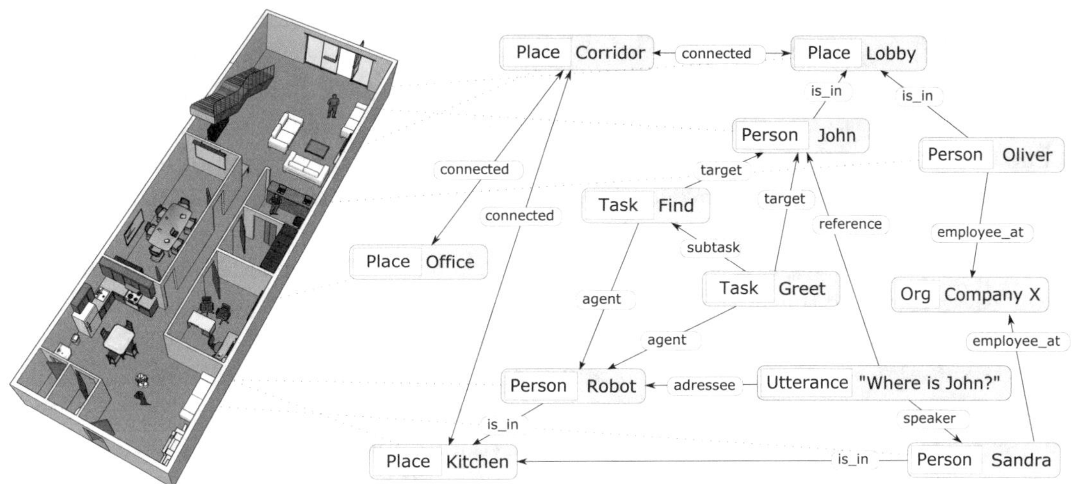

Figure 6.2: Knowledge graph for a human-robot interaction setting. Used with permission.

6.4 KNOWLEDGE GRAPHS FOR DIALOGUE SYSTEMS

In order to respond intelligently, a dialogue system should be able to draw on information from the real world. In early open-domain dialogue systems the main focus was on generating high-quality responses measured in terms of metrics such as Sensibleness and Specificity. See Section 4.3.1. Generally, the response was conditioned on the previous words in the conversation that constituted the conversation's context. Various additions to the context were reviewed in Chapter 5: for example, representing the Persona of the user or the system in order to improve response consistency [Li et al., 2016a]; including information about emotion to provide more expressive and more human-like responses [Zhou et al., 2018a] and incorporating information from the visual environment (see Section 6.1). Adding external knowledge in this way helps to make dialogue models knowledge-grounded [Gao et al., 2019].

External knowledge can be represented in a knowledge graph that contains interlinked descriptions of entities such as objects, events, and concepts. Google's Knowledge Graph, which was launched in 2012, contains over 500 billion facts about 5 billion entities that have been sourced across the World Wide Web and from various open source and licensed databases. As well as supporting search queries Google's Knowledge Graph is also used in enterprises to maintain facts and relationships within the enterprise and to enable the automatic answering of queries.

Knowledge graphs are used extensively in various question-answering systems [Hao et al., 2017], [Sun et al., 2018], and they are now being adopted by dialogue researchers.

Figure 6.2 is a fragment of a knowledge graph for a human-robot interaction setting from the GraphDial project.[6] The graph connects various entities such as places, persons, tasks and utterances and can be used to answer questions. For example, given Sandra's utterance *where is John?* the answer *I just saw him in the lobby* can be constructed by following the **reference** link to **Person(John)** and then the **is_in** link to **Place(Lobby)**. The overall goal of the GraphDial project is to use probabilistic knowledge graphs to represent and enrich the system's dialogue state.

For Seq2Seq dialogue systems the main issue is how to incorporate information from knowledge graphs into the encoder-decoder architecture. To address this, Ghazvininejad et al. [2018] developed a model with an additional encoder that inserted factual information relevant to the conversation—in their example, restaurant reviews about a restaurant that had been mentioned in the conversation. The system retrieves the information from a large collection of facts using search words extracted from the conversation context. By separating the user's input from the input coming from the environment, the system can generate different responses when the environment changes.

Being able to adapt to a changing environment is crucial for an intelligent dialogue system. Tuan et al. [2019] investigated how to apply dynamic knowledge graphs in a neural conversation model to generate relevant responses using two networks: a Seq2Seq model and a multi-hop reasoning model. The ability of the system to adapt dynamically to new information was benchmarked against other knowledge-grounded baseline systems and was shown to outperform them.

6.5 REASONING AND COLLABORATIVE PROBLEM SOLVING IN DIALOGUE SYSTEMS

In order to be able to act intelligently, a dialogue system should be able to display common sense and have the ability to reason about its own actions and those of its interlocutor. Recent research has been addressing these issues.

In an example discussed in more detail in Section 6.9, Jeon et al. [2016] used information in a commonsense ontology to enable the system to suggest that a window should be closed if the air conditioning is to be switched on. In other work, Liu et al. [2019], Zhou et al. [2018b], and others have shown how commonsense knowledge can be extracted from knowledge graphs to enhance the system's understanding of an input and its response generation.

In order to be able to interact in a collaborative and co-operative manner an intelligent dialogue system needs to be able to reason about its own actions and the actions of its conversational partner. One aspect of this is that in addition to understanding the meaning of the other's utterances, the system should also be able to infer the intentions behind the utterances and then respond in such a way as to address those intentions. These issues were addressed in early

[6] http://graphdial.nr.no/

work on plan-based dialogue [Allen and Perrault, 1980], [Cohen and Perrault, 1979], [Cohen and Levesque, 1990], using symbolic methods and plan recognition algorithms, but they have received little attention in recent work.

One exception is a recent position paper by Cohen [2019] and a discussion by a panel of dialogue experts looking at challenges for multimodal dialogue systems [Allen et al., 2019]. Example 6.2 illustrates.

Example 6.2
A traveller in South Korea for the first time needs to catch a bus to her destination. She approaches an information provider at 10.45 pm.

USER: Do you know when is the next bus to Suwon?

A literal answer to the question would be uncooperative, e.g.,

SYSTEM: Yes, I do know.

as would an answer such as:

SYSTEM: The next bus leaves at 5.00 in the morning.

Instead, if the system has reasoned that the traveller's goal is to be in Suwon that evening and discovers an obstacle to the plan, i.e., that the last direct bus has departed, then the system should look for an alternative plan to help her achieve her goal, for example:

SYSTEM: Sorry, the last bus has left for the evening. You will have to take a bus to Seongnam and then transfer to the bus to Suwon. The bus leaves here from bay number 6 at 11:00 pm.

Being able to respond cooperatively in this way requires explicit representations of plans and actions at a general level of granularity that are independent of the actual plans and actions in a particular situation. See Galescu et al. [2018] for an approach to this issue. Whether these sorts of representation can be incorporated as additional context into an end-to-end neural dialogue system is at the frontiers of research, as discussed in detail in the panel discussion [Allen et al., 2019].

6.6 DISCOURSE AND DIALOGUE PHENOMENA

There are several discourse and dialogue phenomena that pose challenges for dialogue systems research. These include: how to refer to entities and objects; the ability to detect changes in topic and to maintain or select new topics; how to engage in multi-party dialogues; how to process input in an incremental manner; and how manage conversational turn-taking.

6.6.1 MAKING REFERENCE

There are several different ways in which entities can be referred to in a text or dialogue. *Coreference* is when the same entities are mentioned but with different referring expressions. For example, a person might be referred to on one occasion as *John* and on another occasion as *the manager*. *Anaphoric reference* differs from coreference as it describes when an entity that was mentioned previously is referred to using an anaphoric expression such as a pronoun (see Example 2.2). *Exophoric reference* is where the reference is to an entity outside the dialogue, as in Example 2.3. The term *entity linking* is used to describe the task of identifying the correct entity, as in Example 2.3.

There has been a long tradition of rule-based approaches to discourse modeling, for example, Brady and Berwick [1983]. In current work methods based on deep learning are being used, for example, Clark and Manning [2016] and Ng [2017]. Sukthanker et al. [2020] is a comprehensive survey of anaphora and coreference in NLP, reviewing datasets, rule-based and machine learning-based algorithms, and identifying issues for further research, such as: the need for standard evaluation metrics; the need to address confused labeling in datasets due to differences in terms used in different theories of reference; and the need to consider the extent to which world knowledge is required to resolve reference and, if so, how it should be incorporated into the processing.

6.6.2 DETECTING, MAINTAINING, AND CHANGING TOPIC

In an open-domain conversation the participants can talk about a wide variety of topics. Engaging effectively in a conversation requires the ability to detect topics raised by the other participant, maintain the topic as required, detect when the topic has changed, and proactively suggest new topics.

As well as being able to track topics and generate relevant responses, a participant in a dialogue should also be able to decide whether to keep on the same topic and when to change to another topic. Wu et al. [2019] used a knowledge graph to enable a dialogue agent to proactively select new topics in a conversation. The knowledge graph contained facts about movies along with comments and synopses. Using a conversation dataset constructed from the knowledge graph, a dialogue system was trained to move between topics while keeping the conversation natural and engaging.

Khatri et al. [2018b] describe methods used by the socialbots in the Alexa Prize to identify topics in open-domain dialogues and transition between topics and entities listed in a knowledge graph. For example, the socialbot Alana used the Coherence bot, one of the bots in its bot ensemble, to switch topic if the conversation demanded it, i.e., if it looked like the conversation was coming to a halt [Cercas Curry et al., 2018]. In the case of a returning user, Alana used its user model of that user to suggest a topic that it knew the user liked, saying for example, *since I remember that you like movies …*, or *since I know you like books …*.

Work in the area of topic maintenance and change is still in its infancy and there are still many challenges to be addressed, particularly for end-to-end neural dialogue systems, as it is difficult to incorporate long-distance context into the input of an encoder.

6.6.3 MULTI-PARTY DIALOGUE

Multi-party dialogue is when several people are involved in a conversation with a dialogue system, as, for example, in interactions between robots or avatars and several human participants, or in situations where several people interact with a smart speaker [Porcheron et al., 2018].

Multi-party dialogue raises a number of issues that are not present or less obvious in two-party dialogues [Traum, 2003]:

- identifying who is being addressed: this can have implications for who takes the next turn;
- identifying who is actively involved in the conversation, as not everyone present in the environment may be actively involved at a given point in time;
- identifying who is the speaker: this applies particularly to robots and avatars with visual capabilities, where cues such as lip movement or gestures are important indicators. In other cases speakers may be differentiated according to their voices;
- managing turn-taking (see Section 6.6.5); and
- distinguishing between multiple topics and multiple conversations, as in multi-party dialogue several topics and even several conversations might be ongoing at the same time.

Although these issues were raised by Traum [2003] in 2003 and investigated in a project in which virtual humans were used to help train decision-making in a team context, there has been little research since then on multi-party dialogue. Richter et al. [2016] describe experiments with a robot in multi-party dialogues where the task for the robot was to distinguish between utterances directed at it and talk between the humans in the environment. Attention management involving mutual gaze and detection of lip movements was found to be an important factor in the recognition of potential addressees, especially when it was not possible for the robot to see all of the participants in the interaction at the same time.

In another study, Porcheron et al. [2018] recorded families interacting with a smart speaker (Amazon Echo) in their homes. However, in this study the focus was on how the human participants interacted with the smart speaker and embedded these interactions into multi-party conversations within the family. The study did not investigate how the smart speaker was able to manage interactions in multi-party dialogues.

Many of the issues related to multi-party dialogues are still open areas for research and will be the focus of investigation in a new European Union (EU) funded project SPRING[7] that

[7] https://spring-h2020.eu/

aims to develop social robots that can engage in multi-person interactions and open-domain dialogue.

6.6.4 INCREMENTAL PROCESSING IN DIALOGUE

In interactions with dialogue systems the user is often able to interrupt the output of the dialogue agent using *barge-in*. This causes the system to stop speaking and to listen to the user's input. The system is not able to do this. Instead it waits until it believes the user has stopped speaking, as indicated by silence. This is known as *endpoint detection* and is also relevant in conversational turn-taking (see Section 6.6.5).

However, human-human dialogue is different as speakers often engage in incremental processing where they anticipate what the other speaker is going to say [Tanenhaus, 2006]. Recent versions of Google Voice Search make use of incremental speech processing by showing words as they are being recognized without waiting until the user has finished speaking.

As well as processing the input incrementally, participants in dialogues often cut in on the ongoing utterance to offer a completion. Indeed, it was found in a corpus of dialogues that almost one-fifth of all turns involved completions, also known as joint productions [Howes et al., 2011]. See Example 6.3[8]:

Example 6.3

DAUGHTER: Oh here dad, a good way to get those corners out
FATHER: is to stick her finger inside.

With incremental processing a dialogue can be more fluent and more natural. For example, in a study in which incremental and non-incremental versions of a system were compared, it was found that the incremental version was rated as more polite and efficient, as well as better at predicting when to speak [Skantze and Hjalmarsson, 2013]. Systems using incremental processing have also been found to enhance user satisfaction [Rieser and Schlangen, 2011], [Baumann, 2013].

However, implementing incremental processing is technically challenging, particularly in pipeline architectures where the output from one component is only sent to the next component when it is complete. In a system using incremental processing the data has to be processed partially and is subject to revision as a result of subsequent output. DeVault et al. [2009] presented a system that was able to generate a completion of a user's input based on the semantic representation it had built up so far. Schlangen and Skantze [2011] present a general, abstract model of incremental dialogue processing while Baumann [2013] provides a detailed discussion of architectural issues and models for incremental processing across the various components of a spoken dialogue system.

[8]Source: Lerner [1991].

In more recent work reinforcement learning was used to model incremental processing in a fast-paced dialogue game [Manuvinakurike et al., 2017]. See also Devault's Incremental Language Processing website[9] for recent publications and video demos, and the website of Anticipant.ai,[10] a company focused on developing advanced automated conversation and speech processing services.

Some open source software has been made available to developers wishing to implement incremental processing in their spoken dialogue systems. The INPROTK toolkit provides an architecture for incremental processing, including evaluation tools for analyzing timing behavior [Baumann and Schlangen, 2012]. Jindigo[11] is a framework for incremental dialogue systems that is being developed in Sweden at the KTH Royal Institute of Technology. Dylan (Dynamics of Language) is an implementation of dynamic syntax that uses a word-by-word incremental semantic grammar [Eshghi et al., 2012].

There has been little work on incremental processing for neural dialogue systems, which is surprising as neural dialogue systems encode their input on a token-by-token basis but have so far only been used to process completed utterances. Lison and Kennington [2017] created an incremental RNN-based neural model in which the input length was reduced to a single token that was combined with a fixed-size vector representing what had been processed so far in the dialogue. After each token a new vector was output that represented the updated dialogue state. By keeping the history of previous state vectors in memory until their words were confirmed, for example, by other components of the dialogue system, it was possible to go back to previous state vectors if the words needed to be revoked. The approach was tested in an experiment that showed that accuracy increased as more words were processed.

6.6.5 TURN-TAKING IN DIALOGUE

Turn-taking in current spoken dialogue systems is rigid. The system waits until it detects silence longer than a pre-specified threshold to decide that the user has finished speaking, while the user can barge in and terminate the system's output at any time. Turn-taking in human-human conversations operates differently as here the participants actively monitor the ongoing turn to predict its possible completion point, also known as the *transition-relevance place* [Sacks et al., 1978].

Predicting turn completion in interactions with spoken dialogue systems has been investigated in several studies with the aim of making the systems more natural. This is particularly important for interactions with social robots and avatars that are endowed with human-like behaviors. Gravano and Hirschberg [2011] identified specific acoustic and linguistic cues that correlate strongly with the prediction of turn completion points and that can be computed automatically. They also found that turn changing was more likely to occur the greater the number

[9] http://djdsite.org/incremental.html
[10] http://anticipant.ai/
[11] http://www.speech.kth.se/jindigo/

of turn-yielding cues in the ongoing turn. In a similar vein, Raux and Eskenazi [2012] treated turn completion prediction as decision making under uncertainty and developed a Finite-State Turn-Taking Machine (FSTTM) that they evaluated on the CMU Let's Go! dataset (see Section 5.8.1), finding that the FSTTM helped to improve the system's responsiveness.

Roddy et al. [2018] used RNNs to model turn-taking in a continuous manner to predict probability scores for speech features in a future time window. The models outperformed previously reported baselines. This work was extended by Skantze [2017] using an LSTM RNN to predict turn-taking, showing that the model could be extended to other tasks that it was not trained for, i.e., predicting whether a turn change will occur during a pause in the ongoing turn, and predicting at the beginning of a turn whether it will be a longer utterance or a back-channel, i.e., an utterance such as *uhhuh* that gives feedback but is not an attempt to take the floor. It was found in these tasks that the model achieved better performance than human subjects.

Turn-taking in multi-party dialogues brings the challenge of participants competing for the next turn, not knowing who is being addressed, and whether someone is being selected as next speaker. In addition to the verbal cues used in two-party dialogues, participants in multi-party conversations use various non-verbal cues such as gaze and gestures. Bohus and Horvitz [2010] conducted experiments to investigate the mechanisms used by an avatar to manage turn-taking, finding correlations among several variables including gaze, dialogue act type, previous speaker context, presence of deictic expressions, and elapsed time. Johansson and Skantze [2015] studied how a robot took turns in multi-party dialogues about objects. The aim of the study was to develop a data-driven model that the robot could use to decide whether to take a turn. Since the dialogue was about objects in the shared physical space, gaze was less relevant for managing turn-taking as it was also being used to focus on the objects being discussed, i.e., cards in a collaborative card sorting game. The best results were achieved when several modalities were combined that included voice activity, syntax, prosody, head pose, movement of cards, and dialogue context. See also Skantze et al. [2015].

Current research at Amazon Alexa AI is addressing some of the issues discussed here. Among the features announced in September 2020 for the new Amazon Alexa Show 10 is natural turn-taking.[12] Natural turn-taking, which is due to become available in 2021, will make conversations with Alexa more natural.[13] Recall that in multi-party conversations one of the main problems for an AI conversational agent such as Alexa is to know when speech is being directed toward them and when not, also who was speaking and who is to be addressed next. The new technology, known as multi-sensory AI, addresses this problem by combining acoustic, linguistic, and visual information and feeding it into a fusion model.[14]

- Acoustic cues help to distinguish ambient sounds from human speech using sound source localization (SSL).

[12] https://blog.aboutamazon.com/devices/ai-advances-make-alexa-more-natural-conversational-and-useful
[13] https://www.amazon.science/blog/change-to-alexa-wake-word-process-adds-natural-turn-taking
[14] https://www.amazon.science/blog/the-science-behind-echo-show-10

- Linguistic cues help to distinguish between questions that are likely to have been addressed to Alexa as opposed to those addressed to another human user.
- Visual cues, based on information from computer vision (CV) algorithms, identify humans and objects in the field of vision and determine whether people are looking at each other or at the device.

It will be interesting to see how well these exciting new features work when they are released and used by the general public and whether they will help to make conversations with Alexa more engaging and more natural.

6.7 HYBRID DIALOGUE SYSTEMS

Throughout this book, rule-based, statistical data-driven, and neural dialogue approaches have been presented as distinct and apparently mutually exclusive approaches in dialogue technology. However, there have been various efforts to develop hybrid approaches that leverage the best from each approach.

Selecting a dialogue strategy in rule-based systems requires detailed handcrafting, while statistical approaches require large amounts of data to learn a dialogue policy. Statistical approaches also suffer from the problem of dimensionality in large state-action spaces. One approach to this problem was to combine optimization of dialogue policies using RL with knowledge from experts [Heeman, 2007], [Williams, 2008]. This idea was taken further by Lison [2015] who developed a hybrid approach using probabilistic rules integrated into the statistical model. These rules were defined as structured mappings between logical conditions and probabilistic effects. In this way a system designer is able to express the internal structure of a dialogue domain in a set of rules that encode expert domain knowledge. The approach was investigated in an experiment in which it was found that the framework with probabilistic rules outperformed rule-based and statistical approaches on a range of subjective and objective metrics. The framework has been implemented in the OpenDial toolkit[15] [Lison and Kennington, 2016].

End-to-end neural dialogue systems often suffer from issues such as generating repetitive and generic utterances and lacking commonsense. Incorporating rules and knowledge into end-to-end systems is a way to address these issues. Razumovskaia and Eskenazi [2019] incorporated rules into the encoding of the dialogue context, finding that this produced more diverse output in comparisons with baseline systems. Madotto et al. [2018] addressed the issue of incorporating knowledge bases into task-oriented end-to-end neural dialogue systems using a memory-to-sequence (Mem2Seq) model in which words from the dialogue history or knowledge bases are inserted into the encoder and read by the decoder to generate a response. The Mem2Seq model showed state-of-the art performance on three task-oriented dialogue datasets. Liang et al. [2020] used a hybrid approach to the problem of data sparseness by incorporating information from the NLU, DM, and NLG components into an encoder-decoder architecture.

[15]The toolkit and its documentation are available at http://opendial-toolkit.net.

Trained on reduced amounts of data the model outperformed state-of-the-art models on the CamRest676 dataset [Wen et al., 2017].

Hybrid approaches are likely to feature strongly in future research as attention focuses on how to incorporate external knowledge, address intelligent behaviors such as collaborative problem solving, and model interactions in situated environments. In these cases advanced forms of representation are required that cannot easily be integrated into systems that learn purely from datasets of dialogues.

6.8 DIALOGUE WITH SOCIAL ROBOTS

There are several different types of robot. Service robots perform automated tasks in industries such as car manufacture but generally they do not have the ability to communicate. WITAS[16] is an exception. WITAS is a small robotic helicopter that can be controlled in a dialogue with human operators to carry out activities that it could not otherwise complete on its own. Lemon et al. [2002] developed a dialogue context model that could support multi-tasking and collaborative planning with WITAS in a robust and flexible way.

Social robots are designed specifically to engage in communication with humans. Social robots can be found in many places such as supermarkets, museums, airports, schools, and homes. For example, the Pepper and Nao robots are being used in schools to help students develop problem solving and analytical skills and develop and improve social and emotional skills.[17] They can also offer help to customers by describing services in stores, in schools they can be used as teaching tools, and in homes they can provide companionship to elderly users [Nap et al., 2018], [Casaccia et al., 2019].

Social robots also provide insight into the nature of face-to-face interaction in situated dialogues that take place in a physical environment and involve a combination of verbal and non-verbal behaviors. Skantze et al. [2019] investigated the role of non-verbal signals such as gaze and head movements in the coordination of conversation, looking in particular at how they affect turn-taking, the grounding of referring expressions, and ways to establish joint attention. Detection of engagement during conversations is a focus of study with the social robot Erica [Lala et al., 2017], [Kawahara, 2018]. Here the aim is to develop a human-like conversational robot that can engage in activities such as attentive listening, displaying backchannels, fillers, laughter, using nonverbal behaviors such as gaze, head movement, and gestures. Models of these behaviors were learned from a large corpus of interactions between humans and Erica.[18]

Nonverbal behaviors such as gestures were also incorporated into the Nao robot as a means of enhancing and exploring communication between humans and social robots [Jokinen and Wilcock, 2014]. Jokinen [2018] presents an architecture that supports the conversational abilities of social robots. In this architecture the social robot operates in two different environments:

[16] https://www.ida.liu.se/ext/witas/

[17] https://www.softbankrobotics.com/emea/en/pepper-and-nao-robots-education

[18] This video shows examples of Erica's conversational behaviors: https://youtu.be/TyJ-xLj9SEE.

- A *micro environment* in which the social robot engages as an agent in face-to-face communication that requires multimodal capabilities.
- A *macro environment* in which the social robot acts like a computer system to access large, dynamic data sources on the web and process information from sensors in the environment.

By being able to act in both these environments social robots can potentially provide a unique conversational experience based on human-like interaction and supported by a rich source of information from the environment in the form of ontologies or knowledge graphs that may contain information about relationships between entities, actions, and activities. Jokinen et al. [2019] describe how a social robot can draw on information about actions and activities in an ontology to explain a correct sequence of actions. The social robot in this example is helping with the care of senior citizens and explains to a new care worker how to change the position of the elderly patient, taking into account the actions required that are represented as tasks and sub-tasks in the ontology.

For further information on social robots and dialogue, see the collections of readings in Mariani et al. [2014] and Jokinen and Wilcock [2017]. Devillers et al. [2020] is a collection of papers from the 2020 Dagstuhl workshop that focused on effective and ethical interactions in spoken dialogues with virtual agents and robots.

6.9 DIALOGUE AND THE INTERNET OF THINGS

There is an ever-increasing number of devices in smart homes, smart offices and other environments to control heating, lights, alarms, and monitor physical aspects of the user such as location, heart rate, etc. These devices are typically connected to the internet, creating a network known as the Internet of Things (IoT). In most cases each device has its own app, but sometimes there is a central controller that integrates the apps.

Dialogue systems provide a more natural interface to devices in IoT. This is still an emerging area and as yet there are few implemented systems. The following example, developed at Samsung Electronics, describes the sorts of interactions that an intelligent dialogue agent could support in an IoT home and what components are required for such a dialogue system [Jeon et al., 2016].

The system was implemented and tested in a real IoT home environment. The most frequent requests were utterances such as *turn on the light*, *turn off the TV in 30 minutes*, and *what's the weather like today?*. These utterances were interpreted by the Spoken Language Understanding component and converted by the Action Planner into a plan in the form of a task tree.

Table 6.2 shows examples of some plans. In the first scenario the Action Planner chooses an external speaker as it offers better sound quality than the TV's internal speaker. In the second scenario it makes an inference from its common sense ontology in the system's knowledge base resulting in a suggestion that the window should be closed if the air conditioning is to be turned on.

Table 6.2: Plans generated by the Action Planner. Source: Jeon et al. [2016, Table 5].

Task	Examples of Planning
Play movie	turn on TV -> choose video content -> set display mode -> turn on external speaker -> connect TV to speaker -> set sound mode -> dim light -> play video
Make it cool	turn on air conditioner -> set cooling mode -> close the window (suggestion)

The Things Manager, which maintains information about each device and monitors the state of the devices, converts the plan from the Action Planner into commands suitable for individual IoT devices. The Things Manager also receives information from the external environment, such as the weather forecast, that could be used to inform the user. Other components are the IoT Control Platform which manages the IoT devices and communicates with the Things Manager about the state of each device; the Context Manager which engages with the external environment, disambiguates requests for actions that are unclear, and locates the required IoT device using contextual information and a context reasoning mechanism; and Knowledge Bases that store personal information about the user and their preferences, as well as a Things ontology that contains information about devices in the smart home.

The dialogue control is mixed initiative, so that in addition to accepting requests from the user to perform some action, the system can initiate a dialogue when it is notified of some event, for example, that the washing machine has completed its cycle.

In this example the dialogue system is supported by a complex set of components to plan and carry out actions using a natural interface to devices in an IoT environment. However, dialogue systems can offer additional functionalities—for example, engaging in clarification dialogues to help recovery from errors caused by misrecognitions and misunderstandings. The following are interactions with a dialogue system in a smart home environment as envisaged by Georgila et al. [2019]. In Example 6.4 the user's request is underspecified and the system makes a clarification request.

Example 6.4

USER1: Play music in ten minutes.
SYSTEM1: In which room shall I play music?
USER2: Bedroom please.

In Example 6.5 the user wants the air-conditioner to be turned on in 10 minutes but the user's request is ambiguous and is misinterpreted by the system.

Example 6.5

USER1: Please turn on the air-conditioner there too.
SYSTEM1: Okay, the air-conditioner in the bedroom is now on.
USER2: Wait, I want the air-conditioner on in 10 minutes, not now.

These examples illustrate the types of situation that an intelligent dialogue system for smart environments needs to be able to handle.

6.10 SOCIAL AND ETHICAL ISSUES

In March 2016, Microsoft launched the chatbot Tay and took it down 16 hours later. Tay was posting offensive tweets in its Twitter account that it had learned from the tweets of some of its users. As a result of this experience researchers in Conversational AI have been alerted to the dangers of dialogue systems learning inappropriate behaviors from interactions with users. Other issues include bias in the data used by machine learning algorithms, outputting fake news, and giving inaccurate or inappropriate advice. On the positive side, researchers are now focusing on issues such as AI for social good, with the aim of creating safer and better-behaved conversational AI models.

Dialogue systems that are available on platforms open to the general public have to deal with a wide variety of inputs. In addition to inputs that are difficult to handle from a technical point of view, as discussed throughout this book, there are also inputs that are offensive and inappropriate. Worswick [2018b] reports that 30% of the input to the chatbot Mitsuku consists of abusive messages, swearing, and sex talk. So-called sensitive content was also a major concern in the Alexa Prize challenges.

There are different ways to deal with inappropriate input. Worswick [2018b] found that a simple list of keywords was not effective as words such as *sex* can be used in a non-offensive way, e.g., *what sex are you?* The approach adopted with Mitsuku was to go through the chat logs to identify inappropriate content and then create AIML categories to handle them, such as diverting to another topic, or after a certain number of occurrences, banning that particular user.

In the Alexa Prize competitions the teams were able to make use of a sensitive content classifier that was provided by the Alexa developers as part of the Cobot toolkit. The teams also implemented their own strategies. For example, if the Alana socialbot detected abusive content, like Mitsuku it attempted to direct the dialogue in a different direction, for example, by changing the topic, appealing to some external authority, or chastising the user [Curry and Rieser, 2018]. Detecting profanity, which accounted for 5% of interactions, involved training an embedding-based abuse detection model that achieved precision of 0.98 on non-abusive content, 0.84 on abusive content, and 1.00 on sexual/hate content.

Preventing offensive output by the socialbots was also a major concern in the Alexa Prize as the socialbots were trained from publicly available data sources such as Reddit and Twitter that contain large amounts of sensitive content. Khatri et al. [2018a] describe how high confidence sensitive and non-sensitive comments were sampled on a classifier and then used to train and fine-tune a Bidirectional Long Short-Term Memory (BiLSTM) classifier that achieved accuracy of 96% and an F1 score of 95.5%. It was found that using a blacklist of offensive words did not scale well and often resulted in false positives. The Alana socialbot included in its ensemble of bots a Profanity bot. When selecting a response to a user's input a Priority list was used in which the Profanity bot was first in the list [Cercas Curry et al., 2018].

In other work, Curry and Rieser [2019] conducted a crowd-based evaluation of abuse response strategies in conversational systems finding that strategies such as "polite refusal" scored highly. Curry and Rieser [2018] examined the responses of commercial systems to inappropriate content such as bullying and sexual harassment. They collected and annotated a corpus of data (the #MeTooAlexa corpus) based on around 370,000 conversations from the Alexa Prize 2017 and from 11 state-of-the-art systems. Analysis of the corpus found that rule-based systems tended to use deflection strategies, as with Mitsuku, while data-driven systems were often non-coherent or responded in a way that could be interpreted as flirtatious or aggressive. In many cases the systems were trained on "clean" data, which suggests that these inappropriate behaviors were not due to bias in the training data.

Bias is a related issue in Conversational AI and in machine learning in general. A recent UNESCO report revealed that most voice-based conversational assistants on smartphones and smart speakers are female, which can reinforce gender stereotypes of women as submissive and acting in subordinate roles [West et al., 2019]. Maedche [2020] investigated gender-specific cues in the design of 1,375 chatbots listed on the chatbots.org platform.[19] They found that most chatbots had female names, if they had avatars they were female-looking, and they were described as being female.

In addition to issues associated with design that can be easily addressed, there is the problem of bias in training data. This can arise from gaps in the training data, for example, a lack of diversity that excludes females, people of color, and people from different religious and cultural backgrounds. Bias can also be introduced unintentionally by annotators. Bias in Conversational AI is being addressed by the Conversation AI Research Github Organization.[20]

Other relevant issues include the use of bots to spread fake news and disinformation [Gomez-Perez et al., 2020]; the need for explanation in AI to engender trust and transparency [Kuksenok, 2019], [Mueller et al., 2019]; and issues of patient and consumer safety, especially in dialogue systems designed for domains such as healthcare and mental well-being. For example, Miner et al. [2016] investigated the responses of several smartphone-based conversational agents to critical inputs such as *I was raped* and found that several of the popular agents output responses such as *I don't understand what you mean by "I was raped". How about a web search for it?* Similar concerns have been expressed regarding the inability of current dialogue systems

[19] https://chatbots.org/
[20] https://conversationai.github.io/bias.html

to correctly interpret user inputs in critical healthcare conversations and to generate appropriate and helpful responses [Bickmore et al., 2018a], [Bickmore et al., 2018b].

Given these concerns some initiatives have been launched to address issues of safety and interactional behaviors in dialogue systems. The Safety for Conversational Workshop[21] brought together experts from industry and academia to discuss how to improve conversational models in neural dialogue systems.

A related issue is how to develop dialogue systems for social good. Based on research in persuasion in the social sciences, Wang et al. [2019] developed intelligent persuasive conversational agents that could change people's opinions and actions for social good. A large dataset of 1,017 dialogues was collected and annotated and used as a baseline classifier to predict 10 different persuasion strategies that were used in the corpus and to determine which types of persuasion strategy were more successful in a task where one participant was asked to persuade the other to donate to a charity. The strategy that showed the most positive effect on the donation outcome was "Donation Information", which gives the person being persuaded step-by-step instructions on how to donate.

Given that persuasion can be used for evil as well as good causes, the authors raise various ethical concerns such as: which scenarios are appropriate for the use of automated persuasion; the need to keep users informed of the role of the dialogue system; giving the users the option to communicate directly with the humans behind the system; and developing procedures to monitor the responses generated by the system to ensure that they are appropriate and comply with ethical standards.

Summarizing, while there are many technical challenges that remain to be addressed in Conversational AI, there are also social and ethical issues to be considered that are particularly pertinent as conversational agents become more human-like to the extent that they engender engagement and trust in human users.

6.11 THE WAY AHEAD

What capabilities should future dialogue systems have to enable them to engage in truly human-like dialogues? One way to answer this is to examine the Apple Knowledge Navigator video[22] that was produced in 1987 by Apple to be used in a keynote by the then CEO John Sculley. The video was intended to be seen as a realistic vision of what would be feasible at some time in the future.

In the video a university professor returns home and turns on his computer to be greeted by his Personal Digital Assistant (PDA). The PDA appears on the screen and informs the professor that he has several messages and some events on his calendar. The professor engages in a dialogue with the PDA to collect data for an upcoming lecture.

[21] https://safetyforconvai.splashthat.com/
[22] https://youtu.be/umJsITGzXd0

Some of the behaviors of the PDA are possible today, for example, informing about messages, missed calls, and upcoming calendar events. The professor asks the PDA to show some pictures, e.g., *show only universities with geography nodes* and *show Brazil*. Voice search for textual and visual data is also possible with current dialogue systems on smartphones and smart speakers with visual displays.

Consider, however, this interaction in which the professor (Prof) asks the PDA for specific data for his lecture.

Example 6.6

PDA1: You have a lecture at 4.15 on deforestation in the Amazon rainforest.
PROF1: Let me see the lecture notes from last semester.

PDA retrieves the lecture notes and displays them.

PROF2: No that's not enough.
PROF3: I need to review more recent literature.
PROF4: Pull up all the new articles I haven't read yet.
PDA2: Journal articles only?
PROF5: Mm-hmm.
PDA3: Your friend Jill Gilbert has published an article about deforestation in the Amazon and its effect on rainfall in the sub-Sahara, it also covers droughts effect on food production in Africa and increasing imports of food.
PROF6: Contact Jill.
PDA4: She's not available

Some parts of this scenario are possible today, such as asking to call someone (PROF6) and being told that they are not available (PDA4), also finding a particular type of document, i.e., journal article, and reading out its description (PDA3). Other parts are more challenging. For example, retrieving the lecture notes from last semester (PROF1) is underspecified and can only be understood correctly if the PDA maintains the context of the topic of the upcoming lecture (PDA1). The phrase *more recent literature* is also problematic as it involves resolving the expression *more recent* to retrieve documents later than the date of those retrieved. Finally, pulling up documents that the professor hasn't read yet requires a user model that contains a list of what the professor has read in this area and omitting them from the list of recent and new articles.

Most of these challenges affect the Natural Language Understanding (NLU) component, not so much in terms of understanding literal content but more in terms of interpreting discourse phenomena such as underspecified reference. Current NLU systems require input that is more specific and explicit in order for the system to be able to locate the requested items in its search.

In summary, examining the Knowledge Navigator shows how far Conversational AI has come but also what has still to be achieved.

SUMMARY

This chapter has examined some future directions for research in dialogue systems. Ten different challenges were reviewed: dealing with multimodality; visual dialogue that requires integration of information from Computer Vision with textual descriptions; learning from sparse data; using external knowledge; reasoning and engaging in collaborative problem solving; dealing with a range of discourse and dialogue phenomena, such as coreference, topic handling, multiparty dialogues, incremental processing, and turn-taking; developing hybrid architectures; supporting interactions with social robots and in situated contexts; and dealing with social and ethical issues.

Given these challenges there is still much work ahead for researchers in Conversational AI toward the goal of the ultimate intelligent dialogue system.

APPENDIX A

Toolkits for Developing Dialogue Systems

TOOLKITS THAT DO NOT REQUIRE CODING

Botmock	https://botmock.com/
Botpress	https://botpress.com/
Botsify	https://botsify.com/
Botsociety	https://botsociety.io/
Chatbase	https://chatbase.com/
Chatfuel	http://chatfuel.com/
Chatlayer	http://chatlayer.ai/
Dashbot	https://www.dashbot.io/
Engati	https://www.engati.com/
Flow.ai	https://flow.ai/
FlowXO	https://flowxo.com/
Gutshup	https://www.gupshup.io/developer/home
HubSpot	https://www.hubspot.com/products/crm/chatbot-builder
ManyChat	https://manychat.com
MobileMonkey	https://mobilemonkey.com/
Morph.ai	https://morph.ai/
Octane AI	https://octaneai.com/
Sequel	https://www.onsequel.com/
Voiceflow	https://www.voiceflow.com/

TOOLKITS FOR SCRIPTING DIALOGUE SYSTEMS

Botkit	https://botkit.ai/getstarted.html
Chatscript	http://chatscript.sourceforge.net/
Pandorabots	https://home.pandorabots.com/home.html/

ADVANCED COMMERCIAL TOOLKITS

Amazon Alexa Skills	https://developer.amazon.com/en-US/alexa/alexa-skills-kit/
Amazon Lex	https://aws.amazon.com/lex/
DialogFlow	https://cloud.google.com/dialogflow/
Facebook Messenger Platform	https://developers.facebook.com/docs/messenger-platform
Haptik Conversational AI Toolkit	https://haptik.ai/technology/
IBM Watson Assistant	https://www.ibm.com/cloud/watson-assistant/
Microsoft Bot Framework	https://dev.botframework.com/
Oracle Digital Assistant	https://www.oracle.com/solutions/chatbots/
Rasa	https://rasa.com/
SAP Conversational AI	https://www.sap.com/products/conversational-ai.html
Teneo (Artificial Solutions)	https://www.teneo.ai/
Wit.ai	https://wit.ai/

RESEARCH TOOLKITS

ConvLab	https://github.com/ConvLab/ConvLab
DeepPavlov	http://deeppavlov.ai/
Olympus	http://wiki.speech.cs.cmu.edu/olympus/index.php/Olympus
OpenDial	https://github.com/plison/opendial
ParlAI (Facebook AI Research)	https://github.com/facebookresearch/ParlAI
Plato (Uber AI)	https://eng.uber.com/plato-research-dialogue-system/
Pydial	https://bitbucket.org/dialoguesystems/pydial/src/master/
Virtual Human Toolkit	https://vhtoolkit.ict.usc.edu/

Bibliography

Daniel Adiwardana, Minh-Thang Luong, David R. So, Jamie Hall, Noah Fiedel, Romal Thoppilan, Zi Yang, Apoorv Kulshreshtha, Gaurav Nemade, Yifeng Lu, and Quoc V. Le. Towards a human-like open-domain chatbot. *ArXiv Preprint ArXiv:2001.09977*, 2020. 21, 35, 39, 106, 141

Shubham Agarwal, Ondřej Dušek, Ioannis Konstas, and Verena Rieser. Improving context modelling in multimodal dialogue generation. In *Proc. of the 11th International Conference on Natural Language Generation*, pages 129–134, Association for Computational Linguistics, Tilburg University, The Netherlands, November 2018. https://www.aclweb.org/anthology/W18-6514 DOI: 10.18653/v1/w18-6514 161, 162

Hua Ai and Diane Litman. Assessing dialog system user simulation evaluation measures using human judges. In *Proc. of ACL-08: HLT*, pages 622–629, 2008. https://www.aclweb.org/anthology/P08-1071 95

Hua Ai, Antoine Raux, Dan Bohus, Maxine Eskenazi, and Diane Litman. Comparing spoken dialog corpora collected with recruited subjects versus real users. In *Proc. of the 8th SIGdial Workshop on Discourse and Dialogue*, pages 124–131, September 2007. https://www.sigdial.org/files/workshops/workshop8/Proceedings/SIGdial23.pdf 93

Rahul P. Akolkar. Beyond the form interpretation algorithm: Towards flexible dialog management for conversational voice and multi-modal applications. In *Proc. of Workshop on Conversational Applications—Use Cases and Requirements for New Models of Human Language to Support Mobile Conversational Systems*, June 2010. https://www.w3.org/2010/02/convapps/Papers/ConvApps10.pdf 67

Samer Al Moubayed, Jonas Beskow, Gabriel Skantze, and Björn Granström. Furhat: A back-projected human-like robot head for multiparty human-machine interaction. In Anna Esposito, Antonietta M. Esposito, Alessandro Vinciarelli, Rüdiger Hoffmann, and Vincent Müller, Eds., *Cognitive Behavioural Systems: COST International Training School*, pages 114–130, Springer, Berlin, Heidelberg, 2012. DOI: 10.1007/978-3-642-34584-5_9 12, 23

Jan Alexandersson, Ralf Engel, Michael Kipp, Stephan Koch, Uwe Küssner, Norbert Reithinger, and Manfred Stede. Modeling negotiation dialogs. In Wolfgang Wahlster, Ed., *Verbmobil: Foundations of Speech-to-Speech Translation*, pages 441–451, Springer Berlin Heidelberg, Berlin, Heidelberg, 2000. DOI: 10.1007/978-3-662-04230-4_32 152

James Allen. *Natural Language Understanding*. Pearson, 1995. 16

James Allen, Elisabeth André, Philip R. Cohen, Dilek Hakkani-Tür, Ronald Kaplan, Oliver Lemon, and David Traum. Challenge discussion: Advancing multimodal dialogue. In Sharon Oviatt, Björn Schuller, Philip R. Cohen, Daniel Sonntag, Gerasimos Potamianos, and Antonio Krüger, Eds., *The Handbook of Multimodal-Multisensor Interfaces: Language Processing, Software, Commercialization, and Emerging Directions-Volume 3*, pages 191–217, Association for Computing Machinery (ACM) and Morgan & Claypool, 2019. DOI: 10.1145/3233795.3233802 169

James F. Allen and Mark Core. *Draft of DAMSL: Dialog Act Markup in Several Layers*. The Multiparty Discourse Group, University of Rochester, Rochester, 1997. http://www.cs.rochester.edu/research/cisd/resources/damsl/RevisedManual/ 48

James F. Allen and C. Raymond Perrault. Analyzing intention in utterances. *Artificial Intelligence*, 15(3):143–178, 1980. DOI: 10.1016/0004-3702(80)90042-9 16, 169

James F. Allen, Donna K. Byron, Myroslava Dzikovska, George Ferguson, Lucian Galescu, and Amanda Stent. Toward conversational human-computer interaction. *AI Magazine*, 22(4):27–38, 2001. DOI: 10.1609/aimag.v22i4.1590 16

Elisabeth André and Catherine Pelachaud. Interacting with embodied conversational agents. In Fang Chen and Kristiina Jokinen, Eds., *Speech Technology*, pages 123–149, Springer, 2010. DOI: 10.1007/978-0-387-73819-2_8 22

Elisabeth André, Matthias Rehm, Wolfgang Minker, and Dirk Bühler. Endowing spoken language dialogue systems with emotional intelligence. In *Tutorial and Research Workshop on Affective Dialogue Systems*, pages 178–187, Springer, 2004. DOI: 10.1007/978-3-540-24842-2_17 149

Nabiha Asghar, Pascal Poupart, Jesse Hoey, Xin Jiang, and Lili Mou. Affective neural response generation. In *European Conference on Information Retrieval*, pages 154–166, Springer, 2018. https://arxiv.org/abs/1709.03968 DOI: 10.1007/978-3-319-76941-7_12 149

John Langshaw Austin. *How to do Things with Words*. Oxford University Press, 1962. DOI: 10.1093/acprof:oso/9780198245537.001.0001 15

Dzmitry Bahdanau, Kyunghyun Cho, and Yoshua Bengio. Neural machine translation by jointly learning to align and translate. *ArXiv Preprint ArXiv:1409.0473*, 2014. 126, 136

Tadas Baltrušaitis, Chaitanya Ahuja, and Louis-Philippe Morency. Challenges and applications in multimodal machine learning. In Sharon Oviatt, Björn Schuller, Philip R. Cohen, Daniel

Sonntag, Gerasimos Potamianos, and Antonio Krüger, Eds., *The Handbook of Multimodal-Multisensor Interfaces: Signal Processing, Architectures, and Detection of Emotion and Cognition-Volume 2*, pages 17–48, Association for Computing Machinery (ACM) and Morgan & Claypool, 2018. DOI: 10.1145/3107990.3107993 161

Rafael E. Banchs. Movie-dic: A movie dialogue corpus for research and development. In *Proc. of the 50th Annual Meeting of the Association for Computational Linguistics: Short Papers - Volume 2, ACL*, pages 203–207, Association for Computational Linguistics, 2012. https://www.aclweb.org/anthology/P12-204 105, 153

Rachel Batish. *Voicebot and Chatbot Design: Flexible Conversational Interfaces with Amazon Alexa, Google Home, and Facebook Messenger*. Packt Publishing Ltd., 2018. 26, 40

T. Baumann and D. Schlangen. The inprotk 2012 release: A toolkit for incremental spoken dialogue processing. In *Speech Communication; 10. ITG Symposium*, pages 1–4, 2012. 173

Timo Baumann. Incremental spoken dialogue processing: Architecture and lower-level components. Ph.D. thesis, Angewandte Computerlinguistik, Germany, 2013. https://pub.uni-bielefeld.de/record/2581910 172

Samy Bengio, Hanna M. Wallach, Hugo Larochelle, Kristen Grauman, Nicolò Cesa-Bianchi, and Roman Garnet, Eds. *NIPS'18: Proc. of the 32nd International Conference on Neural Information Processing Systems*, Curran Associates Inc., Red Hook, NY, 2018. 158

Christina Bennett and Alexander I. Rudnicky. The Carnegie Mellon communicator corpus. In *Proc. of the 7th International Conference on Spoken Language Processing (ICSLP)*, pages 341–344, International Speech Communication Association, Denver, CO, September 2002. https://www.isca-speech.org/archive/icslp_2002/i02_0341.html 151

Nicole Beringer, Ute Kartal, Katerina Louka, Florian Schiel, Uli Türk, and Uli Trk. Promise: A procedure for multimodal interactive system evaluation. In *Proc. of the LREC Workshop on Multimodal Resources and Multimodal Systems Evaluation*, pages 77–80, Las Palmas, Spain, 2002. 114

Timothy Bickmore and Justine Cassell. Social dialongue with embodied conversational agents. In Jan van Kuppevelt, Laila Dybkjær, and Niels Ole Bernsen, Eds., *Advances in Natural Multimodal Dialogue Systems*, pages 23–54, Springer, 2005. DOI: 10.1007/1-4020-3933-6_2 22

Timothy Bickmore, Ha Trinh, Reza Asadi, and Stefan Olafsson. Safety first: Conversational agents for health care. In Robert J. Moore, Margaret H. Szymanski, Raphael Arar, and Guang-Jie Ren, Eds., *Studies in Conversational UX Design*, Springer International Publishing, 2018a. DOI: 10.1007/978-3-319-95579-7_3 181

Timothy W. Bickmore, Ha Trinh, Stefan Olafsson, Teresa K. O'Leary, Reza Asadi, Nathaniel M. Rickles, and Ricardo Cruz. Patient and consumer safety risks when using conversational assistants for medical information: An observational study of Siri, Alexa, and Google assistant. *Journal of Medical Internet Research (JMIR)*, 20(9):e11510, September 2018b. http://www.jmir.org/2018/9/e11510/ DOI: 10.2196/11510 181

Alan W. Black and Keiichi Tokuda. The blizzard challenge-2005: evaluating corpus-based speech synthesis on common datasets. In *9th European Conference on Speech Communication and Technology*, 2005. https://www.isca-speech.org/archive/interspeech_2005/i05_0077.html 100

Alan W. Black, Susanne Burger, Alistair Conkie, Helen Hastie, Simon Keizer, Oliver Lemon, Nicolas Merigaud, Gabriel Parent, Gabriel Schubiner, Blaise Thomson, Jason D. Williams, Kai Yu, Steve Young, and Maxine Eskenazi. Spoken dialog challenge 2010: Comparison of live and control test results. In *Proc. of the SIGDIAL Conference*, pages 2–7, Association for Computational Linguistics, Portland, OR, June 2011. https://www.aclweb.org/anthology/W11-2002/ 84, 92, 93

Daniel G. Bobrow, Ronald M. Kaplan, Martin Kay, Donald A. Norman, Henry S. Thompson, and Terry Winograd. Gus, a frame-driven dialog system. *Artificial Intelligence*, 8:155–173, 1977. DOI: 10.1016/0004-3702(77)90018-2 14

Dan Bohus. Error awareness and recovery in conversational spoken language interfaces. Ph.D. Thesis, Computer Science, 2007. 17

Dan Bohus and Eric Horvitz. Facilitating multiparty dialog with gaze, gesture, and speech. In Wen Gao, Chin-Hui Lee, Jie Yang, Xilin Chen, Maxine Eskénazi, and Zhengyou Zhang, Eds., *International Conference on Multimodal Interfaces and the Workshop on Machine Learning for Multimodal Interaction*, pages 1–8, November 2010. DOI: 10.1145/1891903.1891910 174

Dan Bohus and Eric Horvitz. Situated interaction. In *The Handbook of Multimodal-Multisensor Interfaces: Language Processing, Software, Commercialization, and Emerging Directions-Volume 3*, pages 105–143, Association for Computing Machinery (ACM) and Morgan & Claypool, 2019. DOI: 10.1145/3233795.3233800 160

Dan Bohus and Alexander I. Rudnicky. The RavenClaw dialog management framework: Architecture and systems. *Computer Speech & Language*, 23(3):332–361, 2009. DOI: 10.1016/j.csl.2008.10.001 16

Piotr Bojanowski, Edouard Grave, Armand Joulin, and Tomas Mikolov. Enriching word vectors with subword information. *Transactions of the Association for Computational Linguistics*, 5:135–146, 2017. https://www.aclweb.org/anthology/Q17-1010 DOI: 10.1162/tacl_a_00051 130

Antoine Bordes and Jason Weston. Learning end-to-end goal-oriented dialog. *ArXiv Preprint ArXiv:1605.07683*, 2016. 138, 152, 154

Johan Bos, Ewan Klein, Oliver Lemon, and Tetsushi Oka. DIPPER: Description and formalisation of an information-state update dialogue system architecture. In *Proc. of the 4th SIGdial Workshop of Discourse and Dialogue*, pages 115–124, 2003. https://www.aclweb.org/anthology/W03-2123 18

Michael Brady and Robert C. Berwick. *Computational Models of Discourse*. MIT Press, 1983. 65, 170

Tom B. Brown, Benjamin Mann, Nick Ryder, Melanie Subbiah, Jared Kaplan, Prafulla Dhariwal, Arvind Neelakantan, Pranav Shyam, Girish Sastry, Amanda Askell, Sandhini Agarwal, Ariel Herbert-Voss, Gretchen Krueger, Tom Henighan, Rewon Child, Aditya Ramesh, Daniel M. Ziegler, Jeffrey Wu, Clemens Winter, Christopher Hesse, Mark Chen, Eric Sigler, Mateusz Litwin, Scott Gray, Benjamin Chess, Jack Clark, Christopher Berner, Sam McCandlish, Alec Radford, Ilya Sutskever, and Dario Amodei. Language models are few-shot learners. *ArXiv Preprint ArXiv:2005.14165*, 2020. 144, 145

Paweł Budzianowski, Tsung-Hsien Wen, Bo-Hsiang Tseng, I nigo Casanueva, Stefan Ultes, Osman Ramadan, and Milica Gašić. MultiWOZ—a large-scale multi-domain wizard-of-Oz dataset for task-oriented dialogue modelling. In *Proc. of the Conference on Empirical Methods in Natural Language Processing*, pages 5016–5026, Association for Computational Linguistics, Brussels, Belgium, October–November 2018. https://www.aclweb.org/anthology/D18-1547 DOI: 10.18653/v1/d18-1547 78, 152

Harry Bunt, Volha Petukhova, David Traum, and Jan Alexandersson. Dialogue act annotation with the ISO 24617-2 standard. In *Multimodal Interaction with W3C Standards*, pages 109–135, Springer, 2017. DOI: 10.1007/978-3-319-42816-1_6 48

Rafael A. Calvo, Sidney D'Mello, Jonathan Matthew Gratch, and Arvid Kappas. *The Oxford Handbook of Affective Computing*. Oxford University Press, 2015. DOI: 10.1093/oxfordhb/9780199942237.001.0001 149

Gillian Cameron, David Cameron, Gavin Megaw, Raymond Bond, Maurice Mulvenna, Siobhan O'Neill, Cherie Armour, and Michael McTear. Assessing the usability of a chatbot for mental health care. In *International Conference on Internet Science*, pages 121–132, Springer, 2018. DOI: 10.1007/978-3-030-17705-8_11 25

Sara Casaccia, Gian Marco Revel, Lorenzo Scalise, Roberta Bevilacqua, Lorena Rossi, Robert A. Paauwe, Irek Karkowsky, Ilaria Ercoli, J. Artur Serrano, Sandra Suijkerbuijk, Dirk Lukkien, and Henk Herman Nap. Social robot and sensor network in support of activity of daily living for people with dementia. In Rens Brankaert and Wijnand IJsselsteijn, Eds.,

Dementia Lab 2019. Making Design Work: Engaging with Dementia in Context, pages 128–135, Springer International Publishing, Cham, 2019. DOI: 10.1007/978-3-030-33540-3_12 176

Justine Cassell, Joseph Sullivan, Elizabeth Churchill, and Scott Prevost. *Embodied Conversational Agents*. MIT Press, 2000. DOI: 10.7551/mitpress/2697.001.0001 22

Thiago Castro Ferreira, Chris van der Lee, Emiel van Miltenburg, and Emiel Krahmer. Neural data-to-text generation: A comparison between pipeline and end-to-end architectures. In *Proc. of the Conference on Empirical Methods in Natural Language Processing and the 9th International Joint Conference on Natural Language Processing (EMNLP-IJCNLP)*, pages 552–562, Association for Computational Linguistics, Hong Kong, China, November 2019. https://www.aclweb.org/anthology/D19-1052 DOI: 10.18653/v1/d19-1052 81

Roberta Catizone, Andrea Setzer, and Yorick Wilks. Multimodal dialogue management in the comic project. In *Proc. of the EACL Workshop on Dialogue Systems: Interaction, Adaptation and Styles of Management*, 2003. 160

Asli Celikyilmaz, Li Deng, and Dilek Hakkani-Tür. Deep learning in spoken and text-based dialog systems. In Li Deng and Yang Liu, Eds., *Deep Learning in Natural Language Processing*, pages 49–78, Springer, 2018. DOI: 10.1007/978-981-10-5209-5_3 19, 158

Amanda Cercas Curry, Ioannis Papaioannou, Alessandro Suglia, Shubham Agarwal, Igor Shalyminov, Xu Xinnuo, Ondrej Dusek, Arash Eshghi, Ioannis Konstas, Verena Rieser, and Oliver Lemon. Alana v2: Entertaining and informative open-domain social dialogue using ontologies and entity linking. In *Alexa Prize Proceedings*, 2018. https://s3.amazonaws.com/dex-microsites-prod/alexaprize/2018/papers/Alana.pdf 38, 68, 69, 170, 180

Hongshen Chen, Xiaorui Liu, Dawei Yin, and Jiliang Tang. A survey on dialogue systems: Recent advances and new frontiers. *ACM Sigkdd Explorations Newsletter*, 19(2):25–35, 2017. DOI: 10.1145/3166054.3166058 13, 158

Kyunghyun Cho, Bart Van Merriënboer, Dzmitry Bahdanau, and Yoshua Bengio. On the properties of neural machine translation: Encoder-decoder approaches. *ArXiv Preprint ArXiv:1409.1259*, 2014a. DOI: 10.3115/v1/w14-4012 126, 136

Kyunghyun Cho, Bart Van Merriënboer, Caglar Gulcehre, Dzmitry Bahdanau, Fethi Bougares, Holger Schwenk, and Yoshua Bengio. Learning phrase representations using RNN encoder-decoder for statistical machine translation. *ArXiv Preprint ArXiv:1406.1078*, 2014b. DOI: 10.3115/v1/d14-1179 126, 135

Herbert H. Clark and Susan E. Brennan. Grounding in communication. In S. D. Teasley L. B. Resnick, J. M. Levine, Ed., *Perspectives on Socially Shared Cognition*, pages 127–149, American Psychological Association, 1991. DOI: 10.1037/10096-006 164

Kevin Clark and Christopher D. Manning. Improving coreference resolution by learning entity-level distributed representations. *ArXiv Preprint ArXiv:1606.01323*, 2016. DOI: 10.18653/v1/p16-1061 170

Michael H. Cohen, James P. Giangola, and Jennifer Balogh. *Voice User Interface Design*. Addison-Wesley Professional, 2004. 20

Philip R. Cohen. Back to the future—a position paper. In *Deep-Dial: The 2nd AAAI Workshop on Reasoning and Learning for Human-Machine Dialogues*, Association for the Advancement of Artificial Intelligence (AAAI), Hawaii, January 2019. https://arxiv.org/abs/1812.01144 169

Philip R. Cohen and Hector J. Levesque. Intention is choice with commitment. *Artificial Intelligence*, 42(2–3):213–261, 1990. DOI: 10.1016/0004-3702(90)90055-5 169

Philip R. Cohen and C. Raymond Perrault. Elements of a plan-based theory of speech acts. *Cognitive Science*, 3(3):177–212, 1979. DOI: 10.1016/S0364-0213(79)80006-3 16, 169

Ron Cole. Tools for research and education in speech science. In *Proc. of the International Conference of Phonetic Sciences*, 1:277–1, Citeseer, 1999. 18

Ronan Collobert and Jason Weston. A unified architecture for natural language processing: Deep neural networks with multitask learning. In *Proc. of the 25th International Conference on Machine Learning*, pages 160–167, 2008. DOI: 10.1145/1390156.1390177 76

Heriberto Cuayáhuitl, Steve Renals, Oliver Lemon, and Hiroshi Shimodaira. Human-computer dialogue simulation using hidden Markov models. In *IEEE Workshop on Automatic Speech Recognition and Understanding*, pages 290–295, IEEE, 2005. DOI: 10.1109/asru.2005.1566485 76

Heriberto Cuayáhuitl, Simon Keizer, and Oliver Lemon. Strategic dialogue management via deep reinforcement learning. *ArXiv Preprint ArXiv:1511.08099*, 2015. 87

Amanda Cercas Curry and Verena Rieser. #MeToo Alexa: How conversational systems respond to sexual harassment. In *Proc. of the 2nd ACL Workshop on Ethics in Natural Language Processing*, pages 7–14, Association for Computational Linguistics, New Orleans, LA, June 2018. https://www.aclweb.org/anthology/W18-0802 DOI: 10.18653/v1/w18-0802 179, 180

Amanda Cercas Curry and Verena Rieser. A crowd-based evaluation of abuse response strategies in conversational agents. *ArXiv Preprint ArXiv:1909.04387*, 2019. DOI: 10.18653/v1/w19-5942 180

Deborah A. Dahl. *Multimodal Interaction with W3C Standards*. Springer, 2017. DOI: 10.1007/978-3-319-42816-1 20, 22, 67

Morena Danieli and Elisabetta Gerbino. Metrics for evaluating dialogue strategies in a spoken language system. In *Proc. of the AAAI Spring Symposium on Empirical Methods in Discourse Interpretation and Generation*, 16:34–39, 1995. https://arxiv.org/abs/cmp-lg/9612003 115

Abhishek Das, Satwik Kottur, Khushi Gupta, Avi Singh, Deshraj Yadav, José M. F. Moura, Devi Parikh, and Dhruv Batra. Visual dialog. *ArXiv Preprint ArXiv:1611.08669*, 2017. 163

Harm de Vries, Florian Strub, Sarath Chandar, Olivier Pietquin, Hugo Larochelle, and Aaron C. Courville. Guesswhat?! visual object discovery through multi-modal dialogue. *ArXiv Preprint ArXiv:1611. 08481*, 2016. DOI: 10.1109/cvpr.2017.475 164

Harm de Vries, Kurt Shuster, Dhruv Batra, Devi Parikh, Jason Weston, and Douwe Kiela. Talk the walk: Navigating New York City through grounded dialogue. *ArXiv Preprint ArXiv: 1807.03367*, 2018. 163

Jan Deriu, Alvaro Rodrigo, Arantxa Otegi, Guillermo Echegoyen, Sophie Rosset, Eneko Agirre, and Mark Cieliebak. Survey on evaluation methods for dialogue systems. *Artificial Intelligence Review*, 2020. DOI: 10.1007/s10462-020-09866-x 91

David DeVault, Kenji Sagae, and David Traum. Can I finish? learning when to respond to incremental interpretation results in interactive dialogue. In *Proc. of the SIGDIAL Conference*, pages 11–20, Association for Computational Linguistics, London, UK, September 2009. https://www.aclweb.org/anthology/W09-3902 DOI: 10.3115/1708376.1708378 172

Laurence Devillers, Tatsuya Kawahara, Roger K. Moore, and Matthias Scheutz. Spoken language interaction with virtual agents and robots (SLIVAR): Towards effective and ethical interaction (Dagstuhl Seminar). *Dagstuhl Reports*, 10(1):1–51, 2020. https://drops.dagstuhl.de/opus/volltexte/2020/12400 DOI: 10.4230/DagRep.10.1.1 177

Jacob Devlin, Ming-Wei Chang, Kenton Lee, and Kristina Toutanova. Bert: Pre-training of deep bidirectional transformers for language understanding. *ArXiv Preprint ArXiv:1810.04805*, 2018. 130

Emily Dinan, Varvara Logacheva, Valentin Malykh, Alexander Miller, Kurt Shuster, Jack Urbanek, Douwe Kiela, Arthur Szlam, Iulian Serban, Ryan Lowe, Shrimai Prabhumoye, Alan W. Black, Alexander Rudnicky, Jason Williams, Joelle Pineau, Mikhail Burtsev, and Jason Weston. The second conversational intelligence challenge (convai2). *ArXiv Preprint ArXiv:1902.00098*, 2019a. DOI: 10.1007/978-3-030-29135-8_7 91, 112, 157

Emily Dinan, Stephen Roller, Kurt Shuster, Angela Fan, Michael Auli, and Jason Weston. Wizard of Wikipedia: Knowledge-powered conversational agents. In *International Conference on Learning Representations*, 2019b. https://openreview.net/forum?id=r1l73iRqKm 143

Jesse Dodge, Andreea Gane, Xiang Zhang, Antoine Bordes, Sumit Chopra, Alexander Miller, Arthur Szlam, and Jason Weston. Evaluating prerequisite qualities for learning end-to-end dialog systems. *ArXiv Preprint ArXiv:1511.06931*, 2015. 154

Ondřej Dušek, Jekaterina Novikova, and Verena Rieser. Evaluating the state-of-the-art of end-to-end natural language generation: The E2E NLG challenge. *Computer Speech & Language*, 59:123–156, 2020. DOI: 10.1016/j.csl.2019.06.009 51, 81, 100

Wieland Eckert, Esther Levin, and Roberto Pieraccini. User modeling for spoken dialogue system evaluation. In *IEEE Workshop on Automatic Speech Recognition and Understanding Proceedings*, pages 80–87, IEEE, 1997. DOI: 10.1109/asru.1997.658991 94

Layla El Asri, Jing He, and Kaheer Suleman. A sequence-to-sequence model for user simulation in spoken dialogue systems. In *Interspeech*, pages 1151–1155, 2016. http://dx.doi.org/10.21437/Interspeech.2016-1175 DOI: 10.21437/interspeech.2016-1175 94

Layla El Asri, Hannes Schulz, Shikhar Sharma, Jeremie Zumer, Justin Harris, Emery Fine, Rahul Mehrotra, and Kaheer Suleman. Frames: A corpus for adding memory to goal-oriented dialogue systems. In *Proc. of the 18th Annual SIGdial Meeting on Discourse and Dialogue*, pages 207–219, Association for Computational Linguistics, Saarbrücken, Germany, August 2017. https://www.aclweb.org/anthology/W17-5526 DOI: 10.18653/v1/w17-5526 151

Klaus-Peter Engelbrecht, Michael Kruppa, Sebastian Möller, and Michael Quade. Memo workbench for semi-automated usability testing. In *Proc. of Interspeech, 9th Annual Conference of the International Speech Communication Association*, pages 1662–1665, Brisbane, Australia, September 2008. https://www.isca-speech.org/archive/interspeech_2008/i08_1662.html 94

Klaus-Peter Engelbrecht, Michael Quade, and Sebastian Möller. Analysis of a new simulation approach to dialog system evaluation. *Speech Communication*, 51(12):1234–1252, 2009. DOI: 10.1016/j.specom.2009.06.007 95

Mihail Eric, Lakshmi Krishnan, Francois Charette, and Christopher D. Manning. Key-value retrieval networks for task-oriented dialogue. In *Proc. of the 18th Annual SIGdial Meeting on Discourse and Dialogue*, pages 37–49, Association for Computational Linguistics, Saarbrücken, Germany, August 2017. https://www.aclweb.org/anthology/W17-5506 DOI: 10.18653/v1/w17-5506 78, 152, 166

Mihail Eric, Rahul Goel, Shachi Paul, Abhishek Sethi, Sanchit Agarwal, Shuyang Gao, Adarsh Kumar, Anuj Goyal, Peter Ku, and Dilek Hakkani-Tür. MultiWOZ 2.1: A consolidated multi-domain dialogue dataset with state corrections and state tracking baselines. In *Proc. of the 12th Language Resources and Evaluation Conference*, pages 422–428, European Language Resources Association, Marseille, France, May 2020. https://www.aclweb.org/anthology/2020.lrec-1.53 78, 152

Arash Eshghi, Julian Hough, Matthew Purver, Ruth Kempson, and Eleni Gregoromichelaki. Conversational interactions: Capturing dialogue dynamics. *From Quantification to Conversation: Festschrift for Robin Cooper on the Occasion of his 65th Birthday*, 19:325–349, 2012. 173

Maxine Eskenazi, Gina-Anne Levow, Helen Meng, Gabriel Parent, and David Suendermann. *Crowdsourcing for Speech Processing: Applications to Data Collection, Transcription and Assessment*. John Wiley & Sons, 2013. DOI: 10.1002/9781118541241 95

Keelen Evanini, Phillip Hunter, Jackson Liscombe, David Suendermann, Krishna Dayanidhi, and Roberto Pieraccini. Caller experience: A method for evaluating dialog systems and its automatic prediction. In *Proc. of the IEEE Spoken Language Technology Workshop*, pages 129–132, Goa, India, December 2008. DOI: 10.1109/slt.2008.4777857 92

Mary Ellen Foster. Interleaved preparation and output in the COMIC fission module. In *Proc. of Workshop on Software*, pages 34–46, Association for Computational Linguistics, Ann Arbor, MI, June 2005. https://www.aclweb.org/anthology/W05-1103 DOI: 10.3115/1626315.1626318 162

Mary Ellen Foster, Bart Craenen, Amol Deshmukh, Oliver Lemon, Emanuele Bastianelli, Christian Dondrup, Ioannis Papaioannou, Andrea Vanzo, Jean-Marc Odobez, Olivier Canévet, Yuanzhouhan Cao, Weipeng He, Angel Martínez-González, Petr Motlicek, Rémy Siegfried, Rachid Alami, Kathleen Belhassein, Guilhem Buisan, Aurélie Clodic, Amandine Mayima, Yoan Sallami, Guillaume Sarthou, Phani-Teja Singamaneni, Jules Waldhart, Alexandre Mazel, Maxime Caniot, Marketta Niemelä, Päivi Heikkilä, Hanna Lammi, and Antti Tammela. MuMMER: Socially intelligent human-robot interaction in public spaces. In *Proc. of AI-HRI*, September 2019. https://arxiv.org/abs/1909.06749 23

Norman M. Fraser and G. Nigel Gilbert. Simulating speech systems. *Computer Speech & Language*, 5(1):81–99, 1991. DOI: 10.1016/0885-2308(91)90019-m 53

Raefer Gabriel, Yang Liu, Anna Gottardi, Eric Mihail, Anju Khatri, Anjali Chadha, Qinlang Chen, Behnam Hedayatnia, Pankaj Rajan, Ali Bincili, Shui Hu, Karthik Gopalakrishnan, Seokhwan Kim, Lauren Stubel, Kate Bland, Arindam Mandal, and Dilek Hakkani-Tür. Further advances in open domain dialog systems in the third Alexa Prize Social Bot Grand Challenge, July 2020. https://m.media-amazon.com/images/G/01/mobile-apps/dex/alexa/alexaprize/assets/challenge3/proceedings/Alexa-Prize-Technical-Paper-2020_Final.pdf 140, 141

Lucian Galescu, Choh Man Teng, James Allen, and Ian Perera. Cogent: A generic dialogue system shell based on a collaborative problem solving model. In *Proc. of the 19th Annual SIGdial Meeting on Discourse and Dialogue*, pages 400–409, Association for Computational Linguistics, Melbourne, Australia, July 2018. https://www.aclweb.org/anthology/W18-5048 DOI: 10.18653/v1/w18-5048 169

Jianfeng Gao, Michel Galley, and Lihong Li. *Neural Approaches to Conversational AI: Question Answering, Task-Oriented Dialogues and Social Chatbots*. Now Foundations and Trends, 2019. DOI: 10.1561/1500000074 19, 158, 167

Milica Gašić and Steve Young. Gaussian processes for POMDP-based dialogue manager optimization. *IEEE/ACM Transactions on Audio, Speech, and Language Processing*, 22(1):28–40, 2013. DOI: 10.1109/tasl.2013.2282190 88

Milica Gašić, Filip Jurčíček, Blaise Thomson, Kai Yu, and Steve Young. On-line policy optimisation of spoken dialogue systems via live interaction with human subjects. In *Proc. of the IEEE Workshop on Automatic Speech Recognition and Understanding*, pages 312–317, IEEE, 2011. DOI: 10.1109/asru.2011.6163950 93

Kallirroi Georgila, Carla Gordon, Hyungtak Choi, Jill Boberg, Heesik Jeon, and David Traum. Toward low-cost automated evaluation metrics for internet of things dialogues. In *9th International Workshop on Spoken Dialogue System Technology*, pages 161–175, Springer, 2019. DOI: 10.1007/978-981-13-9443-0_14 178

Marjan Ghazvininejad, Chris Brockett, Ming-Wei Chang, Bill Dolan, Jianfeng Gao, Wen-tau Yih, and Michel Galley. A knowledge-grounded neural conversation model. In *32nd AAAI Conference on Artificial Intelligence*, 2018. https://arxiv.org/abs/1702.01932 168

Sayan Ghosh, Mathieu Chollet, Eugene Laksana, Louis-Philippe Morency, and Stefan Scherer. Affect-LM: A neural language model for customizable affective text generation. *ArXiv Preprint ArXiv:1704.06851*, 2017. DOI: 10.18653/v1/p17-1059 149, 150

Jose Manuel Gomez-Perez, Ronald Denaux, and Andres Garcia-Silva. *A Practical Guide to Hybrid Natural Language Processing: Combining Neural Models and Knowledge Graphs for NLP*. Springer Nature, 2020. DOI: 10.1007/978-3-030-44830-1 180

Allen L. Gorin, Giuseppe Riccardi, and Jeremy H. Wright. How may I help you? *Speech Communication*, 23:113–127, 1997. DOI: 10.1016/s0167-6393(97)00040-x 19

Maartje Ma De Graaf, Somaya Ben allouch, and Tineke Klamer. Sharing a life with Harvey: Exploring the acceptance of and relationship-building with a social robot. *Computers in Human Behavior*, 43:1–14, 2015. DOI: 10.1016/j.chb.2014.10.030 23

Jonathan Gratch, Arno Hartholt, Morteza Dehghani, and Stacy Marsella. Virtual humans: A new toolkit for cognitive science research. In *Proc. of the Annual Meeting of the Cognitive Science Society*, 35, 2013. 22

Agustín Gravano and Julia Hirschberg. Turn-taking cues in task-oriented dialogue. *Computer Speech & Language*, 25(3):601–634, 2011. DOI: 10.1016/j.csl.2010.10.003 173

Bert F. Green, Alice K. Wolf, Carol Chomsky, and Kenneth Laughery. Baseball: An automatic question-answerer. In *Western Joint IRE-AIEE-ACM Computer Conference, IRE-AIEE-ACM, (Western)*, pages 219–224, Association for Computing Machinery, New York, May 9–11, 1961. DOI: 10.1145/1460690.1460714 14

H. P. Grice. Logic and conversation. In Peter Cole and Jerry L. Morgan, Eds., *Syntax and Semantics: Volume 3: Speech Acts*, pages 41–58, Academic Press, New York, 1975. 15

David Griol, Lluís F. Hurtado, Encarna Segarra, and Emilio Sanchis. A statistical approach to spoken dialog systems design and evaluation. *Speech Communication*, 50(8-9):666–682, 2008. DOI: 10.1016/j.specom.2008.04.001 76, 77

David Griol, Zoraida Callejas, Ramón López-Cózar, and Giuseppe Riccardi. A domain-independent statistical methodology for dialog management in spoken dialog systems. *Computer Speech & Language*, 28(3):743–768, 2014. DOI: 10.1016/j.csl.2013.09.002 76, 78

Barbara Grosz and Candace L. Sidner. Attention, intentions, and the structure of discourse. *Computational Linguistics*, 1986. 65

Fenfei Guo, Angeliki Metallinou, Chandra Khatri, Anirudh Raju, Anu Venkatesh, and Ashwin Ram. Topic-based evaluation for conversational bots. *ArXiv Preprint ArXiv:1801.03622*, 2018. 35, 108

Isabelle Guyon, Ulrike von Luxburg, Samy Bengio, Hanna M. Wallach, Rob Fergus, S. V. N. Vishwanathan, and Roman Garnett, Eds. *Advances in Neural Information Processing Systems 30: Annual Conference on Neural Information Processing Systems*, December 2017. https://papers.nips.cc/book/advances-in-neural-information-processing-systems-30-2017 158

Stefan Hahn, Marco Dinarelli, Christian Raymond, Fabrice Lefevre, Patrick Lehnen, Renato De Mori, Alessandro Moschitti, Hermann Ney, and Giuseppe Riccardi. Comparing stochastic approaches to spoken language understanding in multiple languages. *IEEE Transactions on Audio, Speech, and Language Processing*, 19(6):1569–1583, 2010. DOI: 10.1109/tasl.2010.2093520 75

Dilek Hakkani-Tür, Gökhan Tür, Asli Celikyilmaz, Yun-Nung Chen, Jianfeng Gao, Li Deng, and Ye-Yi Wang. Multi-domain joint semantic frame parsing using bi-directional RNN-LSTM. In *Interspeech*, pages 715–719, 2016. DOI: 10.21437/interspeech.2016-402 76

Yanchao Hao, Yuanzhe Zhang, Kang Liu, Shizhu He, Zhanyi Liu, Hua Wu, and Jun Zhao. An end-to-end model for question answering over knowledge base with cross-attention combining global knowledge. In *Proc. of the 55th Annual Meeting of the Association for Computational Linguistics (Volume 1: Long Papers)*, pages 221–231, 2017. DOI: 10.18653/v1/p17-1021 167

Helen Hastie. Metrics and evaluation of spoken dialogue systems. In Oliver Lemon and Olivier Pietquin, Eds., *Data-Driven Methods for Adaptive Spoken Dialogue Systems: Computational Learning for Conversational Interfaces*, pages 131–150, Springer, New York, 2012. DOI: 10.1007/978-1-4614-4803-7_7 91

Peter A. Heeman. Combining reinforcement learning with information-state update rules. In *Human Language Technologies: The Conference of the North American Chapter of the Association for Computational Linguistics; Proceedings of the Main Conference*, pages 268–275, 2007. https://www.aclweb.org/anthology/N07-1034.pdf 85, 175

Charles T. Hemphill, John J. Godfrey, and George R. Doddington. The ATIS spoken language systems pilot corpus. In *Speech and Natural Language: Proceedings of a Workshop on*, Hidden Valley, PA, June 24–27, 1990. https://www.aclweb.org/anthology/H90-1021 DOI: 10.3115/116580.116613 16, 151

James Henderson and Filip Jurčíček. Data-driven methods for spoken language understanding. In Oliver Lemon and Olivier Pietquin, Eds., *Data-Driven Methods for Adaptive Spoken Dialogue Systems*, pages 19–38, Springer, 2012. DOI: 10.1007/978-1-4614-4803-7_3 75

James Henderson, Oliver Lemon, and Kallirroi Georgila. Hybrid reinforcement/supervised learning of dialogue policies from fixed data sets. *Computational Linguistics*, 34(4):487–511, 2008. DOI: 10.1162/coli.2008.07-028-r2-05-82 88

Matthew Henderson. Machine learning for dialog state tracking: A review. In *Proc. of the 1st International Workshop on Machine Learning in Spoken Language Processing*, Aizu-Wakamatsu city, Fukushima, Japan, September 2015. https://static.googleusercontent.com/media/research.google.com/en//pubs/archive/44018.pdf 85, 99

Matthew Henderson, Blaise Thomson, and Steve Young. Deep neural network approach for the dialog state tracking challenge. In *Proc. of the SIGDIAL Conference*, pages 467–471, Metz, France, August 2013. https://www.aclweb.org/anthology/W13-4073.pdf 85

Matthew Henderson, Blaise Thomson, and Jason D. Williams. The second dialog state tracking challenge. In *Proc. of the 15th Annual Meeting of the Special Interest Group on Discourse and Dialogue (SIGDIAL)*, pages 263–272, Association for Computational Linguistics, Philadelphia, PA, June 2014a. https://www.aclweb.org/anthology/W14-4337 DOI: 10.3115/v1/W14-4337 86, 153, 155

Matthew Henderson, Blaise Thomson, and Jason D. Williams. The third dialog state tracking challenge. In *IEEE Spoken Language Technology Workshop (SLT)*, pages 324–329, 2014b. DOI: 10.1109/slt.2014.7078595 86, 153, 155

Dan Hendrycks, Collin Burns, Steven Basart, Andy Zou, Mantas Mazeika, Dawn Song, and Jacob Steinhardt. Measuring massive multitask language understanding. *ArXiv Preprint ArXiv: 2009.03300*, 2020. 145

Ryuichiro Higashinaka, Kotaro Funakoshi, Yuka Kobayashi, and Michimasa Inaba. The dialogue breakdown detection challenge: Task description, datasets, and evaluation metrics. In *Proc. of the 10th International Conference on Language Resources and Evaluation (LREC'16)*, pages 3146–3150, 2016. 157

Ryuichiro Higashinaka, Kotaro Funakoshi, Michimasa Inaba, Yuiko Tsunomori, Tetsuro Takahashi, and Nobuhiro Kaji. Overview of dialogue breakdown detection challenge 3. *Proc. of Dialog System Technology Challenge*, 6, 2017. 110, 157

Erhard W. Hinrichs, Julia Bartels, Yasuhiro Kawata, Valia Kordoni, and Heike Telljohann. The Tübingen treebanks for spoken German, English, and Japanese. In Wolfgang Wahlster, Ed., *Verbmobil: Foundations of Speech-to-Speech Translation*, pages 550–574, Springer Berlin Heidelberg, Berlin, Heidelberg, 2000. DOI: 10.1007/978-3-662-04230-4_40 152

Geoffrey Hinton, Li Deng, Dong Yu, George E. Dahl, Abdel-rahman Mohamed, Navdeep Jaitly, Andrew Senior, Vincent Vanhoucke, Patrick Nguyen, Tara N. Sainath, and Brian Kingsbury. Deep neural networks for acoustic modeling in speech recognition: The shared views of four research groups. *IEEE Signal Processing Magazine*, 29(6):82–97, 2012. DOI: 10.1109/msp.2012.2205597 45

Geoffrey E. Hinton, Simon Osindero, and Yee-Whye Teh. A fast learning algorithm for deep belief nets. *Neural Computation*, 18(7):1527–1554, 2006. DOI: 10.1162/neco.2006.18.7.1527 75

Sepp Hochreiter and Jürgen Schmidhuber. Long short-term memory. *Neural Computation*, 9(8):1735–1780, 1997. DOI: 10.1162/neco.1997.9.8.1735 134

Samuel Holmes, Anne Moorhead, Raymond Bond, Huiru Zheng, Vivien Coates, and Michael F. McTear. Usability testing of a healthcare chatbot: Can we use conventional methods to assess conversational user interfaces? In Maurice Mulvenna and Raymond Bond, Eds., *Proc. of the 31st European Conference on Cognitive Ergonomics*, pages 207–214. Association for Computing Machinery, New York, 2019. DOI: 10.1145/3335082.3335094 103

Kate S. Hone and Robert Graham. Towards a tool for the subjective assessment of speech system interfaces (sassi). *Natural Language Engineering*, 6(3-4):287–303, 2000. DOI: 10.1017/s1351324900002497 102

Chiori Hori, Julien Perez, Ryuichiro Higashinaka, Takaaki Hori, Y-Lan Boureau, Michimasa Inaba, Yuiko Tsunomori, Tetsuro Takahashi, Koichiro Yoshino, and Seokhwan Kim.

Overview of the sixth dialog system technology challenge: DSTC6. *Computer Speech & Language*, 55:1–25, 2019. DOI: 10.1016/j.csl.2018.09.004 155

Christine Howes, Matthew Purver, Patrick G. T. Healey, Greg J. Mills, and Eleni Gregoromichelaki. On incrementality in dialogue: Evidence from compound contributions. *Dialogue and Discourse*, 2(1):279—311, 2011. http://journals.linguisticsociety.org/elanguage/dad/article/view/362/1462.html DOI: 10.5087/dad.2011.111 172

Baotian Hu, Zhengdong Lu, Hang Li, and Qingcai Chen. Convolutional neural network architectures for matching natural language sentences. In *Advances in Neural Information Processing Systems*, pages 2042–2050, 2014. https://arxiv.org/abs/1503.03244 137

Susan L. Hura. Usability testing of spoken conversational systems. *Journal of Usability Studies*, 12(4):155–163, 2017. 20

Lluıs F. Hurtado, David Griol, Emilio Sanchis, and Encarna Segarra. A stochastic approach to dialog management. In *IEEE Workshop on Automatic Speech Recognition and Understanding*, pages 226–231, 2005. DOI: 10.1109/asru.2005.1566518 77, 78

Lluís F. Hurtado, David Griol, Encarna Segarra, and Emilio Sanchis. A stochastic approach for dialog management based on neural networks. In *9th International Conference on Spoken Language Processing*, 2006. https://www.isca-speech.org/archive/interspeech_2006/i06_1206.html 78

Srinivasan Janarthanam, Helen Hastie, Oliver Lemon, and Xingkun Liu. The day after the day after tomorrow? A machine learning approach to adaptive temporal expression generation: Training and evaluation with real users. In *Proc. of the SIGDIAL Conference*, pages 142–151, Association for Computational Linguistics, Portland, OR, June 2011. https://www.aclweb.org/anthology/W11-2017 84

Heesik Jeon, Hyung Rai Oh, Inchul Hwang, and Jihie Kim. An intelligent dialogue agent for the IoT home. In Bruno Bouchard, Sylvain Giroux, Abdenour Bouzouane, and Sebastien Gaboury, Eds., *Artificial Intelligence Applied to Assistive Technologies and Smart Environments, AAAI Workshop*, Phoenix, AZ, February 2016. http://www.aaai.org/ocs/index.php/WS/AAAIW16/paper/view/12596 168, 177, 178

Martin Johansson and Gabriel Skantze. Opportunities and obligations to take turns in collaborative multi-party human-robot interaction. In *Proc. of the 16th Annual Meeting of the Special Interest Group on Discourse and Dialogue*, pages 305–314, Association for Computational Linguistics, Prague, Czech Republic, September 2015. https://www.aclweb.org/anthology/W15-4642 DOI: 10.18653/v1/w15-4642 174

Michael Johnston. Multimodal integration for interactive conversational systems. In Sharon Oviatt, Björn Schuller, Philip R. Cohen, Daniel Sonntag, Gerasimos Potamianos, and Antonio Krüger, editors, *The Handbook of Multimodal-Multisensor Interfaces: Language Processing, Software, Commercialization, and Emerging Directions - Volume 3*, pages 21–76, Association for Computing Machinery and Morgan & Claypool, 2019. DOI: 10.1145/3233795.3233798 160, 161

Michael Johnston, Srinivas Bangalore, Gunaranjan Vasireddy, Amanda Stent, Patrick Ehlen, Marilyn Walker, Steve Whittaker, and Preetam Maloor. Match: An architecture for multimodal dialogue systems. In *Proc. of the 40th Annual Meeting of the Association for Computational Linguistics*, pages 376–383, 2002. DOI: 10.3115/1073083.1073146 160, 162

Kristiina Jokinen. *Constructive Dialogue Modelling: Speech Interaction and Rational Agents*, vol. 10. John Wiley & Sons, 2009. DOI: 10.1002/9780470511275 16

Kristiina Jokinen. Dialogue models for socially intelligent robots. In *International Conference on Social Robotics*, pages 127–138, Springer, 2018. DOI: 10.1007/978-3-030-05204-1_13 176

Kristiina Jokinen and Michael F. McTear. *Spoken Dialogue Systems*. Morgan & Claypool Publishers, 2009. DOI: 10.2200/s00204ed1v01y200910hlt005 19

Kristiina Jokinen and Catherine Pelachaud. From annotation to multimodal behaviour. In Matej Rojc and Nick Campbell, Eds., *Coverbal Synchrony in Human-Machine Interaction*, pages 203–222, CRC Press, Taylor & Francis Group, 2013. DOI: 10.1201/b15477-9 22

Kristiina Jokinen and Graham Wilcock. Multimodal open-domain conversations with the Nao robot. In Joseph Mariani, Sophie Rosset, Martine Garnier-Rizet, and Laurence Devillers, Eds., *Natural Interaction with Robots, Knowbots and Smartphones*, pages 213–224, Springer, 2014. DOI: 10.1007/978-1-4614-8280-2_19 176

Kristiina Jokinen and Graham Wilcock, Eds. *Dialogues with Social Robots: Enablements, Analyses, and Evaluation*. Springer, 2017. DOI: 10.1007/978-981-10-2585-3 177

Kristiina Jokinen, Satoshi Nishimura, Kentaro Watanabe, and Nishimura Takuichi. Human-robot dialogues for explaining activities. In Luis Fernando D'Haro, Rafael E. Banchs, and Haizhou Li, Eds., *9th International Workshop on Spoken Dialogue System Technology. Lecture Notes in Electrical Engineering*, 579:239–251, Springer, 2019. DOI: 10.1007/978-981-13-9443-0_20 177

Rafal Jozefowicz, Wojciech Zaremba, and Ilya Sutskever. An empirical exploration of recurrent network architectures. In *International Conference on Machine Learning*, pages 2342–2350, 2015. https://dl.acm.org/citation.cfm?id=3045367 135

Sangkeun Jung, Cheongjae Lee, Kyungduk Kim, Minwoo Jeong, and Gary Geunbae Lee. Data-driven user simulation for automated evaluation of spoken dialog systems. *Computer Speech & Language*, 23(4):479–509, 2009. DOI: 10.1016/j.csl.2009.03.002 94

Dan Jurafsky and James H. Martin. Speech and language processing (3rd ed. draft). Under development, 2020. https://web.stanford.edu/jurafsky/slp3/ 13, 19, 45, 74, 75, 134

Daniel Jurafsky and James H. Martin. *Speech and Language Processing: An Introduction to Natural Language Processing, Computational Linguistics, and Speech Recognition*, 2nd ed., Pearson Prentice Hall, Upper Saddle River, NJ, 2009. 19

Juraj Juraska, Panagiotis Karagiannis, Kevin Bowden, and Marilyn Walker. A deep ensemble model with slot alignment for sequence-to-sequence natural language generation. In *Proc. of the Conference of the North American Chapter of the Association for Computational Linguistics: Human Language Technologies, Volume 1 (Long Papers)*, pages 152–162, New Orleans, LA, June 2018. https://www.aclweb.org/anthology/N18-1014 DOI: 10.18653/v1/n18-1014 100

Filip Jurčíček, Simon Keizer, Milica Gašić, François Mairesse, Blaise Thomson, Kai Yu, and Steve Young. Real user evaluation of spoken dialogue systems using Amazon mechanical turk. In *INTERSPEECH, 12th Annual Conference of the International Speech Communication Association*, pages 3061–3064, August 2011. https://www.isca-speech.org/archive/interspeech_2011/i11_3061.html 95

Anjuli Kannan, Karol Kurach, Sujith Ravi, Tobias Kaufman, Balint Miklos, Greg Corrado, Andrew Tomkins, Laszlo Lukacs, Marina Ganea, Peter Young, and Vivek Ramavajjala. Smart reply: Automated response suggestion for email. In *Proc. of the ACM SIGKDD Conference on Knowledge Discovery and Data Mining (KDD)*, 2016. https://arxiv.org/abs/1606.04870 DOI: 10.1145/2939672.2939801 126

Tatsuya Kawahara. Spoken dialogue system for a human-like conversational robot ERICA. In Luis Fernando D'Haro, Rafael E. Banchs, and Haizhou Li, Eds., *9th International Workshop on Spoken Dialogue System Technology, IWSDS*, Singapore, April 18–20, 2018, volume 579 of *Lecture Notes in Electrical Engineering*, pages 65–75, Springer, 2018. DOI: 10.1007/978-981-13-9443-0_6 176

Simon Keizer, Stéphane Rossignol, Senthilkumar Chandramohan, and Olivier Pietquin. User simulation in the development of statistical spoken dialogue systems. In Oliver Lemon and Olivier Pietquin, Eds., *Data-Driven Methods for Adaptive Spoken Dialogue Systems*, pages 39–73, Springer, New York, 2012. DOI: 10.1007/978-1-4614-4803-7_4 94

Gil Keren, Amr El-Desoky Mousa, Olivier Pietquin, Stefanos Zafeiriou, and Björn Schuller. Deep learning for multisensorial and multimodal interaction. In Sharon Oviatt, Björn Schuller, Philip R. Cohen, Daniel Sonntag, Gerasimos Potamianos, and Antonio Krüger,

Eds., *The Handbook of Multimodal-Multisensor Interfaces: Signal Processing, Architectures, and Detection of Emotion and Cognition - Volume 2*, pages 99–128, Association for Computing Machinery and Morgan & Claypool, 2018. DOI: 10.1145/3107990.3107996 161

Chandra Khatri, Behnam Hedayatnia, Anu Venkatesh, Jeff Nunn, Yi Pan, Qing Liu, Han Song, Anna Gottardi, Sanjeev Kwatra, Sanju Pancholi, Ming Cheng, Qinglang Chen, Lauren Stubel, Karthik Gopalakrishnan, Kate Bland, Raefer Gabriel, Arindam Mandal, Dilek Hakkani-Tür, Gene Hwang, Nate Michel, Eric King, and Rohit Prasad. Advancing the state of the art in open domain dialog systems through the Alexa prize. *ArXiv Preprint ArXiv:1812.10757*, 2018a. xv, 32, 38, 112, 140, 180

Chandra Khatri, Anu Venkatesh, Behnam Hedayatnia, Raefer Gabriel, Ashwin Ram, and Rohit Prasad. Alexa prize—state of the art in conversational AI. *AI Magazine*, 39(3):40–55, 2018b. DOI: 10.1609/aimag.v39i3.2810 38, 112, 148, 170

Seokhwan Kim, Luis Fernando D'Haro, Rafael E. Banchs, Jason D. Williams, Matthew Henderson, and Koichiro Yoshino. The fifth dialog state tracking challenge. In *Proc. of IEEE Spoken Language Technology Workshop (SLT)*, pages 511–517, San Diego, CA, December 2016. DOI: 10.1109/slt.2016.7846311 155

Seokhwan Kim, Luis Fernando D'Haro, Rafael E. Banchs, Jason D. Williams, and Matthew Henderson. The fourth dialog state tracking challenge. In Kristiina Jokinen and Graham Wilcock, Eds., *Dialogues with Social Robots—Enablements, Analyses, and Evaluation*, pages 435–449, Springer, New York, 2017. DOI: 10.1007/978-981-10-2585-3_36 155

Alfred Kobsa and Wolfgang Wahlster, Eds. *User Models in Dialog Systems*. Springer, Berlin, 1989. DOI: 10.1007/978-3-642-83230-7 149

A. Baki Kocaballi, Liliana Laranjo da Silva, and Enrico Coiera. Measuring user experience in conversational interfaces: A comparison of six questionnaires. In Raymond Bond, Maurice Mulvenna, Jonathan Wallace, and Michaela Black, Eds., *Proc. of 32nd BCS Human Computer Interaction Conference (HCI)*, pages 1–12, BCS, The Chartered Institute for IT, Belfast, UK, November 2018. DOI: 10.14236/ewic/hci2018.21 103

Kit Kuksenok. Why (and how) explainable AI matters for chatbot design. *Medium*, September 2019. https://medium.com/jobpal-dev/why-and-how-explainable-ai-matters-for-chatbot-design-21d3089b33dc 180

Divesh Lala, Koji Inoue, Pierrick Milhorat, and Tatsuya Kawahara. Detection of social signals for recognizing engagement in human-robot interaction. *ArXiv Preprint ArXiv:1709.10257*, 2017. 176

James A. Larson. Ten criteria for measuring effective voice user interfaces. *Speech Technology Magazine*, November 2005. https://www.speechtechmag.com/Articles/Editorial/Feature/Ten-Criteria-for-Measuring-Effective-Voice-User-Interfaces-29443.aspx 96

Stefan Larson, Anish Mahendran, Joseph J. Peper, Christopher Clarke, Andrew Lee, Parker Hill, Jonathan K. Kummerfeld, Kevin Leach, Michael A. Laurenzano, Lingjia Tang, and Jason Mars. An evaluation dataset for intent classification and out-of-scope prediction. In *Proc. of the Conference on Empirical Methods in Natural Language Processing and the 9th International Joint Conference on Natural Language Processing (EMNLP-IJCNLP)*, pages 1311–1316, Association for Computational Linguistics, Hong Kong, China, November 2019. https://www.aclweb.org/anthology/D19-1131 DOI: 10.18653/v1/d19-1131 75

Staffan Larsson and David R. Traum. Information state and dialogue management in the TRINDI dialogue move engine toolkit. *Natural Language Engineering*, 6(3–4):323–340, September 2000. DOI: 10.1017/s1351324900002539 18, 85

Quoc Le and Tomas Mikolov. Distributed representations of sentences and documents. In *Proc. of the 31st International Conference on International Conference on Machine Learning - Volume 32, ICML'14*, pages II–1188–II–1196, JMLR.org, 2014. https://arxiv.org/abs/1405.4053v2 132

Yann LeCun, Yoshua Bengio, and Geoffrey Hinton. Deep learning. *Nature*, 521(7553):436–444, 2015. DOI: 10.1038/nature14539 133

Cheongjae Lee, Sangkeun Jung, Seokhwan Kim, and Gary Geunbae Lee. Example-based dialog modeling for practical multi-domain dialog system. *Speech Communication*, 51(5):466–484, 2009. DOI: 10.1016/j.specom.2009.01.008 76

Cheongjae Lee, Sangkeun Jung, Kyungduk Kim, Donghyeon Lee, and Gary Geunbae Lee. Recent approaches to dialog management for spoken dialog systems. *Journal of Computing Science and Engineering*, 4(1):1–22, 2010. DOI: 10.5626/jcse.2010.4.1.001 49

Oliver Lemon. Learning what to say and how to say it: Joint optimisation of spoken dialogue management and natural language generation. *Computer Speech & Language*, 25(2):210–221, September 2011. DOI: 10.1016/j.csl.2010.04.005 51, 79, 126

Oliver Lemon. Statistical approaches to adaptive natural language generation. In Oliver Lemon and Olivier Pietquin, Eds., *Data-Driven Methods for Adaptive Spoken Dialogue Systems: Computational Learning for Conversational Interfaces*, pages 103–130, Springer, New York, 2012. DOI: 10.1007/978-1-4614-4803-7_6 51, 72, 79, 80

Oliver Lemon and Alexander Gruenstein. Multithreaded context for robust conversational interfaces: Context-sensitive speech recognition and interpretation of corrective fragments.

ACM Transactions on Computer—Human Interaction, 11(3):241–267, September 2004. DOI: 10.1145/1017494.1017496 48

Oliver Lemon and Olivier Pietquin. Machine learning for spoken dialogue systems. In *Proc. of the 8th Annual Conference of the International Speech Communication Association (INTERSPEECH)*, pages 185–186, Antwerp, Belgium, August 2007. https://www.isca-speech.org/archive/interspeech_2007/i07_2685.html 88

Oliver Lemon, Alexander Gruenstein, Alexis Battle, and Stanley Peters. Multi-tasking and collaborative activities in dialogue systems. In *Proc. of the 3rd SIGdial Workshop on Discourse and Dialogue*, pages 113–124, Association for Computational Linguistics, Philadelphia, PA, July 2002. https://www.aclweb.org/anthology/W02-0216 DOI: 10.3115/1118121.1118137 176

Oliver Lemon, Xingkun Liu, Daniel Shapiro, and Carl Tollander. Hierarchical reinforcement learning of dialogue policies in a development environment for dialogue systems: REALL-DUDE. In *BRANDIAL'06, Proc. of the 10th Workshop on the Semantics and Pragmatics of Dialogue*, pages 185–186, 2006. 88

Gene H. Lerner. On the syntax of sentences-in-progress. *Language in Society*, 20(3):441–458, 1991. http://www.jstor.org/stable/4168265 DOI: 10.1017/s0047404500016572 172

Esther Levin, Roberto Pieraccini, and Wieland Eckert. A stochastic model of human-machine interaction for learning dialog strategies. *IEEE Transactions on Speech and Audio Processing*, 8(1):11–23, 2000. DOI: 10.1109/89.817450 81

Stephen C. Levinson. *Pragmatics*. Cambridge Textbooks in Linguistics. Cambridge University Press, 1983. DOI: 10.1017/CBO9780511813313 15

James R. Lewis. *Practical Speech User Interface Design*. CRC Press, Boca Raton, FL, 2016a. DOI: 10.1201/b10461 20

James R. Lewis. Standardized questionnaires for voice interaction design. *Voice Interaction Design*, 1(1), 2016b. 104

Jiwei Li, Michel Galley, Chris Brockett, Jianfeng Gao, and Bill Dolan. A diversity-promoting objective function for neural conversation models. *ArXiv Preprint ArXiv:1510.03055*, 2015. DOI: 10.18653/v1/n16-1014 110, 147, 148

Jiwei Li, Michel Galley, Chris Brockett, Georgios P. Spithourakis, Jianfeng Gao, and Bill Dolan. A persona-based neural conversation model. *ArXiv Preprint ArXiv:1603.06155*, 2016a. DOI: 10.18653/v1/p16-1094 149, 167

Jiwei Li, Alexander H. Miller, Sumit Chopra, Marc'Aurelio Ranzato, and Jason Weston. Dialogue learning with human-in-the-loop. *ArXiv Preprint ArXiv:1611.09823*, 2016b. 154

Margaret Li, Jason Weston, and Stephen Roller. ACUTE-EVAL: Improved dialogue evaluation with optimized questions and multi-turn comparisons. *ArXiv Preprint ArXiv:1909.03087*, 2019. 104, 107

Xiujun Li, Yun-Nung Chen, Lihong Li, Jianfeng Gao, and Asli Celikyilmaz. End-to-end task completion neural dialogue systems. *ArXiv Preprint ArXiv:1703.01008*, 2018a. 138

Xiujun Li, Yu Wang, Siqi Sun, Sarah Panda, Jingjing Liu, and Jianfeng Gao. Microsoft dialogue challenge: Building end-to-end task-completion dialogue systems. *ArXiv Preprint ArXiv:1807.11125*, 2018b. 95

Weixin Liang, Youzhi Tian, Chengcai Chen, and Zhou Yu. MOSS: End-to-end dialog system framework with modular supervision. In *Proc. of the AAAI Conference on Artificial Intelligence*, pages 8327–8335, AAAI Press, February 2020. https://aaai.org/ojs/index.php/AAAI/article/view/6349 DOI: 10.1609/aaai.v34i05.6349 175

Lizi Liao, Yunshan Ma, Xiangnan He, Richang Hong, and Tat-Seng Chua. Knowledge-aware multimodal dialogue systems. In *Proc. of the 26th ACM International Conference on Multimedia*, pages 801–809, Association for Computing Machinery, New York, 2018. DOI: 10.1145/3240508.3240605 162

Tsung-Yi Lin, Michael Maire, Serge Belongie, James Hays, Pietro Perona, Deva Ramanan, Piotr Dollár, and C. Lawrence Zitnick. Microsoft COCO: Common objects in context. In *European Conference on Computer Vision*, pages 740–755, Springer, 2014. DOI: 10.1007/978-3-319-10602-1_48 164, 165

Pierre Lison. A hybrid approach to dialogue management based on probabilistic rules. *Computer Speech & Language*, 34(1):232–255, 2015. DOI: 10.1016/j.csl.2015.01.001 175

Pierre Lison and Casey Kennington. OpenDial: A toolkit for developing spoken dialogue systems with probabilistic rules. In *Proc. of ACL System Demonstrations*, pages 67–72, Association for Computational Linguistics, Berlin, Germany, August 2016. https://www.aclweb.org/anthology/P16-4012 DOI: 10.18653/v1/p16-4012 18, 175

Pierre Lison and Casey Kennington. Incremental processing for neural conversation models. In *Proc. SEMDIAL (SaarDial) Workshop on the Semantics and Pragmatics of Dialogue*, pages 154–155, Saarbrücken, Germany, August 2017. http://semdial.org/anthology/Z17-Lison_semdial_0023.pdf 173

Bing Liu and Ian Lane. An end-to-end trainable neural network model with belief tracking for task-oriented dialog. In *Proc. of the 18th Annual Meeting of the International Speech Communication Association (INTERSPEECH)*, pages 2506–2510, Stockholm, Sweden, August 2017. DOI: 10.21437/interspeech.2017-1326 139

Chia-Wei Liu, Ryan Lowe, Iulian Serban, Mike Noseworthy, Laurent Charlin, and Joelle Pineau. How not to evaluate your dialogue system: An empirical study of unsupervised evaluation metrics for dialogue response generation. In *Proc. of the Conference on Empirical Methods in Natural Language Processing*, pages 2122–2132, Association for Computational Linguistics, Austin, TX, November 2016. https://www.aclweb.org/anthology/D16-1230 DOI: 10.18653/v1/d16-1230 105, 110

Zhibin Liu, Zheng-Yu Niu, Hua Wu, and Haifeng Wang. Knowledge aware conversation generation with explainable reasoning over augmented graphs. In *Proc. of the Conference on Empirical Methods in Natural Language Processing and the 9th International Joint Conference on Natural Language Processing (EMNLP-IJCNLP)*, pages 1782–1792, Association for Computational Linguistics, Hong Kong, China, November 2019. https://www.aclweb.org/anthology/D19-1187 DOI: 10.18653/v1/d19-1187 168

Hugh Loebner. How to hold a turing test contest. In Robert Epstein, Gary Roberts, and Grace Beber, Eds., *Parsing the Turing Test*, pages 173–179, Springer, Dordrecht, 2009. DOI: 10.1007/978-1-4020-6710-5_12 111

Ramón López-Cózar and Masahiro Araki. *Spoken, Multilingual and Multimodal Dialogue Systems: Development and Assessment*. John Wiley & Sons, 2007. DOI: 10.1002/0470021578 160

Ramón López-Cózar and Zoraida Callejas. ASR post-correction for spoken dialogue systems based on semantic, syntactic, lexical and contextual information. *Speech Communication*, 50(8–9):745–766, August 2008. DOI: 10.1016/j.specom.2008.03.008 48

Ramón López-Cózar, A. De la Torre, José C. Segura, and Antonio J. Rubio. Assessment of dialogue systems by means of a new simulation technique. *Speech Communication*, 40(3):387–407, 2003. DOI: 10.1016/s0167-6393(02)00126-7 94

Ramón López-Cózar, Zoraida Callejas, and Michael F. McTear. Testing the performance of spoken dialogue systems by means of an artificially simulated user. *Artificial Intelligence Review*, 26(4):291–323, 2006. DOI: 10.1007/s10462-007-9059-9 94

Ramón López-Cózar, Zoraida Callejas, David Griol, and José F. Quesada. Review of spoken dialogue systems. *Loquens*, 1(2):1–15, 2014. DOI: 10.3989/loquens.2014.012 49

Ryan Lowe, Nissan Pow, Iulian Serban, Laurent Charlin, and Joelle Pineau. Incorporating unstructured textual knowledge sources into neural dialogue systems. In *Neural Information Processing Systems Workshop on Machine Learning for Spoken Language Understanding*, 2015a. 105

Ryan Lowe, Nissan Pow, Iulian Serban, and Joelle Pineau. The ubuntu dialogue corpus: A large dataset for research in unstructured multi-turn dialogue systems. *ArXiv Preprint ArXiv:1506.08909*, 2015b. DOI: 10.18653/v1/w15-4640 138, 152

Ryan Lowe, Iulian V. Serban, Mike Noseworthy, Laurent Charlin, and Joelle Pineau. On the evaluation of dialogue systems with next utterance classification. *ArXiv Preprint ArXiv:1605.05414*, 2016. DOI: 10.18653/v1/w16-3634 96, 105

Yi Luan, Chris Brockett, Bill Dolan, Jianfeng Gao, and Michel Galley. Multi-task learning for speaker-role adaptation in neural conversation models. *ArXiv Preprint ArXiv:1710.07388*, 2017. 149

Nikita Lukianets. 50+ platforms for chatbot design, development and analytics—less is more. *Medium*, July 2019. https://medium.com/voice-tech-podcast/50-platforms-for-chatbot-design-development-and-analytics-less-is-more-a8677ab2b7d5 54

Andrea Madotto, Chien-Sheng Wu, and Pascale Fung. Mem2Seq: Effectively incorporating knowledge bases into end-to-end task-oriented dialog systems. In *Proc. of the 56th Annual Meeting of the Association for Computational Linguistics (Volume 1: Long Papers)*, pages 1468–1478, Association for Computational Linguistics, Melbourne, Australia, July 2018. https://www.aclweb.org/anthology/P18-1136 DOI: 10.18653/v1/p18-1136 175

Alexander Maedche. Gender bias in chatbot design. In *Chatbot Research and Design: 3rd International Workshop, CONVERSATIONS, Revised Selected Papers*, 11970:79, Springer, November 2020. DOI: 10.1007/978-3-030-39540-7_6 180

François Mairesse and Steve Young. Stochastic language generation in dialogue using factored language models. *Computational Linguistics*, 40(4):763–799, 2014. DOI: 10.1162/coli_a_00199 79

Christopher D. Manning, Mihai Surdeanu, John Bauer, Jenny Rose Finkel, Steven Bethard, and David McClosky. The Stanford CoreNLP natural language processing toolkit. In *Proc. of 52nd Annual Meeting of the Association for Computational Linguistics: System Demonstrations*, pages 55–60, Baltimore, MD, 2014. https://www.aclweb.org/anthology/P14-5010 DOI: 10.3115/v1/p14-5010 32

Ramesh Manuvinakurike, David DeVault, and Kallirroi Georgila. Using reinforcement learning to model incrementality in a fast-paced dialogue game. In *Proc. of the 18th Annual SIGdial Meeting on Discourse and Dialogue*, pages 331–341, Association for Computational Linguistics, Saarbrücken, Germany, August 2017. https://www.aclweb.org/anthology/W17-5539 DOI: 10.18653/v1/w17-5539 173

Mitchell Marcus, Beatrice Santorini, and Mary Ann Marcinkiewicz. Building a large annotated corpus of English: The Penn treebank. *Computational Linguistics*, 19(2):313–330, 1993. DOI: 10.21236/ada273556 75

Joseph Mariani, Rosset Sophie, Martine Garnier-Rizet, and Laurence Devillers, Eds. *Natural Interaction with Robots, Knowbots and Smartphones*. Springer, 2014. DOI: 10.1007/978-1-4614-8280-2 177

Yoichi Matsuyama, Arjun Bhardwaj, Ran Zhao, Oscar Romeo, Sushma Akoju, and Justine Cassell. Socially-aware animated intelligent personal assistant agent. In *Proc. of the 17th Annual Meeting of the Special Interest Group on Discourse and Dialogue*, pages 224–227, Association for Computational Linguistics, Los Angeles, September 2016. https://www.aclweb.org/anthology/W16-3628 DOI: 10.18653/v1/w16-3628 23

Adrienne Mayor. *Gods and Robots: Myths, Machines, and Ancient Dreams of Technology*. Princeton University Press, 2018. DOI: 10.2307/j.ctvc779xn 14

Scott McGlashan, Norman Fraser, Nigel Gilbert, Eric Bilange, Paul Heisterkamp, and Nick Youd. Dialogue management for telephone information systems. In *Proc. of the 3rd Conference on Applied Natural Language Processing, ANLC'92*, pages 245–246, Association for Computational Linguistics, 1992. DOI: 10.3115/974499.974549 16

Gary McKeown, Michel F. Valstar, Roderick Cowie, and Maja Pantic. The SEMAINE corpus of emotionally coloured character interactions. In *IEEE International Conference on Multimedia and Expo*, pages 1079–1084, 2010. DOI: 10.1109/icme.2010.5583006 154

Michael F. McTear. *The Articulate Computer*. Blackwell, Oxford, 1987. 15

Michael F. McTear. Using the CSLU toolkit for practicals in spoken dialogue technology. In *MATISSE-ESCA/SOCRATES Workshop on Method and Tool Innovations for Speech Science Education*, pages 113–116, 1999. 18

Michael F. McTear. *Spoken Dialogue Technology: Toward the Conversational User Interface*. Springer Science & Business Media, 2004. DOI: 10.1007/978-0-85729-414-2 19

Michael F. McTear, Zoraida Callejas, and David Griol. *The Conversational Interface: Talking to Smart Devices*. Springer, New York, 2016. DOI: 10.1007/978-3-319-32967-3 13, 19, 22, 28

Helen M. Meng, Carmen Wai, and Roberto Pieraccini. The use of belief networks for mixed-initiative dialog modeling. *IEEE Transactions on Speech and Audio Processing*, 11(6):757–773, 2003. DOI: 10.1109/tsa.2003.814380 76

Grégoire Mesnil, Xiaodong He, Li Deng, and Yoshua Bengio. Investigation of recurrent-neural-network architectures and learning methods for spoken language understanding. In

Proc. of the 14th Annual Meeting of the International Speech Communication Association (INTERSPEECH), pages 3771–3775, Lyon, France, August 2013. https://www.iscaspeech.org/archive/interspeech_2013/i13_3771.html 76

Grégoire Mesnil, Yann Dauphin, Kaisheng Yao, Yoshua Bengio, Li Deng, Dilek Hakkani-Tür, Xiaodong He, and Geoffrey Zweig. Using recurrent neural networks for slot filling in spoken language understanding. *IEEE/ACM Transactions on Audio, Speech, and Language Processing*, 23(3):530–539, 2014. DOI: 10.1109/taslp.2014.2383614 76

Drew Meyer. Introducing Alexa conversations (beta), a new AI-driven approach to providing conversational experiences that feel more natural, July 2020. https://developer.amazon.com/en-US/blogs/alexa/alexa-skills-kit/2020/07/introducing-alexa-conversations-beta-a-new-ai-driven-approach-to-providing-conversational-experiences-that-feel-more-natural 64, 65

Tomas Mikolov, Kai Chen, Greg Corrado, and Jeffrey Dean. Efficient estimation of word representations in vector space. *ArXiv Preprint ArXiv:1301.3781*, 2013a. 130

Tomas Mikolov, Ilya Sutskever, Kai Chen, Greg S. Corrado, and Jeff Dean. Distributed representations of words and phrases and their compositionality. In *Advances in Neural Information Processing Systems*, pages 3111–3119, 2013b. 131, 132

Tomáš Mikolov, Wen-tau Yih, and Geoffrey Zweig. Linguistic regularities in continuous space word representations. In *Proc. of the Conference of the North American Chapter of the Association for Computational Linguistics: Human Language Technologies*, pages 746–751, Atlanta, GA June 2013c. https://www.aclweb.org/anthology/N13-1090 131

Adam S. Miner, Arnold Milstein, Stephen Schueller, Roshini Hegde, Christina Mangurian, and Eleni Linos. Smartphone-based conversational agents and responses to questions about mental health, interpersonal violence, and physical health. *JAMA Internal Medicine*, 176(5):619–625, 2016. DOI: 10.1001/jamainternmed.2016.0400 180

Wolfgang Minker, Dirk Bühler, and Laila Dybkjær. *Spoken Multimodal Human-Computer Dialogue in Mobile Environments*, vol. 28. Springer Science & Business Media, 2006. DOI: 10.1007/1-4020-3075-4 160

Volodymyr Mnih, Koray Kavukcuoglu, David Silver, Alex Graves, Ioannis Antonoglou, Daan Wierstra, and Martin Riedmiller. Playing atari with deep reinforcement learning. *ArXiv Preprint ArXiv:1312.5602*, 2013. 87

Sebastian Möller. *Quality of Telephone-based Spoken Dialogue Systems*. Springer Science & Business Media, 2004. DOI: 10.1007/b100796 117, 118

Sebastian Möller and Friedemann Köster. Review of recent standardization activities in speech quality of experience. *Quality and User Experience*, 2(1), 2017. DOI: 10.1007/s41233-017-0012-7 116

Sebastian Möller, Roman Englert, Klaus Engelbrecht, Verena Hafner, Anthony Jameson, Antti Oulasvirta, Alexander Raake, and Norbert Reithinger. Memo: Towards automatic usability evaluation of spoken dialogue services by user error simulations. In *9th International Conference on Spoken Language Processing*, pages 1786–1789, Pittsburgh, PA, September 2006. https://www.isca-speech.org/archive/interspeech_2006/i06_1131.html 94

Sebastian Möller, Paula Smeele, Heleen Boland, and Jan Krebber. Evaluating spoken dialogue systems according to de-facto standards: A case study. *Computer Speech & Language*, 21(1):26–53, 2007. DOI: 10.1016/j.csl.2005.11.003 118

Sebastian Möller, Klaus-Peter Engelbrecht, Christine Kuhnel, Ina Wechsung, and Benjamin Weiss. A taxonomy of quality of service and quality of experience of multimodal human-machine interaction. In *International Workshop on Quality of Multimedia Experience*, pages 7–12, IEEE, San Diego, CA, July 2009. DOI: 10.1109/qomex.2009.5246986 116, 118

Johanna D. Moore and Peter Wiemer-Hastings. Discourse in computational linguistics and artificial intelligence. *Handbook of Discourse Processes*, pages 439–486, 2003. 65

Robert J. Moore and Raphael Arar. *Conversational UX Design: A Practitioner's Guide to the Natural Conversation Framework*. Association for Computing Machinery, New York, 2019. DOI: 10.1145/3304087 36, 37, 38

Nikola Mrkšić, Diarmuid O Séaghdha, Blaise Thomson, Milica Gašić, Pei-Hao Su, David Vandyke, Tsung-Hsien Wen, and Steve Young. Multi-domain dialog state tracking using recurrent neural networks. *ArXiv Preprint ArXiv:1506.07190*, 2015. DOI: 10.3115/v1/p15-2130 85

Nikola Mrkšić, Diarmuid O Séaghdha, Tsung-Hsien Wen, Blaise Thomson, and Steve Young. Neural belief tracker: Data-driven dialogue state tracking. *ArXiv Preprint ArXiv:1606.03777*, 2016. DOI: 10.18653/v1/p17-1163 85, 86

Shane T. Mueller, Robert R. Hoffman, William Clancey, Abigail Emrey, and Gary Klein. Explanation in human-AI systems: A literature meta-review, synopsis of key ideas and publications, and bibliography for explainable AI. *ArXiv Preprint ArXiv:1902.01876*, 2019. 180

Chetan Naik, Arpit Gupta, Hancheng Ge, Lambert Mathias, and Ruhi Sarikaya. Contextual slot carryover for disparate schemas. *ArXiv Preprint ArXiv:1806.01773*, 2016. DOI: 10.21437/interspeech.2018-1035 63

Henk Nap, Sandra Suijkerbuijk, Dirk Lukkien, Sara Casaccia, Roberta Bevilacqua, Gian Revel, Lorena Rossi, and Lorenzo Scalise. A social robot to support integrated person centered care. *International Journal of Integrated Care*, 18(s2), 2018. DOI: 10.5334/ijic.s2120 176

Vincent Ng. Machine learning for entity coreference resolution: A retrospective look at two decades of research. In *31st AAAI Conference on Artificial Intelligence*, pages 4877–4884, 2017. http://aaai.org/ocs/index.php/AAAI/AAAI17/paper/view/14995 170

Liqiang Nie, Wenjie Wang, Richang Hong, Meng Wang, and Qi Tian. Multimodal dialog system: Generating responses via adaptive decoders. In *Proc. of the 27th ACM International Conference on Multimedia*, Association for Computing Machinery, New York, 2019. DOI: 10.1145/3343031.3350923 162

Radoslaw Niewiadomski, Elisabetta Bevacqua, Maurizio Mancini, and Catherine Pelachaud. Greta: An interactive expressive ECA system. In *Proc. of The 8th International Conference on Autonomous Agents and Multiagent Systems - Volume 2, AAMAS'09*, pages 1399–1400, International Foundation for Autonomous Agents and Multiagent Systems, Richland, SC, 2009. DOI: 10.1145/1558109.1558314 22

Jekaterina Novikova, Ondřej Dušek, Amanda Cercas Curry, and Verena Rieser. Why we need new evaluation metrics for NLG. In *Proc. of the Conference on Empirical Methods in Natural Language Processing*, pages 2241–2252, Association for Computational Linguistics, Copenhagen, Denmark, September 2017. https://www.aclweb.org/anthology/D17-1238 DOI: 10.18653/v1/d17-1238 99

Jekaterina Novikova, Ondřej Dušek, and Verena Rieser. RankME: Reliable human ratings for natural language generation. In *Proc. of the Conference of the North American Chapter of the Association for Computational Linguistics: Human Language Technologies, Volume 2 (Short Papers)*, pages 72–78, New Orleans, LA, June 2018. https://www.aclweb.org/anthology/N18-2012 DOI: 10.18653/v1/n18-2012 100

Alice H. Oh and Alexander I. Rudnicky. Stochastic natural language generation for spoken dialog systems. *Computer Speech & Language*, 16(3–4):387–407, 2002. DOI: 10.1016/s0885-2308(02)00012-8 51, 79

Daniel E. O'Leary. Google's duplex: Pretending to be human. *Intelligent Systems in Accounting, Finance and Management*, 26(1):46–53, 2019. DOI: 10.1002/isaf.1443 14

Aaron van den Oord, Sander Dieleman, Heiga Zen, Karen Simonyan, Oriol Vinyals, Alex Graves, Nal Kalchbrenner, Andrew Senior, and Koray Kavukcuoglu. WaveNet: A generative model for raw audio. *ArXiv Preprint ArXiv:1609.03499*, 2016. 52

Sharon Oviatt and Philip R. Cohen. The paradigm shift to multimodality in contemporary computer interfaces. *Synthesis Lectures on Human-Centered Informatics*, 8(3):1–243, 2015. DOI: 10.2200/s00636ed1v01y201503hci030 160

Sharon Oviatt, Björn Schuller, Philip Cohen, Daniel Sonntag, and Gerasimos Potamianos. *The Handbook of Multimodal-Multisensor Interfaces, Volume 1: Foundations, User Modeling, and Common Modality Combinations*. Morgan & Claypool, 2017. DOI: 10.1145/3015783 160

Sharon Oviatt, Björn Schuller, Philip Cohen, Daniel Sonntag, Gerasimos Potamianos, and Antonio Krüger. *The Handbook of Multimodal-Multisensor Interfaces, Volume 2: Signal Processing, Architectures, and Detection of Emotion and Cognition*. Morgan & Claypool, 2018. DOI: 10.1145/3107990 160

Sharon Oviatt, Björn Schuller, Philip Cohen, Daniel Sonntag, Gerasimos Potamianos, and Antonio Krüger. *The Handbook of Multimodal-Multisensor Interfaces, Volume 3: Language Processing, Software, Commercialization, and Emerging Directions*. Morgan & Claypool, 2019. DOI: 10.1145/3233795 160

Tim Paek and Eric Horvitz. Conversation as action under uncertainty. In *Proc. of the 16th Conference on Uncertainty in Artificial Intelligence, UAI'00*, pages 455–464, Morgan Kaufmann Publishers Inc., San Francisco, CA, 2000. https://arxiv.org/pdf/1301.3883 76

Timothy Paek and Roberto Pieraccini. Automating spoken dialogue management design using machine learning: An industry perspective. *Speech Communication*, 50(8–9):716–729, 2008. DOI: 10.1016/j.specom.2008.03.010 66, 88

Alexandros Papangelis, Yi-Chia Wang, Piero Molino, and Gokhan Tur. Collaborative multi-agent dialogue model training via reinforcement learning. *ArXiv Preprint ArXiv:1907.05507*, 2019. DOI: 10.18653/v1/w19-5912 66

Alexandros Papangelis, Mahdi Namazifar, Chandra Khatri, Yi-Chia Wang, Piero Molino, and Gokhan Tur. Plato dialogue system: A flexible conversational AI research platform. *ArXiv Preprint ArXiv:2001.06463*, 2020. 66

Kishore Papineni, Salim Roukos, Todd Ward, and Wei-Jing Zhu. BLEU: A method for automatic evaluation of machine translation. In *Proc. of the 40th Annual Meeting on Association for Computational Linguistics*, pages 311–318, Association for Computational Linguistics, 2002. DOI: 10.3115/1073083.1073135 104

Stuart R. Patterson. Automated virtual caregiving using voice-first services: Proactive, personalized, wholistic, 24x7 and affordable. In David Metcalf, Teri Tisher, Sandhya Pruthi, and Harry P. Pappas, Eds., *Voice Technology in Healthcare: Leveraging Voice to Enhance Patient and Provider Experiences*, pages 111–147, CRC Press, Boca Raton, FL, 2020. https://voicefirsthealth.com/book/ 34

Cathy Pearl. *Designing Voice User Interfaces: Principles of Conversational Experiences*. O'Reilly Media, Inc., Sebastapol, 2016. 20, 40, 54

Catherine Pelachaud, Ed. *Emotion-Oriented Systems*. John Wiley & Sons, 2013. DOI: 10.1002/9781118601938 149

Jeffrey Pennington, Richard Socher, and Christopher D. Manning. Glove: Global vectors for word representation. In *Proc. of the Conference on Empirical Methods in Natural Language Processing (EMNLP)*, pages 1532–1543, Doha, Qatar, October 2014. DOI: 10.3115/v1/d14-1162 130

Matthew Peters, Mark Neumann, Mohit Iyyer, Matt Gardner, Christopher Clark, Kenton Lee, and Luke Zettlemoyer. Deep contextualized word representations. In *Proc. of the Conference of the North American Chapter of the Association for Computational Linguistics: Human Language Technologies, Volume 1 (Long Papers)*, pages 2227–2237, New Orleans, LA, June 2018. https://www.aclweb.org/anthology/N18-1202 DOI: 10.18653/v1/n18-1202 130

Michael Phi. Illustrated guide to LSTMs and GRUs: A step by step explanation. *Towards Data Science*, September 2018. https://towardsdatascience.com/illustrated-guide-to-lstms-and-gru-s-a-step-by-step-explanation-44e9eb85bf21 135

Rosalind W. Picard. *Affective Computing*. MIT Press, 2000. DOI: 10.7551/mitpress/1140.001.0001 149

Jan Pichl, Petr Marek, Jakub Konrád, Martin Matulík, Hoang Long Nguyen, and Jan Šedivý. Alquist 2.0: Alexa prize socialbot based on sub-dialogue models. *ArXiv Preprint ArXiv:1804.06705*, 2018. 68

Roberto Pieraccini. *The Voice in the Machine: Building Computers that Understand Speech*. MIT Press, Cambridge, MA, 2012. DOI: 10.7551/mitpress/9072.001.0001 14

Olivier Pietquin and Helen Hastie. A survey on metrics for the evaluation of user simulations. *The Knowledge Engineering Review*, 28(1):59–73, 2013. DOI: 10.1017/s0269888912000343 95

Martin Porcheron, Joel E. Fischer, Stuart Reeves, and Sarah Sharples. Voice interfaces in everyday life. In *Proc. of the CHI Conference on Human Factors in Computing Systems, CHI'18*, pages 1–12, Association for Computing Machinery, New York, 2018. DOI: 10.1145/3173574.3174214 171

Helmut Prendinger, Junichiro Mori, and Mitsuru Ishizuka. Using human physiology to evaluate subtle expressivity of a virtual quizmaster in a mathematical game. *International Journal of Human-Computer Studies*, 62(2):231–245, February 2005. DOI: 10.1016/j.ijhcs.2004.11.009 149

Matthew Purver, Florin Ratiu, and Lawrence Cavedon. Robust interpretation in dialogue by combining confidence scores with contextual features. In *Proc. of the 9th International Conference on Spoken Language Processing (INTERSPEECH)*, 2006. https://www.isca-speech.org/archive/interspeech_2006/i06_1314.html 48

Kirk Quimet. Conversations with GPT-3. *Medium*, July 2020. https://medium.com/@kirkouimet/my-mind-blowing-conversations-openais-latest-ai-gpt-3-235ba5fb9453 146

Alec Radford, Jeffrey Wu, Rewon Child, David Luan, Dario Amodei, and Ilya Sutskever. Language models are unsupervised multitask learners. *OpenAI Blog*, 1(8):9, 2019. 130, 140, 144, 166

Vikram Ramanarayanan, David Suendermann-Oeft, Hillary Molloy, Eugene Tsuprun, Patrick Lange, and Keelan Evanini. Crowdsourcing multimodal dialog interactions: Lessons learned from the HALEF case. In *Proc. of the Workshop on Crowdsourcing, Deep Learning and Artificial Intelligence Agents*, pages 423–431, American Association of Artificial Intelligence (AAAI), San Francisco, CA, 2017. https://www.aaai.org/ocs/index.php/WS/AAAIW17/paper/view/15197 95

Hannah Rashkin, Eric Michael Smith, Margaret Li, and Y-Lan Boureau. Towards empathetic open-domain conversation models: A new benchmark and dataset. *ArXiv Preprint ArXiv: 1811.00207*, 2018. DOI: 10.18653/v1/p19-1534 143

Antoine Raux and Maxine Eskenazi. Optimizing the turn-taking behavior of task-oriented spoken dialog systems. *ACM Transactions on Speech and Language Processing (TSLP)*, 9(1):1–23, 2012. DOI: 10.1145/2168748.2168749 174

Antoine Raux, Brian Langner, Dan Bohus, Alan W. Black, and Maxine Eskenazi. Let's go public! taking a spoken dialog system to the real world. In *Proc. of the 8th International Conference on Spoken Language Processing (INTERSPEECH)*, pages 885–888, 2005. https://www.isca-speech.org/archive/interspeech_2005/i05_0885.html 151

Evgeniia Razumovskaia and Maxine Eskenazi. Incorporating rules into end-to-end dialog systems. In *3rd NeurIPS Workshop on Conversational AI*, Vancouver, Canada, December 2019. http://alborz-geramifard.com/workshops/neurips19-Conversational-AI/Papers/43.pdf 175

Ronan G. Reilly, Ed. *Communication Failure in Dialogue and Discourse: Detection and Repair Processes*. Elsevier (North-Holland Publishing Co.), Amsterdam, 1987. 15

Ehud Reiter and Anja Belz. An investigation into the validity of some metrics for automatically evaluating natural language generation systems. *Computational Linguistics*, 35(4):529–558, 2009. DOI: 10.1162/coli.2009.35.4.35405 99

Ehud Reiter and Robert Dale. *Building Natural Language Generation Systems*. Cambridge University Press, Cambridge, 2000. DOI: 10.1017/cbo9780511519857 51

Ehud Reiter, Roma Robertson, and Liesl M. Osman. Lessons from a failure: Generating tailored smoking cessation letters. *Artificial Intelligence*, 144(1-2):41–58, 2003. DOI: 10.1016/s0004-3702(02)00370-3 99

Viktor Richter, Birte Carlmeyer, Florian Lier, Sebastian Meyer Zu Borgsen, David Schlangen, Franz Kummert, Sven Wachsmuth, and Britta Wrede. Are you talking to me? improving the robustness of dialogue systems in a multi party HRI scenario by incorporating gaze direction and lip movement of attendees. In *Proc. of the 4th International Conference on Human Agent Interaction*, pages 43–50, Association for Computing Machinery, New York, 2016. DOI: 10.1145/2974804.2974823 171

Hannes Rieser and David Schlangen. Introduction to the special issue on incremental processing in dialogue. *Dialogue and Discourse*, 2(1), 2011. DOI: 10.5087/dad.2011.001 172

Verena Rieser and Oliver Lemon. Learning and evaluation of dialogue strategies for new applications: Empirical methods for optimization from small data sets. *Computational Linguistics*, 37(1):153–196, 2011a. DOI: 10.1162/coli_a_00038 116

Verena Rieser and Oliver Lemon. *Reinforcement Learning for Adaptive Dialogue Systems: A Data-Driven Methodology for Dialogue Management and Natural Language Generation*. Springer Science & Business Media, 2011b. DOI: 10.1007/978-3-642-24942-6 19, 72, 87, 89

Verena Rieser, Oliver Lemon, and Xingkun Liu. Optimising information presentation for spoken dialogue systems. In *Proc. of the 48th Annual Meeting of the Association for Computational Linguistics*, pages 1009–1018, Association for Computational Linguistics, Uppsala, Sweden, July 2010. https://www.aclweb.org/anthology/P10-1103 51, 79

Verena Rieser, Oliver Lemon, and Simon Keizer. Natural language generation as incremental planning under uncertainty: Adaptive information presentation for statistical dialogue systems. *IEEE/ACM Transactions on Audio, Speech, and Language Processing*, 22(5):979–994, 2014. DOI: 10.1109/tasl.2014.2315271 51, 79, 80, 99

Eric K. Ringger and James F. Allen. Error correction via a post-processor for continuous speech recognition. In *Proc. of the IEEE International Conference on Acoustics, Speech, and Signal Processing*, pages 427–430, 1996. DOI: 10.1109/icassp.1996.541124 48

Alan Ritter, Colin Cherry, and William B. Dolan. Data-driven response generation in social media. In *Proc. of the Conference on Empirical Methods in Natural Language Processing*, pages 583–593, Association for Computational Linguistics, Edinburgh, Scotland, UK, July 2011. https://www.aclweb.org/anthology/D11-1054 153

Jean-Philippe Robichaud, Paul A. Crook, Puyang Xu, Omar Zia Khan, and Ruhi Sarikaya. Hypotheses ranking for robust domain classification and tracking in dialogue systems. In *Proc. of the 15th Annual Conference of the International Speech Communication Association (INTERSPEECH)*. ISCA—International Speech Communication Association, September 2014. https://www.microsoft.com/en-us/research/publication/hypotheses-ranking-for-robust-domain-classification-and-tracking-in-dialogue-systems/ 48

Matthew Roddy, Gabriel Skantze, and Naomi Harte. Investigating speech features for continuous turn-taking prediction using LSTMs. *ArXiv Preprint ArXiv:1806.11461*, 2018. DOI: 10.21437/interspeech.2018-2124 174

Lina Maria Rojas-Barahona and Toni Giorgino. Adaptable dialog architecture and runtime engine (adarte): A framework for rapid prototyping of health dialog systems. *International Journal of Medical Informatics*, 78:S56–S68, 2009. DOI: 10.1016/j.ijmedinf.2008.07.017 67

Stephen Roller, Emily Dinan, Naman Goyal, Da Ju, Mary Williamson, Yinhan Liu, Jing Xu, Myle Ott, Kurt Shuster, Eric M. Smith, Y-Lan Boureau, and Jason Weston. Recipes for building an open-domain chatbot. *ArXiv Preprint ArXiv:2004.13637*, 2020. 21, 142

Harvey Sacks, Emanuel A. Schegloff, and Gail Jefferson. A simplest systematics for the organization of turn taking for conversation. In *Studies in the Organization of Conversational Interaction*, pages 7–55, Elsevier, 1978. 173

Amrita Saha, Mitesh Khapra, and Karthik Sankaranarayanan. Towards building large scale multimodal domain-aware conversation systems. *ArXiv Preprint ArXiv:1704.00200*, 2017. 162

Priyanka Sahu, Mohit Dua, and Ankit Kumar. Challenges and issues in adopting speech recognition. In S. S. Agrawal, Amita Devi, Ritika Wason, and Poonam Bansal, Eds., *Speech and Language Processing for Human-Machine Communications*, pages 209–215, Springer Singapore, Singapore, 2018. DOI: 10.1007/978-981-10-6626-9_23 18

Maha Salem, Stefan Kopp, Ipke Wachsmuth, and Frank Joublin. Towards an integrated model of speech and gesture production for multi-modal robot behavior. In *19th International Symposium in Robot and Human Interactive Communication*, pages 614–619, IEEE, 2010. DOI: 10.1109/roman.2010.5598665 22

Ruhi Sarikaya. The technology behind personal digital assistants: An overview of the system architecture and key components. *IEEE Signal Processing Magazine*, 34(1):67–81, 2017. DOI: 10.1109/msp.2016.2617341 13, 26, 158

Ruhi Sarikaya, Geoffrey E. Hinton, and Anoop Deoras. Application of deep belief networks for natural language understanding. *IEEE/ACM Transactions on Audio, Speech, and Language Processing*, 22(4):778–784, 2014. DOI: 10.1109/taslp.2014.2303296 75

Jost Schatzmann and Steve Young. The hidden agenda user simulation model. *IEEE Transactions on Audio, Speech, and Language Processing*, 17(4):733–747, 2009. DOI: 10.1109/tasl.2008.2012071 94

Jost Schatzmann, Kallirroi Georgila, and Steve Young. Quantitative evaluation of user simulation techniques for spoken dialogue systems. In *6th SIGdial Workshop on Discourse and Dialogue*, 2005. 89

Jost Schatzmann, Karl Weilhammer, Matt Stuttle, and Steve Young. A survey of statistical user simulation techniques for reinforcement-learning of dialogue management strategies. *The Knowledge Engineering Review*, 21(2):97–126, 2006. DOI: 10.1017/s0269888906000944 88, 94

Jost Schatzmann, Blaise Thomson, Karl Weilhammer, Hui Ye, and Steve Young. Agenda-based user simulation for bootstrapping a pomdp dialogue system. In *Human Language Technologies: The Conference of the North American Chapter of the Association for Computational Linguistics; Companion Volume, Short Papers*, pages 149–152, Association for Computational Linguistics, 2007. DOI: 10.3115/1614108.1614146 89

Emanuel A. Schegloff. *Sequence Organization in Interaction: A Primer in Conversation Analysis*, vol. 1. Cambridge University Press, 2007. DOI: 10.1017/cbo9780511791208 36

David Schlangen and Gabriel Skantze. A general, abstract model of incremental dialogue processing. *Dialogue and Discourse*, 2(1):83–111, 2011. DOI: 10.5087/dad.2011.105 172

Alexander Schmitt and Stefan Ultes. Interaction Quality. *Speech Communication*, 74:12–36, November 2015. DOI: 10.1016/j.specom.2015.06.003 93, 118, 119

Alexander Schmitt, Benjamin Schatz, and Wolfgang Minker. Modeling and predicting quality in spoken human-computer interaction. In *Proc. of the 12th SIGdial Workshop on Discourse and Dialogue*, pages 173–184, Association for Computational Linguistics, 2011. https://www.aclweb.org/anthology/W11-2020/ 104, 118

Mike Schuster and Kuldip K. Paliwal. Bidirectional recurrent neural networks. *IEEE Transactions on Signal Processing*, 45(11):2673–2681, 1997. DOI: 10.1109/78.650093 134

Jetze Schuurmans and Flavius Frasincar. Intent classification for dialogue utterances. *IEEE Intelligent Systems*, 35(1):82–88, 2019. DOI: 10.1109/mis.2019.2954966 75

John R. Searle. *Speech Acts: An Essay in the Philosophy of Language*. Cambridge University Press, 1969. DOI: 10.1017/CBO9781139173438 15

João Sedoc, Daphne Ippolito, Arun Kirubarajan, Jai Thirani, Lyle Ungar, and Chris Callison-Burch. ChatEval: A tool for chatbot evaluation. In *Proc. of the Conference of the North American*

Chapter of the Association for Computational Linguistics (Demonstrations), pages 60–65, Association for Computational Linguistics, Minneapolis, MN, June 2019. https://www.aclweb.org/anthology/N19-4011 110

Abigail See, Stephen Roller, Douwe Kiela, and Jason Weston. What makes a good conversation? how controllable attributes affect human judgments. In *Proc. of the Conference of the North American Chapter of the Association for Computational Linguistics: Human Language Technologies, Volume 1 (Long and Short Papers)*, pages 1702–1723, Minneapolis, MN, June 2019. https://www.aclweb.org/anthology/N19-1170 DOI: 10.18653/v1/n19-1170 107, 147

Stephanie Seneff and Joseph Polifroni. Dialogue management in the Mercury flight reservation system. In *ANLP-NAACL Workshop: Conversational Systems*, 2000. https://www.aclweb.org/anthology/W00-0303 DOI: 10.3115/1117562.1117565 16

Iulian V Serban, Alessandro Sordoni, Yoshua Bengio, Aaron Courville, and Joelle Pineau. Building end-to-end dialogue systems using generative hierarchical neural network models. In *Proc. of the 30th AAAI Conference on Artificial Intelligence, AAAI'16*, pages 3776–3783, AAAI Press, 2016. 136, 137

Iulian Vlad Serban, Ryan Lowe, Peter Henderson, Laurent Charlin, and Joelle Pineau. A survey of available corpora for building data-driven dialogue systems. *ArXiv Preprint ArXiv:1512.05742*, 2015. DOI: 10.5087/dad.2018.101 71, 151

Iulian Vlad Serban, Tim Klinger, Gerald Tesauro, Kartik Talamadupula, Bowen Zhou, Yoshua Bengio, and Aaron Courville. Multiresolution recurrent neural networks: An application to dialogue response generation. In *Proc. of the 31st AAAI Conference on Artificial Intelligence*, pages 3288–3294, AAAI Press, 2017a. https://aaai.org/ocs/index.php/AAAI/AAAI17/paper/view/14571 95

Iulian Vlad Serban, Alessandro Sordoni, Ryan Lowe, Laurent Charlin, Joelle Pineau, Aaron Courville, and Yoshua Bengio. A hierarchical latent variable encoder-decoder model for generating dialogues. In *Proc. of the 31st AAAI Conference on Artificial Intelligence*, pages 3295–3301, AAAI Press, 2017b. 136

Igor Shalyminov, Arash Eshghi, and Oliver Lemon. Challenging neural dialogue models with natural data: Memory networks fail on incremental phenomena. *ArXiv Preprint ArXiv:1709.07840*, 2017. DOI: 10.21437/semdial.2017-11 154

Igor Shalyminov, Ondřej Dušek, and Oliver Lemon. Neural response ranking for social conversation: A data-efficient approach. In *Proc. of the EMNLP Workshop SCAI: The 2nd International Workshop on Search-Oriented Conversational AI*, pages 1–8, Association for Computational Linguistics, Brussels, Belgium, October 2018. https://www.aclweb.org/anthology/W18-5701 DOI: 10.18653/v1/w18-5701 69, 138

Igor Shalyminov, Sungjin Lee, Arash Eshghi, and Oliver Lemon. Few-shot dialogue generation without annotated data: A transfer learning approach. In *Proc. of the 20th Annual SIGdial Meeting on Discourse and Dialogue*, pages 32–39, Association for Computational Linguistics, Stockholm, Sweden, September 2019. https://www.aclweb.org/anthology/W19-5904 DOI: 10.18653/v1/w19-5904 78, 166

Igor Shalyminov, Alessandro Sordoni, Adam Atkinson, and Hannes Schulz. Fast domain adaptation for goal-oriented dialogue using a hybrid generative-retrieval transformer. In *IEEE International Conference on Acoustics, Speech and Signal Processing (ICASSP)*, pages 8039–8043, 2020a. DOI: 10.1109/icassp40776.2020.9053599 78, 152

Igor Shalyminov, Alessandro Sordoni, Adam Atkinson, and Hannes Schulz. Hybrid generative-retrieval transformers for dialogue domain adaptation. *ArXiv Preprint ArXiv: 2003.01680*, 2020b. 138, 166

Bayan Abu Shawar and Eric Steven Atwell. Using corpora in machine-learning chatbot systems. *International Journal of Corpus Linguistics*, 10(4):489–516, 2005. DOI: 10.1075/ijcl.10.4.06sha 22

Amir Shevat. *Designing Bots*. O'Reilly, Boston, MA, 2017. 24, 54

Satinder Singh, Diane Litman, Michael Kearns, and Marilyn Walker. Optimizing dialogue management with reinforcement learning: Experiments with the NJFun system. *Journal of Artificial Intelligence Research*, 16(1):105–133, February 2002. DOI: 10.1613/jair.859 82, 84

Gabriel Skantze. Towards a general, continuous model of turn-taking in spoken dialogue using LSTM recurrent neural networks. In *Proc. of the 18th Annual SIGdial Meeting on Discourse and Dialogue*, pages 220–230, 2017. DOI: 10.18653/v1/w17-5527 174

Gabriel Skantze and Anna Hjalmarsson. Towards incremental speech generation in conversational systems. *Computer Speech & Language*, 27(1):243–262, 2013. DOI: 10.1016/j.csl.2012.05.004 172

Gabriel Skantze, Martin Johansson, and J. Beskow. Exploring turn-taking cues in multi-party human-robot discussions about objects. In *ICMI*, 2015. DOI: 10.1145/2818346.2820749 174

Gabriel Skantze, Joakim Gustafson, and Jonas Beskow. Multimodal conversational interaction with robots. In Sharon Oviatt, Björn Schuller, Philip R. Cohen, Daniel Sonntag, Gerasimos Potamianos, and Antonio Krüger, Eds., *The Handbook of Multimodal-Multisensor Interfaces: Language Processing, Software, Commercialization, and Emerging Directions - Volume 3*, pages 77–104, Association for Computing Machinery (ACM) and Morgan & Claypool, 2019. DOI: 10.1145/3233795.3233799 176

Eric Michael Smith, Mary Williamson, Kurt Shuster, Jason Weston, and Y-Lan Boureau. Can you put it all together: Evaluating conversational agents' ability to blend skills. *ArXiv Preprint ArXiv: 2004.08449*, 2020. DOI: 10.18653/v1/2020.acl-main.183 143

David R. So, Quoc V. Le, and Chen Liang. The evolved transformer. In Kamalika Chaudhuri and Ruslan Salakhutdinov, Eds., *Proc. of the 36th International Conference on Machine Learning,(ICML)*, volume 97 of *Proc. of Machine Learning Research*, pages 5877–5886, PMLR, Long Beach, CA, June 2019. http://proceedings.mlr.press/v97/so19a.html 141

Richard Socher, Cliff C. Lin, Chris Manning, and Andrew Y. Ng. Parsing natural scenes and natural language with recursive neural networks. In *Proc. of the 28th International Conference on Machine Learning (ICML-11)*, pages 129–136, 2011. 76

Yiping Song, Rui Yan, Xiang Li, Dongyan Zhao, and Ming Zhang. Two are better than one: An ensemble of retrieval-and generation-based dialog systems. In *Proc. of the 27th International Joint Conference on Artificial Intelligence, (IJCAI-18), Main Track*, pages 4382–4388, International Joint Conferences on Artificial Intelligence (IJCAI). Stockholm, Sweden, July 2016. DOI: 10.24963/ijcai.2018/609 138

Alessandro Sordoni, Michel Galley, Michael Auli, Chris Brockett, Yangfeng Ji, Margaret Mitchell, Jian-Yun Nie, Jianfeng Gao, and Bill Dolan. A neural network approach to context-sensitive generation of conversational responses. *ArXiv Preprint ArXiv:1506.06714*, 2015. DOI: 10.3115/v1/n15-1020 136

Andreas Stolcke, Klaus Ries, Noah Coccaro, Elizabeth Shriberg, Rebecca Bates, Daniel Jurafsky, Paul Taylor, Rachel Martin, Carol Van Ess-Dykema, and Marie Meteer. Dialogue act modeling for automatic tagging and recognition of conversational speech. *Computational Linguistics*, 26(3):339–373, 2000. DOI: 10.1162/089120100561737 48

Alessandro Suglia, Ioannis Konstas, Andrea Vanzo, Emanuele Bastianelli, Desmond Elliott, Stella Frank, and Oliver Lemon. Compguesswhat?!: A multi-task evaluation framework for grounded language learning. *ArXiv Preprint ArXiv: 2006.02174*, 2020. DOI: 10.18653/v1/2020.acl-main.682 165

Rhea Sukthanker, Soujanya Poria, Erik Cambria, and Ramkumar Thirunavukarasu. Anaphora and coreference resolution: A review. *Information Fusion*, 59:139–162, 2020. http://www.sciencedirect.com/science/article/pii/S1566253519303677 DOI: 10.1016/j.inffus.2020.01.010 170

Haitian Sun, Bhuwan Dhingra, Manzil Zaheer, Kathryn Mazaitis, Ruslan Salakhutdinov, and William W. Cohen. Open domain question answering using early fusion of knowledge bases and text. In *Proc. of the Conference on Empirical Methods in Natural Language Processing*, pages 4231–4242, Association for Computational Linguistics, Brussels, Belgium, October–November 2018. DOI: 10.18653/v1/d18-1455 167

Ilya Sutskever, Oriol Vinyals, and Quoc V. Le. Sequence to sequence learning with neural networks. In *Advances in Neural Information Processing Systems*, pages 3104–3112, Montreal, Canada, December 2014. https://dl.acm.org/citation.cfm?id=2969033.2969173 127

Stephen Sutton and Ronald Cole. The CSLU toolkit: Rapid prototyping of spoken language systems. In *Proc. of the 10th annual ACM Symposium on User Interface Software and Technology*, pages 85–86, Banff, Alberta, Canada, October 1997. DOI: 10.1145/263407.263517 18

Michael K. Tanenhaus. Sentence processing. *Encyclopedia of Cognitive Science*, 2006. DOI: 10.1002/0470018860.s00613 172

Blaise Thomson and Steve Young. Bayesian update of dialogue state: A POMDP framework for spoken dialogue systems. *Computer Speech & Language*, 24(4):562–588, 2010. DOI: 10.1016/j.csl.2009.07.003 84, 87

Jörg Tiedemann. Parallel data, tools and interfaces in OPUS. In *Proc. of the 8th International Conference on Language Resources and Evaluation (LREC'12)*, pages 2214–2218, European Language Resources Association (ELRA), Istanbul, Turkey, May 2012. http://www.lrec-conf.org/proceedings/lrec2012/pdf/463_Paper.pdf 153

David Traum. Issues in multiparty dialogues. In Frank Dignum, Ed., *Advances in Agent Communication*, pages 201–211, Springer, July 2003. DOI: 10.1007/978-3-540-24608-4_12 171

David Traum. Computational approaches to dialogue. In Edda Weigand, Ed., *The Routledge Handbook of Language and Dialogue*, pages 143–161, Taylor & Francis, 2017. DOI: 10.4324/9781315750583-10 49

David R. Traum and Staffan Larsson. The information state approach to dialog management. In Jan C. J. van Kuppevelt and Ronnie W. Smith, Eds., *Current and New Directions in Discourse and Dialog*, pages 325–353, Kluwer Academic Publishers, Dordrecht, 2003. DOI: 10.1007/978-94-010-0019-2_15 16

Yi-Lin Tuan, Yun-Nung Chen, and Hung-yi Lee. Dykgchat: Benchmarking dialogue generation grounding on dynamic knowledge graphs. In *Proc. of the Conference on Empirical Methods in Natural Language Processing and the 9th International Joint Conference on Natural Language Processing (EMNLP-IJCNLP)*, pages 1855–1865, Association for Computational Linguistics, Hong Kong, China, November 2019. https://www.aclweb.org/anthology/D19-1194 DOI: 10.18653/v1/d19-1194 168

Gokhan Tur and Renato De Mori. *Spoken Language Understanding: Systems for Extracting Semantic Information from Speech.* John Wiley & Sons, Chichester, 2011. DOI: 10.1002/9781119992691 75

Gokhan Tur, Li Deng, Dilek Hakkani-Tür, and Xiaodong He. Towards deeper understanding: Deep convex networks for semantic utterance classification. In *IEEE International Conference on Acoustics, Speech and Signal Processing (ICASSP)*, pages 5045–5048, Kyoto, Japan, March 2012. DOI: 10.1109/icassp.2012.6289054 76

Gokhan Tur, Asli Celikyilmaz, Xiaodong He, Dilek Hakkani-Tür, and Li Deng. Deep learning in conversational language understanding. In Li Deng and Yang Liu, Eds., *Deep Learning in Natural Language Processing*, pages 23–48, Springer, Singapore, 2018. DOI: 10.1007/978-981-10-5209-5_2 72, 75, 76

Alan Turing. Computing machinery and intelligence. *Mind*, 59(236):433–460, 1950. DOI: 10.1093/mind/LIX.236.433 20, 110

Markku Turunen, Jaakko Hakulinen, and Anssi Kainulainen. Evaluation of a spoken dialogue system with usability tests and long-term pilot studies: Similarities and differences. In *Proc. of the 9th International Conference on Spoken Language Processing (INTERSPEECH)*, Pittsburgh, PA, September 2006. https://www.isca-speech.org/archive/interspeech_2006/i06_1978.html 93

Stefan Ultes and Wolfgang Minker. Interaction quality estimation in spoken dialogue systems using hybrid-hmms. In *Proc. of the 15th Annual Meeting of the Special Interest Group on Discourse and Dialogue (SIGDIAL)*, pages 208–217, 2014. https://www.aclweb.org/anthology/W14-4328.pdf DOI: 10.3115/v1/w14-4328 120

Stefan Ultes, Alexander Schmitt, and Wolfgang Minker. Towards quality-adaptive spoken dialogue management. In *NAACL-HLT Workshop on Future Directions and Needs in the Spoken Dialog Community: Tools and Data*, pages 49–52, Association for Computational Linguistics, Montreal, Canada, June 2012. 120

Stefan Ultes, Alexander Schmitt, and Wolfgang Minker. On quality ratings for spoken dialogue systems—experts vs. users. In *Proc. of the Conference of the North American Chapter of the Association for Computational Linguistics: Human Language Technologies*, pages 569–578, Atlanta, Georgia, June 2013. https://www.aclweb.org/anthology/N13-1064 93, 118

Stefan Ultes, Hüseyin Dikme, and Wolfgang Minker. First insight into quality-adaptive dialogue. In *Proc. of the 9th International Conference on Language Resources and Evaluation (LREC)*, pages 246–251, European Language Resources Association (ELRA), Reykjavik, Iceland, May 2014. http://www.lrec-conf.org/proceedings/lrec2014/pdf/113_Paper.pdf 118, 119, 120

Stefan Ultes, Lina M. Rojas-Barahona, Pei-Hao Su, David Vandyke, Dongho Kim, I nigo Casanueva, Paweł Budzianowski, Nikola Mrkšić, Tsung-Hsien Wen, Milica Gašić, and Steve

Young. PyDial: A multi-domain statistical dialogue system toolkit. In *Proc. of ACL, System Demonstrations*, pages 73–78, Association for Computational Linguistics, Vancouver, Canada, July 2017. https://www.aclweb.org/anthology/P17-4013 DOI: 10.18653/v1/p17-4013 18

Emanuele Vanzo, Andrea Bastianelli, and Oliver Lemon. Hierarchical multi-task natural language understanding for cross-domain conversational AI: HERMIT NLU. In *Proc. of the 20th Annual SIGdial Meeting on Discourse and Dialogue*, pages 254–263, Association for Computational Linguistics, Stockholm, Sweden, September 2019. https://www.aclweb.org/anthology/W19-5931 DOI: 10.18653/v1/w19-5931 76

Ashish Vaswani, Noam Shazeer, Niki Parmar, Jakob Uszkoreit, Llion Jones, Aidan N. Gomez, Lukasz Kaiser, and Illia Polosukhin. Attention is all you need. In *Proc. of the 31st International Conference on Neural Information Processing Systems, NIPS'17*, pages 6000–6010, Curran Associates Inc., Red Hook, NY, 2017. https://arxiv.org/abs/1706.03762 137

Anu Venkatesh, Chandra Khatri, Ashwin Ram, Fenfei Guo, Raefer Gabriel, Ashish Nagar, Rohit Prasad, Ming Cheng, Behnam Hedayatnia, Angeliki Metallinou, et al. On evaluating and comparing conversational agents. *ArXiv Preprint ArXiv:1801.03625*, 4:60–68, 2018. 109, 111

Oriol Vinyals and Quoc Le. A neural conversational model. *ArXiv Preprint ArXiv:1506.05869*, 2015. 127

Vladimir Vlasov, Johannes E. M. Mosig, and Alan Nichol. Dialogue transformers. *ArXiv Preprint ArXiv:1910.00486*, 2019. 137

Petra Wagner, Jonas Beskow, Simon Betz, Jens Edlund, Joakim Gustafson, Eje Henter, Sébastien Le Maguer, Zofia Malisz, Éva Székely, Christina Tånnander, and Jana Voße. Speech synthesis evaluation—state-of-the-art assessment and suggestion for a novel research program. In *Proc. of the 10th ISCA Speech Synthesis Workshop*, pages 105–110, Vienna, Austria, September 2019. DOI: 10.21437/ssw.2019-19 101

Wolfgang Wahlster. *SmartKom: Foundations of Multimodal Dialogue Systems*, vol. 12. Springer, 2006. DOI: 10.1007/3-540-36678-4 22, 160, 162

Marilyn Walker, Candace Kamm, and Diane Litman. Towards developing general models of usability with PARADISE. *Natural Language Engineering*, 6(3–4):363–377, 2000a. DOI: 10.1017/s1351324900002503 114

Marilyn A. Walker, Diane J. Litman, Candace A. Kamm, and Alicia Abella. PARADISE: A framework for evaluating spoken dialogue agents. In *35th Annual Meeting of the Association for Computational Linguistics and 8th Conference of the European Chapter of the Association for*

Computational Linguistics, pages 271–280, Madrid, Spain, July 1997. https://www.aclweb.org/anthology/P97-1035 DOI: 10.3115/976909.979652 82, 114, 115

Marilyn A. Walker, Diane J. Litman, Candace A. Kamm, and Alicia Abella. Evaluating spoken dialogue agents with PARADISE: Two case studies. *Computer Speech & Language*, 12(4):317–347, 1998. DOI: 10.1006/csla.1998.0110 114

Marilyn A. Walker, Lynette Hirschman, and John S. Aberdeen. Evaluation for Darpa Communicator spoken dialogue systems. In *Proc. of the 2nd International Conference on Language Resources and Evaluation (LREC'00)*, Athens, Greece, May 2000b. https://www.aclweb.org/anthology/L00-1143/ 91

Marilyn A. Walker, Jiohn S. Aberdeen, Julie E. Boland, Elizabeth Bratt, John S. Garofolo, Lynette Hirschman, Audrey N. Le, Sungbok Lee, Shrikanth S. Narayanan, Kishore Papineni, Bryan L. Pellom, Joseph Polifroni, Alexandros Potamianos, P. Prabhu, Alexander J. Rudnicky, Gregory A. Sanders, Stephanie Seneff, David Stallard, and Steve Whittaker. DARPA communicator dialog travel planning systems: The June 2000 data collection. In *Proc. of the 7th European Conference on Speech Communication and Technology (Eurospeech)*, pages 1371–1374, Aalborg, Denmark, September 2001. http://www.isca-speech.org/archive/eurospeech2001/e011371.html 16

Marilyn A. Walker, Irene Langkilde-Geary, Helen Wright Hastie, Jerry Wright, and Allen Gorin. Automatically training a problematic dialogue predictor for the HMIHY spoken dialogue system. *Journal of Artificial Intelligence Research*, 16:293–319, 2002. DOI: 10.1613/jair.971 19, 82

Richard Wallace. The elements of AIML style, 2004. http://www.alicebot.org/style.pdf 58

Richard Wallace. The anatomy of A.L.I.C.E. In Robert Epstein, Gary Roberts, and Grace Beber, Eds., *Parsing the Turing Test: Philosophical and Methodological Issues in the Quest for the Thinking Computer*, pages 181–210, Springer, New York, 2009. DOI: 10.1007/978-1-4020-6710-5_13 58

Hanna M. Wallach, Hugo Larochelle, Alina Beygelzimer, Florence d'Alché-Buc, Emily B. Fox, and Roman Garnett, Eds. *Advances in Neural Information Processing Systems 32: Annual Conference on Neural Information Processing Systems, NeurIPS*, December 2019. http://papers.nips.cc/book/advances-in-neural-information-processing-systems-32-2019 158

Haixun Wang. An annotated reading list of conversational AI. *Medium*, April 2018. https://medium.com/gobeyond-ai/a-reading-list-and-mini-survey-of-conversational-ai-32fceea97180 158

Xuewei Wang, Weiyan Shi, Richard Kim, Yoojung Oh, Sijia Yang, Jingwen Zhang, and Zhou Yu. Persuasion for good: Towards a personalized persuasive dialogue system for social good. *ArXiv Preprint ArXiv:1906.06725*, 2019. DOI: 10.18653/v1/p19-1566 181

Ye-Yi Wang, Li Deng, and Alex Acero. Semantic frame-based spoken language understanding. In Gokhan Tur and Renato De Mori, Eds., *Spoken Language Understanding: Systems for Extracting Information from Speech*, chapter 3, pages 41–91, John Wiley & Sons, Ltd., 2011. https://onlinelibrary.wiley.com/doi/abs/10.1002/9781119992691.ch3 DOI: 10.1002/9781119992691.ch3 75

Wayne Ward and Sunil Issar. Recent improvements in the CMU spoken language understanding system. In *Proc. of the Workshop on Human Language Technology*, pages 213–216, Association for Computational Linguistics, Plainsboro, NJ, March 1994. DOI: 10.3115/1075812.1075857 47

Bonnie Webber. Computational perspectives on discourse and dialogue. *The Handbook of Discourse Analysis*. Blackwell Publishers Ltd., 2001. DOI: 10.1002/9780470753460.ch42 65

Zhuxiaona Wei and James A. Landay. Evaluating speech-based smart devices using new usability heuristics. *IEEE Pervasive Computing*, 17(2):84–96, 2018. DOI: 10.1109/mprv.2018.022511249 103

Joseph Weizenbaum. ELIZA—a computer program for the study of natural language communication between man and machine. *Communications of the ACM*, 9(1):36–45, January 1966. DOI: 10.1145/365153.365168 20

Tsung-Hsien Wen, Milica Gašić, Nikola Mrkšić, Pei-Hao Su, David Vandyke, and Steve Young. Semantically conditioned LSTM-based natural language generation for spoken dialogue systems. In *Proc. of the Conference on Empirical Methods in Natural Language Processing*, pages 1711–1721, Association for Computational Linguistics, Lisbon, Portugal, September 2015. https://www.aclweb.org/anthology/D15-1199 DOI: 10.18653/v1/d15-1199 80

Tsung-Hsien Wen, Milica Gašić, Nikola Mrkšić, Lina M. Rojas-Barahona, Pei-Hao Su, David Vandyke, and Steve Young. Multi-domain neural network language generation for spoken dialogue systems. In *Proc. of the Conference of the North American Chapter of the Association for Computational Linguistics: Human Language Technologies*, pages 120–129, San Diego, CA, June 2016. https://www.aclweb.org/anthology/N16-1015 DOI: 10.18653/v1/n16-1015 80

Tsung-Hsien Wen, David Vandyke, Nikola Mrkšić, Milica Gašić, Lina M. Rojas-Barahona, Pei-Hao Su, Stefan Ultes, and Steve Young. A network-based end-to-end trainable task-oriented dialogue system. In *Proc. of the 15th Conference of the European Chapter of the Association for Computational Linguistics: Volume 1, Long Papers*, pages 438–449, Valencia, Spain, April 2017. https://www.aclweb.org/anthology/E17-1042 DOI: 10.18653/v1/e17-1042 95, 139, 176

Mark West, Rebecca Kraut, and Han Ei Chew. I'd blush if I could: Closing gender divides in digital skills through education, 2019. https://unesdoc.unesco.org/ark:/48223/pf0000367416 180

Jason Weston, Sumit Chopra, and Antoine Bordes. Memory networks. *ArXiv Preprint ArXiv:1410.3916*, 2015. DOI: 10.1145/3109859.3109868 138

Jason E. Weston. Dialog-based language learning. In *Advances in Neural Information Processing Systems*, pages 829–837, 2016. https://arxiv.org/abs/1604.06045 154

Yorick Wilks, Roberta Catizone, Simon Worgan, and Markku Turunen. Some background on dialogue management and conversational speech for dialogue systems. *Computer Speech & Language*, 25(2):128–139, April 2011. DOI: 10.1016/j.csl.2010.03.001 49

Jason Williams, Antoine Raux, Deepak Ramachandran, and Alan Black. The dialog state tracking challenge. In *Proc. of the 14th Annual SIGdial Meeting on Discourse and Dialogue*, pages 404–413, Association for Computational Linguistics, Metz, France, August 2013. https://www.aclweb.org/anthology/W13-4065 DOI: 10.5087/dad.2016.301 86, 154

Jason D. Williams. Applying POMDPs to dialog systems in the troubleshooting domain. In *Proc. of the Workshop on Bridging the Gap: Academic and Industrial Research in Dialog Technologies, NAACL-HLT-Dialog'07*, pages 1–8, Association for Computational Linguistics, 2007. DOI: 10.3115/1556328.1556329 84, 88

Jason D. Williams. The best of both worlds: Unifying conventional dialog systems and POMDPs. In *INTERSPEECH, 9th Annual Conference of the International Speech Communication Association (ISCA)*, pages 1173–1176, Brisbane, Australia, September 2008. http://www.iscaspeech.org/archive/interspeech_2008/i08_1173.html 175

Jason D. Williams. An empirical evaluation of a statistical dialog system in public use. In *Proc. of the 12th Annual SIGdial Meeting on Discourse and Dialogue*, pages 130–141, Association for Computational Linguistics, Portland, OR, June 2011. https://www.aclweb.org/anthology/W11-2016 84

Jason D. Williams. A belief tracking challenge task for spoken dialog systems. In *NAACL-HLT Workshop on Future Directions and Needs in the Spoken Dialog Community: Tools and Data (SDCTD)*, pages 23–24, Montreal, Canada, June 2012. https://www.aclweb.org/anthology/W12-1812 86

Jason D. Williams and Steve Young. Scaling up POMDPs for dialog management: The "summary POMDP" method. In *Proc. of the IEEE Workshop on Automatic Speech Recognition and Understanding*, pages 177–182, San Juan, Puerto Rico, 2005. DOI: 10.1109/asru.2005.1566498 87

Jason D. Williams and Steve Young. Partially observable Markov decision processes for spoken dialog systems. *Computer Speech & Language*, 21(2):393–422, 2007. DOI: 10.1016/j.csl.2006.06.008 83, 84, 85, 151

Jason D. Williams and Geoffrey Zweig. End-to-end LSTM-based dialog control optimized with supervised and reinforcement learning. *ArXiv Preprint ArXiv:1606.01269*, 2016. 139

Jason D. Williams, Kavosh Asadi, and Geoffrey Zweig. Hybrid code networks: Practical and efficient end-to-end dialog control with supervised and reinforcement learning. *ArXiv Preprint ArXiv:1702.03274*, 2017. DOI: 10.18653/v1/p17-1062 69, 88

Terry Winograd. *Understanding Natural Language*. Academic Press, New York, 1972. 14

Steve Worswick. Can you eat a chair? *Medium*, June 2018a. https://medium.com/@steve.worswick/can-you-eat-a-chair-2e6c865e757e 59

Steve Worswick. The curse of the chatbot users. *Medium*, August 2018b. https://medium.com/pandorabots-blog/the-curse-of-the-chatbot-users-8142f517f8d2 179

Steve Worswick. Wildcards in AIML. *Medium*, July 2018c. https://medium.com/pandorabots-blog/wildcards-in-aiml-da7f4a29f42e 59

Steve Worswick. Dealing with off topic input. *Medium*, September 2019. https://medium.com/pandorabots-blog/dealing-with-off-topic-input-3857af3e5024 67

Wenquan Wu, Zhen Guo, Xiangyang Zhou, Hua Wu, Xiyuan Zhang, Rongzhong Lian, and Haifeng Wang. Proactive human-machine conversation with explicit conversation goals. *ArXiv Preprint ArXiv: 1906.05572*, 2019. DOI: 10.18653/v1/p19-1369 170

Guanghao Xu, Hyungjung Lee, Myoung-Wan Koo, and Jungyun Seo. Optimizing policy via deep reinforcement learning for dialogue management. In *IEEE International Conference on Big Data and Smart Computing (BigComp)*, pages 582–589, Shanghai, China, January 2018. DOI: 10.1109/bigcomp.2018.00101 99

Puyang Xu and Ruhi Sarikaya. Contextual domain classification in spoken language understanding systems using recurrent neural network. In *IEEE International Conference on Acoustics, Speech and Signal Processing (ICASSP)*, pages 136–140, Florence, Italy, May 2014. DOI: 10.1109/icassp.2014.6853573 48

Rui Yan. Chitty-Chitty-Chat Bot: Deep learning for conversational AI. In *Proc. of the 27th International Joint Conference on Artificial Intelligence, IJCAI-18*, pages 5520–5526, International Joint Conferences on Artificial Intelligence Organization, July 2018. DOI: 10.24963/ijcai.2018/778 158

Zhaojun Yang, Baichuan Li, Yi Zhu, Irwin King, Gina Levow, and Helen Meng. Collection of user judgments on spoken dialog system with crowdsourcing. In *IEEE Spoken Language Technology Workshop*, pages 277–282, 2010. DOI: 10.1109/slt.2010.5700864 95

Mariya Yao. 10 important research papers in conversational AI from 2019, November 2019a. https://www.topbots.com/top-conversational-ai-research-papers-2019/ 158

Mariya Yao. Top research papers in conversational AI for chatbots and intelligent agents, February 2019b. https://www.topbots.com/most-important-conversational-ai-research/ 158

Sanghyun Yi, Rahul Goel, Chandra Khatri, Tagyoung Chung, Behnam Hedayatnia, Anu Venkatesh, Raefer Gabriel, and Dilek Hakkani-Tür. Towards coherent and engaging spoken dialog response generation using automatic conversation evaluators. In *Proc. of the 12th International Conference on Natural Language Generation (INLG)*, Tokyo, Japan, October–November 2019. https://www.aclweb.org/anthology/W19-8608 DOI: 10.18653/v1/w19-8608 147, 148

Koichiro Yoshino, Chiori Hori, Julien Perez, Luis Fernando D'Haro, Lazaros Polymenakos, Chulaka Gunasekara, Walter S. Lasecki, Jonathan K. Kummerfeld, Michel Galley, Chris Brockett, Jianfeng Gao, Bill Dolan, Xiang Gao, Huda Alamari, Tim K. Marks, Devi Parikh, and Dhruv Batra. Dialog system technology challenge 7. *ArXiv Preprint ArXiv:1901.03461*, 2015. 155

Steve Young. Probabilistic methods in spoken dialogue systems. *Philosophical Transactions of the Royal Society of London. Series A: Mathematical, Physical and Engineering Sciences*, 358(1769):1389–1402, 2000. DOI: 10.1098/rsta.2000.0593 72

Steve Young, Milica Gašić, Simon Keizer, François Mairesse, Jost Schatzmann, Blaise Thomson, and Kai Yu. The hidden information state model: A practical framework for pomdp-based spoken dialogue management. *Computer Speech & Language*, 24(2):150–174, 2010. DOI: 10.1016/j.csl.2009.04.001 84, 87

Steve Young, Milica Gašić, Blaise Thomson, and Jason D. Williams. POMDP-based statistical spoken dialog systems: A review. *Proc. of the IEEE*, 101(5):1160–1179, 2013. DOI: 10.1109/jproc.2012.2225812 83

Dian Yu, Michelle Cohn, Yi Mang Yang, Chun-Yen Chen, Weiming Wen, Jiaping Zhang, Mingyang Zhou, Kevin Jesse, Austin Chau, Antara Bhowmick, Shreenath Iyer, Giritheja Sreenivasulu, Sam Davidson, Ashwin Bhandare, and Zhou Yu. Gunrock: Building a human-like social bot by leveraging large scale real user data. In *Alexa Prize Proceedings*, 2018. https://arxiv.org/abs/1910.03042 68

Dong Yu and Li Deng. *Automatic Speech Recognition*. Springer, New York, 2016. DOI: 10.1007/978-1-4471-5779-3 45

Idris Yusupov and Yurii Kuratov. NIPS conversational intelligence challenge 2017 winner system: Skill-based conversational agent with supervised dialog manager. In *Proc. of the 27th International Conference on Computational Linguistics*, pages 3681–3692, Santa Fe, New Mexico, 2018. https://www.aclweb.org/anthology/C18-1312 157

Saizheng Zhang, Emily Dinan, Jack Urbanek, Arthur Szlam, Douwe Kiela, and Jason Weston. Personalizing dialogue agents: I have a dog, do you have pets too? *ArXiv Preprint ArXiv:1801.07243*, 2018. DOI: 10.18653/v1/p18-1205 110, 112, 143, 154

Yizhe Zhang, Siqi Sun, Michel Galley, Yen-Chun Chen, Chris Brockett, Xiang Gao, Jianfeng Gao, Jingjing Liu, and Bill Dolan. Dialogpt: Large-scale generative pre-training for conversational response generation. *ArXiv Preprint ArXiv:1911.00536*, 2019. DOI: 10.18653/v1/2020.acl-demos.30 141

Tiancheng Zhao and Maxine Eskenazi. Towards end-to-end learning for dialog state tracking and management using deep reinforcement learning. In *Proc. of the 17th Annual Meeting of the Special Interest Group on Discourse and Dialogue*, pages 1–10, Association for Computational Linguistics, Los Angeles, September 2016. https://www.aclweb.org/anthology/W16-3601 DOI: 10.18653/v1/w16-3601 126

Tiancheng Zhao and Maxine Eskenazi. Zero-shot dialog generation with cross-domain latent actions. In *Proc. of the 19th Annual SIGdial Meeting on Discourse and Dialogue*, pages 1–10, Association for Computational Linguistics, Melbourne, Australia, July 2018. https://www.aclweb.org/anthology/W18-5001 DOI: 10.18653/v1/w18-5001 166

Tiancheng Zhao, Kyusong Lee, and Maxine Eskenazi. Unsupervised discrete sentence representation learning for interpretable neural dialog generation. In *Proc. of the 56th Annual Meeting of the Association for Computational Linguistics (Volume 1: Long Papers)*, pages 1098–1107, Association for Computational Linguistics, Melbourne, Australia, July 2018. https://www.aclweb.org/anthology/P18-1101 DOI: 10.18653/v1/p18-1101 166

Hao Zhou, Minlie Huang, Tianyang Zhang, Xiaoyan Zhu, and Bing Liu. Emotional chatting machine: Emotional conversation generation with internal and external memory. In *32nd AAAI Conference on Artificial Intelligence*, New Orleans, LA, February 2018a. https://arxiv.org/abs/1704.01074 149, 150, 167

Hao Zhou, Tom Young, Minlie Huang, Haizhou Zhao, Jingfang Xu, and Xiaoyan Zhu. Commonsense knowledge aware conversation generation with graph attention. In *Proc. of the 27th International Joint Conference on Artificial Intelligence (IJCAI-18)*, pages 4623–4629, Stockholm, Sweden, July 2018b. DOI: 10.24963/ijcai.2018/643 168

Li Zhou, Jianfeng Gao, Di Li, and Heung-Yeung Shum. The design and implementation of Xiaoice, an empathetic social chatbot. *Computational Linguistics*, 46(1):53–93, 2020. DOI: 10.1162/coli_a_00368 30, 141

Author's Biography

MICHAEL MCTEAR

Michael McTear is an Emeritus Professor at Ulster University with a special interest in spoken language technologies and conversational interfaces. He has authored several books, including *Spoken Dialogue Technology: Toward the Conversational User Interface* (Springer, 2004), *Spoken Dialogue Systems* (Morgan Claypool, 2010, with Kristiina Jokinen), and *The Conversational Interface: Talking to Smart Devices* (Springer, 2016, with Zoraida Callejas and David Griol). Michael has delivered keynote addresses and tutorials at many academic conferences and at industrial conferences, including SpeechTEK, the Conversational Interaction conference, RE-WORK AI Assistant Summit, and ProjectVoice. Currently, he is involved in several projects where he is applying Conversational AI to areas such as mental health support and the home monitoring of the elderly.

Printed in the United States
by Baker & Taylor Publisher Services